PRAISE FOR *JESUS, CONTRADICTED*

This book provides a detailed investigation of how literary works were composed in antiquity. By comparing the Evangelists to other writers in history, Licona encourages his readers to widen their understanding and adopt a new, more nuanced approach to reading the Gospels that takes into account ancient compositional practices when investigating the concept of scriptural authority and inerrancy. Licona takes this challenging topic and makes it accessible, offering in-text definitions, summaries, and "questions for further thought" for each chapter. For those who want an informed and approachable discussion of variations in the Gospels from a faith perspective, this book is for you.

—**SEAN A. ADAMS**, professor of New Testament and ancient culture, University of Glasgow

While we disagree over the nature of Scripture, Licona and I concur 100 percent on the importance of comparing like with like. And carefully comparing the canonical gospels with Greco-Roman biographies, which they resemble in so many important ways, generates a plethora of insights. At every turn readers will experience new and improved ideas supplanting old and inferior ones.

—**DALE C. ALLISON JR.**, Richard J. Dearborn Professor of New Testament Studies, Princeton Theological Seminary

In this lucid and readable book addressing the similarities and differences between the Gospels, Michael Licona solves most of these biblical riddles by explaining how the Gospels were written and how they also are related to each other. When viewed in the genre of contemporary Greco-Roman biography, distinctive features are seen to be rooted in the particulars of historical memory, theological interests of the Evangelists, and the audiences for which they were writing. In explaining how and why the Gospels were written, their authority comes through for believers and skeptics alike.

—**PAUL N. ANDERSON**, author of *From Crisis to Christ*, *The Christology of the Fourth Gospel*, *The Fourth Gospel and the Quest for Jesus*, *The Riddles of the Fourth Gospel*, and *Following Jesus*

Michael Licona is a preeminent Christian apologist who shows us not merely that the Gospels are true but how they are true! Sceptics like to point out alleged contradictions and discrepancies among the Gospels. Licona points out that the Gospels are intended to be history, but history as the ancients understood it, which gave the storyteller a great deal of room for narrative variability and literary vision. This book will help readers make sense of how the Gospels combine fact and faith, history and hermeneutics, authenticity and artistry.

—**MICHAEL F. BIRD**, deputy principal, Ridley College Melbourne, Australia

Licona takes up hard questions about differences in the Gospels' stories and offers comprehensive answers based on extensive research and a commitment to the authority and trustworthiness of the Bible. In easy-to-understand prose, Licona lays out cogent, compelling arguments for reading the Gospels through the lens of first-century biographies. *Jesus, Contradicted* is a must read for every curious Christian.

—**LYNN H. COHICK**, distinguished professor of New Testament, director, Houston Theological Seminary, Houston Christian University

Jesus, Contradicted will be a huge help for people who take the New Testament Gospels seriously but wonder why there are differences when two or more Gospels tell the same story or report the same sayings of Jesus. Michael Licona solves the problem by showing that writers of history in antiquity went about their task with very different assumptions and goals. Readers will find that the New Testament Gospels are reliable after all. I highly recommend this well written book.

—**CRAIG A. EVANS**, John Bisagno Distinguished Professor of Christian Origins, Houston Christian University

We need to respect the shape of the Scripture God has given us over our preconceived, humanly shaped ideas of what that should look like. Licona effectively makes the case that Gospel differences do not undermine Scripture's authority and invites us to respect Scripture enough to let its own approach guide how we define that authority. The differences between ancient and modern biographies go a long way toward explaining many of the differences we find in our Gospels, and we approach the Gospels to our peril if we insist on conforming them to standards of a genre that did not yet exist. Patiently unfolding his argument in the clearest possible manner, Licona offers a methodologically informed work suitable not only for fellow scholars and preachers but even for undergraduates or ordinary readers.

—**CRAIG S. KEENER**, F. M. and Ada Thompson Professor of Biblical Studies, Asbury Theological Seminary

I believe the Bible is true. What the word *true* means must be determined by what the Bible says and what the Bible says about itself. There is no better way to determine what the Bible says than by reading it over and over, carefully and with precision. When it comes to the Gospels, which is a specialty for Michael Licona, it means underlining a synopsis of the Gospels because only by doing so does one experience the particular realities of the Gospels themselves. Underlining the Gospels can shatter expectations and disrupt one's confirmation biases. Instead, underlining permits us to understand the truth God wants us to know. Michael Licona's fresh approach to the nature of Scripture as revealed in the Gospels is nothing less than a godsend for those of us who specialize in the Gospels. The book clearly combines reverence for the text of Scripture and a fearless willingness to describe what is actually there.

—**SCOT MCKNIGHT**, professor of New Testament

Mike Licona spent twelve weeks with a group of executives from the front office of the Atlanta Braves, walking us through the contents of this book. Our group absolutely loved learning from Mike as he explained a fresh approach for understanding and even embracing the differences in the Gospels. I am elated to endorse *Jesus, Contradicted* because I believe your faith will be strengthened as you read it and that you will gain a new appreciation for the reliability of God's Word.

—**JAY MCSWAIN**, chaplain, Atlanta Braves

We talk of "gospel truth," and yet the Gospels themselves do not always agree. How can that be if they are all divinely inspired? In an earlier book Michael Licona explored these contradictions in the light of techniques used by Greek and Latin authors and found the striking feature to be the Gospels' consistency rather than their differences. Now he faces that question of inspiration head-on and in this exemplary and accessible study argues that inspiration can take different forms and allow for a large amount of human agency. Christians can still believe that the Gospels reveal a single harmonious truth and that it comes from God.

—**CHRISTOPHER PELLING**, emeritus regius professor of Greek, Christ Church, Oxford

Context is king for the evaluation of historical evidence, and what body of evidence has greater potential relevance to our relationship with God than the Gospels? In this book, New Testament scholar Michael R. Licona makes accessible the context required to take the proper measure of the various apparent contradictions in the overlapping biblical accounts of the life and teachings of Jesus. Every reader of the New Testament will gain a valuable, fresh perspective from reading this book.

—**JOHN T. RAMSEY**, professor of classics emeritus,
University of Illinois at Chicago

In this important work, Licona expands upon his earlier work on Gospel differences by drawing out its implications with reference to the inspiration and inerrancy of Scripture. While most evangelical statements on inerrancy make sweeping assertions based on what they want Scripture to be, Licona calls for a definition based on the actual phenomenon of Scripture and the nature of the Gospels as Greco-Roman biographies. This groundbreaking volume deserves careful consideration in the ongoing discussions on the nature and significance of biblical authority.

—**MARK L. STRAUSS**, university professor of New
Testament, Bethel Seminary of Bethel University, vice-
chair, NIV Committee on Bible Translation

JESUS, CONTRADICTED

JESUS, CONTRADICTED

WHY THE GOSPELS TELL THE SAME STORY DIFFERENTLY

MICHAEL R. LICONA

ZONDERVAN ACADEMIC

ZONDERVAN ACADEMIC

Jesus, Contradicted

Published in Grand Rapids, Michigan, by Zondervan. Zondervan is a registered trademark of The Zondervan Corporation, L.L.C., a wholly owned subsidiary of HarperCollins Christian Publishing, Inc.

Requests for information should be addressed to customercare@harpercollins.com.

Zondervan titles may be purchased in bulk for educational, business, fundraising, or sales promotional use. For information, please email SpecialMarkets@Zondervan.com.

ISBN 978-0-310-15962-9 (audio)

Library of Congress Cataloging-in-Publication Data

Names: Licona, Mike, 1961- author.
Title: Jesus, contradicted : why the Gospels tell the same story differently / Michael R. Licona.
Description: Grand Rapids, Michigan : Zondervan, 2024. | Includes bibliographical references and index.
Identifiers: LCCN 2023042128 (print) | LCCN 2023042129 (ebook) | ISBN 9780310159599 (hardcover) | ISBN 9780310159605 (ebook)
Subjects: LCSH: Bible. Gospels—Criticism, interpretation, etc. | Biography—To 500. | Biography as a literary form. | BISAC: RELIGION / Biblical Studies / New Testament / Jesus, the Gospels & Acts | RELIGION / Biblical Commentary / New Testament / Jesus, the Gospels & Acts
Classification: LCC BS2555.52 .L524 2024 (print) | LCC BS2555.52 (ebook) | DDC 226/.06—dc23/eng/20240117
LC record available at https://lccn.loc.gov/2023042128
LC ebook record available at https://lccn.loc.gov/2023042129

Unless otherwise indicated, Scripture quotations are the author's translation.

Italics or underlining in Scripture quotations indicate emphasis added by the author unless otherwise indicated.

Cover design: Thinkpen Design
Interior design: Kait Lamphere

Printed in the United States of America

24 25 26 27 28 LBC 5 4 3 2 1

To Ron Sauer, from whom I learned to read the Greek New Testament.
Still, I learned so much more from his exemplary life.

To Richard Burridge, whose research on ancient biography
made the contents of this book possible.

CONTENTS

ACKNOWLEDGMENTS

I have drawn ideas from so many others and benefitted from their criticisms and suggestions that I list their names with great hesitancy, knowing that I will unintentionally omit some important people. Nevertheless, I will attempt to be thorough and apologize in advance to those I have overlooked. My mention of the names that follow does not suggest they agree with everything in this book.

The following people read through portions or all of various drafts and provided criticisms and ideas that proved helpful: William Lane Craig, Sharon Elander, Kurt Jaros, Jonathan Kendall, Ed Komoszewski, Debbie Licona, Sean McDowell, Bill Pratt, and Tim Stratton. I am also indebted to Paul Brinkerhoff and Lois Stück of Grace and Truth Communications, who provided many keen editorial comments before I submitted my manuscript to Zondervan.

In addition to those listed above, the following people provided comments over the years that helped form the ideas in this book: Darrell Bock, Richard Burridge, Kobus Erasmus, Craig Evans, Leighton Flowers, Gary Habermas, J. P. Holding, Braxton Hunter, Douglas Jacoby, Craig Keener, Alex McFarland, Greg Monette, Nick Peters, Mark Strauss, Frank Turek, Dan Wallace, and Scott Willingham.

I am grateful to Jay McSwain (front office chaplain for the Atlanta Braves), Jim Allen (Senior VP for the Atlanta Braves), and Scott Cunningham (VP for the Atlanta Braves), for inviting me to use their Wednesday morning Bible study group for front office personnel as a focus group in order to fine-tune the content of this book for use as a group study. I am grateful to Jeff Smith and the Harvesters Sunday School class at Perimeter Church in Johns Creek, Georgia, for inviting me to speak to their group for eleven weeks as a second and final focus group. Encouraging comments and helpful suggestions for improving the presentation from members of both focus groups made what follows better.

ABBREVIATIONS

In the text and notes, references to ancient authors and their works when abbreviated follow the abbreviations used in the *SBL Handbook of Style* (2nd ed.), supplemented by the *Oxford Classical Dictionary* (4th ed.), as are references to journals and other works of classical and biblical scholarship. Some alternate abbreviations are also included parenthetically as they appear in quoted material. All references to Jewish, intertestamental, Greco-Roman, and patristic literature not mentioned below are given in full.

All English translations of Plutarch and other quotations of ancient authors are from volumes in the Loeb Classical Library unless otherwise indicated. I use the verse numbering found in Loeb unless otherwise indicated, since the Loeb Greek text is readily available to so many. All English translations of Theon are from George A. Kennedy's *Progymnasmata* unless otherwise indicated. All Scripture quotations of the New Testament and Septuagint (LXX) are the author's translation unless otherwise indicated. Other English translation of quotations from ancient sources is indicated as such if translated by the author.

To avoid abbreviating too concisely for readers who are not specialists in classical or biblical studies, author names and works are generally referenced in full when they are first mentioned. Whether abbreviated or used in full, other frequently cited works appear as follows (entries are grouped by category with works alphabetized by abbreviation under an author's name):

GENERAL AND BIBLIOGRAPHIC

BDAG	Danker, Frederick W., Walter Bauer, William F. Arndt, and F. Wilbur Gingrich. *Greek-English Lexicon of the New Testament and Other Early Christian Literature*. 3rd ed. Chicago: University of Chicago Press, 2000
Gk.	Greek
LCL	Loeb Classical Library

LXX	Septuagint
MS	manuscript
NET	New English Translation
NIV	New International Version
NT	New Testament
Q	*Quelle*, which means "source" in German; used to represent hypothetical sources or traditions used by Matthew and Luke

HEBREW BIBLE / OLD TESTAMENT (INCLUDING SEPTUAGINT)

Exod.	Exodus
Num.	Numbers
Deut.	Deuteronomy
Judg.	Judges
2 Sam.	2 Samuel
2 Kgs.	2 Kings
1 Chron.	1 Chronicles
Neh.	Nehemiah
Ps(s).	Psalm(s)
Eccl.	Ecclesiastes
Jer.	Jeremiah
Dan.	Daniel
Zech.	Zechariah

NEW TESTAMENT

Matt.	Matthew
Rom.	Romans
1 Cor.	1 Corinthians
2 Cor.	2 Corinthians
Gal.	Galatians
Phil.	Philippians
Col.	Colossians
2 Thess.	2 Thessalonians
Heb.	Hebrews
1 Pet.	1 Peter
1 John	1 John
Jude	Jude

OLD TESTAMENT PSEUDEPIGRAPHA

4 Ezra	4 Ezra

OTHER ANCIENT SOURCES

Augustine

Cons.	*De consensu evangelistarum* (*Harmony of the Gospels*)
Serm.	*Sermons*
Faust.	*Contra Faustum Manichaeum* (*Against Faustus the Manichaean*)
Ep.	*Letter to Jerome*

Barnabas

Barn.	*Letter of Barnabas*

Chrysostom (John Chrysostom)

Hom. Matt.	*Homiliae in Matthaeum*

Cicero (Marcus Tullius)

Fam.	*Epistulae ad familiares* (*Letters to Friends*)

Clement of Rome

1 Clem.	1 Clement

Eusebius

Hist. eccl.	*Historia ecclesiastica* (*Ecclesiastical History*)

Ignatius

Ign. *Eph.*	Ignatius, *To the Ephesians*
Ign. *Magn.*	Ignatius, *To the Magnesians*

Irenaeus

Adv. Haer.	*Adversus Haereses* (*Against Heresies*)

Josephus

Ant.	*Jewish Antiquities*
Life	*The Life*

Lucian

Hist. conscr. *Quomodo historia conscribenda sit* (*How to Write History*)
Peregr. *De morte Peregrini* (*The Passing of Peregrinus*)

Papias

Frag. *Fragments of Papias*

Plutarch

Alex. *Life of Alexander*
Ant. *Life of Antony*
Brut. *Life of Brutus*
Cat. Min. *Life of Cato Minor*
Caes. *Life of Caesar*
Cic. *Life of Cicero*
Cim. *Life of Cimon*
Crass. *Life of Crassus*
Luc. *Life of Lucullus*
Nic. *Life of Nicias*
Pomp. *Life of Pompey*

Polybius

Hist. *Historiae* (*Histories*)

Quintilian

Inst. *Institutio oratoria* (*Institutes of Oratory*)

Tertullian

Marc. *Adversus Marcionem* (*Against Marcion*)

Theon (Aelius Theon of Alexandria)

Prog. *Progymnasmata*

Valerius Maximus

Mem. *Facta et dicta memorabilia* (*Memorable Deeds and Sayings*)

CHAPTER 1

THE QUEST FOR A BETTER ANSWER

During my undergraduate studies, the Christian university I attended had a program whereby students could volunteer three months of their summer to work out of a participating church. In return, the student would receive free tuition, room, and board for the following academic year. Just say no to student loans, right? Sounded great! I applied for the summer following my sophomore year and was accepted. So I spent the summer of 1981 working for a small church in Philadelphia. Then after my junior year, I spent the summer in a medium-size church in Manhattan. Every person on those summer ministry teams was a committed follower of Jesus. (Well, we also needed some financial help to afford college.) Those summers were a time of tiring service involving evangelism, discipleship, and personal growth. We spent time every day in Bible study and prayer, and we fasted every Wednesday. (Now I'm beginning to sound like the Pharisee in Luke 18:11–12!)

MY FIRST ENCOUNTER WITH GOSPEL DIFFERENCES

I will never forget what happened one morning during my summer in Philadelphia. Dave, one of my teammates, said he wanted to show me something in the Bible. I had come to respect Dave that summer. He was a few inches taller than me, was a year older, and had a superior knowledge of the Bible. We sat down, just the two of us, and he opened his Bible. He showed me Matthew 26:34 where Jesus says to Peter, "Truly I say to you that this very night, before a rooster crows, you will deny me three times."

I was familiar with the passage. He then read Luke 22:34 and John 13:38, both of which have Jesus giving a similar prediction. "Okay, Dave. What's up? They're all saying the same thing."

"I'm not finished," he quickly replied. Dave then read Mark 14:30: "And Jesus said to him, 'Truly I say to you, that this very night, before a rooster crows twice, you yourself will deny me three times.' Did you notice any difference?"

"Yeah. In Mark, Jesus tells Peter he will deny him three times before a rooster crows twice. But in the other Gospels he tells him he will deny him three times before a rooster crows. No big deal. The others could have had multiple 'crowings' in mind."

"No, Mike. They didn't. Take a closer look."

We then looked at the broader context in Mark:

> Now while Peter was below in the courtyard, one of the servant-girls of the high priest came, and seeing Peter warming himself, she looked at him and said, "You also were with Jesus the Nazarene." But he denied it, saying, "I do not know or understand what you are talking about." And he went out to the gateway, and a rooster crowed.[1] The servant-girl saw him and began again to say to the bystanders, "This is one of them!" But again he denied it. And after a little while the bystanders were again saying to Peter, "Truly you are one of them, for you are also a Galilean." But he began to curse and swear, "I do not know this man you are talking about!" Immediately a rooster crowed a second time. And Peter remembered that Jesus had said to him, "Before a rooster crows twice, you will deny me three times." And he broke down and wept. (Mark 14:66–72)

In Matthew, Luke, and John, Jesus tells Peter that he will deny him three times that night *before* the rooster crows. Those Gospels then proceed to narrate Peter denying Jesus three times followed by a rooster crowing. Everything's consistent. However, in Mark, Jesus tells Peter he will deny him three times before the rooster crows twice. Mark then narrates Peter denying Jesus, which is followed by a rooster crowing, which is then followed by Peter denying Jesus twice more, which is followed by a rooster crowing a second time. In Matthew, Luke, and John, a rooster does not crow until Peter denies Jesus three times, just as he predicted in those Gospels. However, in Mark's Gospel, a rooster crows after Peter denies Jesus the first time then again after the third time. This doesn't jibe with Jesus's statement in the other Gospels, "Truly I say to you that tonight,

---

1. Some manuscripts lack the words "and a rooster crowed" in Mark 14:68. The manuscript evidence for their inclusion is slightly better than that for their omission. Of all the most popular English translations, only the NIV omits it.

before a rooster crows, you will deny me three times" (Matt. 26:34; cf. Luke 22:34; John 13:38), because in Mark the rooster crowed after Peter denied him *the first time*.

When Dave finished showing me this, I felt somewhat confused and said, "Well, the Bible is God's Word. So there can't be a contradiction. How do you explain the difference?"

Dave looked at me and said, "I don't know. Maybe it is a contradiction. How would you explain it?"

Although I had not yet seen the 1939 movie *Gone with the Wind*, little did I know I'd respond the same way Scarlett O'Hara did when she was faced with a perplexing situation: "I won't think about that today. I'll think about that tomorrow." Tomorrow came twenty-seven years later.

MY DEBATE WITH A SKEPTIC

It was 2008 and I faced the prominent skeptical New Testament scholar Bart Ehrman in a public debate at Midwestern Baptist Theological Seminary in Kansas City, Missouri. An animated speaker, Ehrman has turned more churchgoers away from Christianity than perhaps anyone else in the Western world. In that debate, Professor Ehrman spent a lot of time criticizing the Gospels with a special focus on Gospel differences. He asked audience members whether Jesus was crucified before or after the Passover meal. He then answered that it depends which Gospel you read. Did Simon of Cyrene carry Jesus's cross, or did Jesus carry it all the way? It depends which Gospel you read. Did both thieves being crucified next to Jesus curse him, or did one repent? It depends which Gospel you read. On Sunday morning, how many women went to the tomb? It depends which Gospel you read. When they got there, how many angels did they see? It depends which Gospel you read. Did Jesus first appear to the group of his male disciples in Jerusalem or Galilee? It depends which Gospel you read. And on and on and on. Ehrman contends that these differences disqualify the Gospels as reliable historical sources about Jesus.

There was a great deal of rhetorical power behind Ehrman's words. His rapid-fire list of Gospel differences followed by "It depends which Gospel you read" each time served as a sort of machine-gun attack aimed at killing trust in the Gospels as reliable sources about Jesus. By the time he is finished, many Christians hearing him are thinking to themselves, "Say it ain't so!" And the carnage is noticeable, not from dead bodies in churches but from an increasing number of vacant seats in them.

This led me to ask some questions: Can these texts be reasonably harmonized? Do any of these differences truly amount to a contradiction? Could a divinely inspired text include contradictions? If God inspired the authors of the Bible, how did he do it? Did he dictate the text to the authors word-for-word? Or did he give them the ideas and allow them to communicate according to their own abilities? Would God allow them to record something that was not true? Did he care if the Gospels included a few inaccurate details that are of little-to-no significance?

"THE BALTIMORE CALL"

Although I had many questions, by the time of that debate with Ehrman, Gospel differences had ceased bothering me. Before I would even broach the topic of differences in a serious manner, I had spent a decade in focused research on the question pertaining to whether Jesus had risen from the dead. During that time, I had seen that a strong historical case can be made to support the New Testament reports that Jesus rose from the dead. In fact, the explanation that Jesus rose from the dead was, in my opinion, far superior to any competing explanation. Moreover, a telephone conversation I had with Christian philosopher Gary Habermas nearly twenty years earlier had provided significant direction. Professor Habermas refers to that conversation as "the Baltimore call."

It was 1989. My wife, Debbie, and I were living in Baltimore, and I was having a crisis of faith. This was before email, so I called Gary. The call went something like this:

> "Doc! You know, many scholars don't think Matthew, Mark, Luke, and John wrote the Gospels. They say we have no idea who wrote them. If they're right, then we don't know anything about the authors. So there's no way of knowing if what they're claiming about Jesus is true. I'm really struggling with this and starting to question if Christianity is true."
>
> Gary listened patiently and then asked, "Did Jesus rise from the dead?"
>
> I said, "Yes."
>
> Then he asked, "Why do you think that?"
>
> I answered, "Because what you call the 'minimal facts' that nearly all scholars grant can only be reasonably accounted for by Jesus rising from the dead. So a strong historical case can be made for Jesus's resurrection."
>
> Gary said, "That's right. And, Mike, there are some reasons for thinking Matthew, Mark, Luke, and John wrote the Gospels. But let's assume

for a moment that we don't know who wrote them. Does that change the fact that Jesus rose from the dead?"

I said, "No, because the apostles were proclaiming the gospel message throughout the Roman Empire long before the first of the New Testament literature was written. If salvation was available to others by believing the gospel message before it was articulated in literature, the truth of the gospel message cannot be contingent on the Gospels being written by their traditional authors."

"That's right, Mike. So why are you letting the matter of Gospel authorship cause you to question whether Christianity itself is true?"

". . . Well, . . . okay, that makes sense. . . . But what about the supposed contradictions in the Gospels?"

"Mike, did Jesus rise from the dead?"

"Yes."

He said, "There are numerous answers offered to explain differences between the Gospels. But let's say for a moment that there are some errors in the Gospels. Is Christianity still true given Jesus's resurrection?"

"Yes."

"Then why are you letting this bother you so much? Mike, I'm not saying these matters aren't important. They are important. But you need to put things in their proper position of importance. If Jesus rose from the dead, Christianity is true, right?"

"Yes. . . . I think I see what you're saying, Doc, but what about the genocide texts in the Old Testament?"

"Mike, did—Jesus—rise—from—the—dead?"

That was a life-changing phone call for me. You see, these other matters are important. But they do not change the answer to the ultimate question of whether Christianity is true. If Jesus rose from the dead, it's game, set, match. Christianity is true—*period*! Why? Because when Jesus's critics challenged him for a sign to confirm his claims, he offered the sign of his resurrection from the dead (Matt. 16:1–4 // Luke 11:29–30; John 2:18–22).[2] So if Jesus rose, he did so to confirm his claims. I now felt a freedom to investigate these other matters with an open mind because even if the answers turned out differently than I had hoped, Christianity is still true.

---

2. For reasons to hold that the historical Jesus predicted his imminent death and resurrection, see Michael R. Licona, *The Resurrection of Jesus: A New Historiographical Approach* (Downers Grove, IL: IVP Academic, 2010), 284–302. The "//" separating references (e.g., Matt. 16:1–4 // Luke 11:29–30) signifies parallel texts.

I want to reiterate that I am not suggesting that differences in how the Gospels report the same events are unimportant. If that was my thinking, I would not have written my previous book on the topic.[3] And you would not be reading this book because I would not have written it either. But I do want to suggest that many people are bothered by Gospel differences far more than they should be. Since Jesus rose from the dead, Christianity is true. And it remains true even if it turns out there are errors and contradictions in the Gospels. Once I understood that principle, a lot changed for me. Many things that had troubled me either no longer did or did to a much lesser extent.

Of course, this conclusion can be taken too far. For if the Gospels were hopelessly mistaken on countless matters, our ability to know the Christianity verified by Jesus's resurrection would be greatly impaired. Fortunately, the Gospels are not in such a predicament. Although this book will not be addressing the historical reliability of the Gospels—that will come in a later volume—I will be showing here that the claim that the Gospels are *not* reliable accounts of Jesus because of their many contradictions should be abandoned.

HOW DAMAGING ARE CONTRADICTIONS?

Those who have studied the practice of history, and even many who have not, recognize that when differences occur in the peripheral details, they do not necessarily call the historicity of the main event into question. When the *Titanic* sank in 1912, some survivors reported that the ship broke in two prior to sinking while others reported that it went down intact. How are such conflicting reports even possible? For the survivors, I think we would be safe in saying this was the most terrifying event of their lives. They were nearly in the middle of the cold Atlantic Ocean. Because the moon was absent in the sky that April evening, only starlight from the mortally wounded ship provided some illumination.

We can only speculate why the survivors provided contradictory reports. Were those who thought the ship went down intact viewing it from a different angle? Did the company that built the *Titanic* pay some survivors to give false testimony in order to give the impression that the ship was stronger than it actually was? Or is this merely an example of

3. Michael R. Licona, *Why Are There Differences in the Gospels? What We Can Learn from Ancient Biography* (New York: Oxford University Press, 2017).

flawed memory? Regardless of how these contradictory reports came to be, no one proposed that the *Titanic* did not sink!

Tacitus, Suetonius, and Cassius Dio are the three primary sources reporting the burning of Rome. They contain discrepancies in a few minor details. Did Nero openly enlist thugs to torch the city? Or did he do it in secret? Or was he not involved in the event? We might mimic Ehrman and answer, "It depends which ancient source you read." Did Nero view the fire from his palace rooftop, from the tower of Maecenas, or from the city of Antium, which was thirty-five miles away? It depends which ancient source you read. Tacitus, Suetonius, and Dio contradict one another on these peripheral details. Yet no one would contend that the fire itself did not occur. We know that it occurred, for some of the ashes remain to this day.[4]

The bottom line: Contradictions offer a challenge to the historical reliability of the Gospels and to some versions of the doctrine of biblical inerrancy. However, they do not necessarily call into question the truth of the Christian faith. So if Ehrman's rhetoric troubles you, take a deep breath and relax. Things are not nearly as horrible as Ehrman and others would have us believe. If you are a Christian who worries every time someone brings up a Gospel difference or something in the Old Testament that disturbs you, remember this principle: *since Jesus rose from the dead, Christianity is true—period!* You will be keeping matters in their proper perspective. And you will sleep better at night.[5]

AWARENESS OF GOSPEL DIFFERENCES IS OLD NEWS

Some of those in the early church were concerned by the differences they observed among the Gospels. In the middle of the second century, Justin Martyr (c. AD 160) asserted that when he cannot explain what appears

4. I am indebted to Paul Maier for this example. See Paul L. Maier, *In the Fullness of Time: A Historian Looks at Christmas, Easter, and the Early Church* (1991; repr., Grand Rapids: Kregel, 1997), 180. See also Suetonius, *Nero* 38.1–2; Cassius Dio, *Hist. rom.* 62.16.2; 62.18.1; Tacitus, *Annals: The Reigns of Tiberius, Claudius, and Nero*, trans. J. C. Yardley (New York: Oxford University Press, 2008), 15.38–39.

5. One may rightly ask why we should believe Jesus rose from the dead. Many books have been written on the topic. For those readers with no previous exposure to the topic, I suggest reading Gary R. Habermas and Michael R. Licona, *The Case for the Resurrection of Jesus* (Grand Rapids: Kregel, 2004); and William Lane Craig, *The Son Rises: Historical Evidence for the Resurrection of Jesus* (1981; repr., Eugene, OR: Wipf and Stock, 2000). For a more thorough read, I suggest Licona, *The Resurrection of Jesus*; Gary R. Habermas, *On the Resurrection*, vol. 1, *Evidences* (Nashville: B&H Academic, 2024).

to be a contradiction, he will admit that he does not understand the text (*Dialogue with Trypho*, 65).

Fairly early in the third century, Origen wrote, "[We must, however, set before the reader] that the truth of these accounts lies in the spiritual meanings, [because] if the discrepancy is not solved, [many] dismiss credence in the Gospels as not true, or not written by a divine spirit, or not successfully recorded."[6] Origen acknowledged the existence of a dizzying number of surface discrepancies in the Gospels.[7] However, he and others did not think the differences rose to the level of casting doubt on the divine inspiration and reliability of the Gospels. And they proposed a number of ways to view the differences. A few paragraphs later Origen adds,

> But I do not condemn, I suppose, the fact that they have also made some minor changes in what happened so far as history is concerned, with a view to the usefulness of the mystical object of [those matters]. Consequently, they have related what happened in [this] place as though it happened in another, or what happened at this time as though at another time, and they have composed what is reported in this manner with a certain degree of distortion.
>
> For their intention was to speak the truth spiritually and materially at the same time where that was possible but, where it was not possible in both ways, to prefer the spiritual to the material. The spiritual truth is often preserved in the material falsehood, so to speak.[8]

In the late fourth and early fifth centuries, Augustine took a position very close to that of Justin, asserting it is not allowable to resolve an apparent contradiction in the Scriptures by saying the author was mistaken. For the real solution lay in either a faulty manuscript, a poor translation,

6. Origen, *Commentary on the Gospel according to John, Books 1–10*, trans. Ronald E. Heine, The Fathers of the Church, vol. 80 (Washington, DC: Catholic University of America Press, 1989), 256, par. 10.

7. Origen, *Commentary on the Gospel according to John, Books 1–10*, 80:257, book 10, par. 14 (Heine). For the Greek text, see Origen, *Origenous ta euriskomena panta = Origenis opera omnia, patrologiae cursus completus, series graeca*, t. 13 (Paris: Migne, 1862). Those interested may access this Greek and Latin text at https://bit.ly/2o9mlRS and scroll to page 312, 2.68. The Greek term translated "dizzying" is *skotodiniasas*.

8. Origen, *Commentary on the Gospel according to John, Books 1–10*, 80:259, book 10, par. 19–20 (Heine). For the Greek text, see Origen, *Origenous ta euriskomena panta*, 4.74–75, p. 313. The Greek term translated "falsehood" in this text is *pseudeiōs*. A similar statement was made in the fourth century by John Chrysostom (*Hom. Matt.* [*Homilies on Matthew*] 1.6).

or the reader does not understand what is being stated (*Faust.* 11.5).[9] Yet Augustine sounded more like Origen when commenting on how Mark and Luke used different words to recall Jesus's warning against blaspheming the Holy Spirit (Mark 3:28–29 // Luke 12:10). Augustine contends that while words are used to communicate a message, it is the message rather than the words that ultimately matters.

> For indeed there is no other reason why the Evangelists do not relate the same things in the same way, but that we may learn thereby to prefer things to words, not words to things, and to seek for nothing else in the speaker, but for his intention, to convey which only the words are used. For what real difference is there whether it is said, "Blasphemy of the Spirit shall not be forgiven;" or "He that blasphemeth against the Holy Ghost, it shall not be forgiven him."[10]

Augustine also wrote a lengthy book titled *The Harmony of the Gospels.* In it, he employs harmonization to resolve many Gospel differences. When he comments on the differences present in the Gospels pertaining to Jesus telling Peter that he will deny him three times, Augustine prefers to harmonize the Gospels and thinks Jesus told Peter on three different occasions that he will deny him! That said, Augustine contends that we cannot determine what Jesus's actual words were pertaining to this matter and that it is unreasonable to try. Notwithstanding, the message matters more than the words.

> But if they seek the actual words that the Lord said to Peter, it is impossible to find them and useless to try, for his meaning, which is what he wanted to make known through saying these words, can be completely understood even through the diverse words of the evangelists. Either Peter, moved at different points in the Lord's discourse, made his presumptuous statement at three separate times, and three times the Lord predicted his denial, which is more probable, based on our investigation, or else the records

9. Augustine makes a similar statement in his *Letter to Jerome* (*Ep.* 82.1.3.).

10. Augustine, *Serm.* 21.13 (NPNF[1]). Augustine of Hippo, "Sermons on Selected Lessons of the New Testament," in *Saint Augustine: Sermon on the Mount, Harmony of the Gospels, Homilies on the Gospels*, ed. Philip Schaff, trans. R. G. MacMullen, *A Select Library of the Nicene and Post-Nicene Fathers of the Christian Church*, 1st series, vol. 6 (New York: Christian Literature Company, 1888), 322. See also Origen, *Commentary on the Gospel according to John, Books 1–10*, 80:259, book 10, par. 19–20 (Heine).

> of all the evangelists could be reduced to one version with some other narrative order, so that it could be shown that there was one occasion on which Peter made his presumptuous statement and the Lord made his prediction that he would deny him. But in either case no inconsistency among the evangelists can be shown, for there is none.[11]

Augustine almost always preferred to harmonize and occasionally went to an extreme length when doing so. However, as he states, what matters is that Jesus made the prediction and Peter denied Jesus three times, regardless of how the prediction and the event actually played out.

Around the same time as Augustine and perhaps a little earlier (ca. AD 390), John Chrysostom contended that the differences between the Gospels are

> a great proof of their truth. For if they accurately agreed in all things, including time, place, and wording, no enemies would believe them but would rather suppose that they came together by some human agreement to write what they did. For such agreement could not stem from sincerity. But as it is now, even the discord in minor matters removes them from all suspicion and clearly defends the character of the writers.[12]

Chrysostom acknowledges that the Gospels sometimes appear to contradict one another pertaining to the times, locations, and wordings they report. But he adds that this suggests they did not collude with one another.

COMMON CHRISTIAN RESPONSES TO GOSPEL DIFFERENCES

Even today, many Christians struggle with how to address different versions of the same stories in the Gospels. Some do not think the differences pose a serious challenge to the general reliability of the accounts. However, those who hold that the Bible contains no errors whatsoever often take one of the following three approaches to the differences between the Gospels:

---

11. Augustine, *Cons.* (*Harmony among the Gospels*) 3.2.8. All quoted translations from Augustine, "Agreement among the Evangelists (*De consensu Evangelistarum*)," trans. Kim Paffenroth, in *Saint Augustine, The New Testament: I and II*, ed. Boniface Ramsey, The Works of Saint Augustine, part 1, vols. 15–16 (Hyde Park, NY: New City, 2014), 261.

12. Chrysostom, *Hom. Matt.* 1.6, PG 57.16.

1. **Ostrich:** "Yes, I've noticed some differences, but it bothers me to think about them. So I don't." (These people simply stick their heads in the ground to avoid dealing with the issue.)
2. **Peacemaker (Harmonizer):** "All of the details can be made to fit. Can't we all just get along?" Harmonization is the preferred approach of today's evangelicals for dealing with Gospel differences, although not always resorting to Augustine's rigid commitment to it.
3. **Cruel Interrogator:** This is the harmonizer who goes much too far. "I can compel these texts to tell the same story, even if it involves twisting and stretching them until they tell me what I want them to say." Cruel interrogators are willing to do violence to the biblical texts because it allows them to keep their particular view of biblical inerrancy intact. ("Since the Bible is God's Word, I know that it does not contain contradictions. There are resolutions to all of the differences in the Gospels. In some cases, I may not know what they are yet. But I know they exist because the Bible is God's Word and God does not contradict himself.")

Recall my first exposure to a Gospel difference. It pertained to when the rooster crowed after Peter denied Jesus and the number of times it crowed. A classic example of harmonization efforts going awry can be observed when Harold Lindsell attempted to solve the difference. While Matthew 26:74, Luke 22:60, and John 18:27 report that the rooster crowed only after Peter had denied Jesus three times, Mark 14:68 and 72 report that it crowed once after Peter's initial denial and then crowed a second time after his third denial. In order to harmonize the difference, Lindsell suggested that the rooster crowed once after Peter had denied Jesus three times then crowed a second time after Peter had denied Jesus another three times. In all, Peter denied Jesus six times.[13] Lindsell's hypothesis is wrong because Mark says the rooster crowed after Peter's *first* denial. Even if that was not a problem, his hypothesis certainly has the appearance of being an ad hoc construction to address a difference that challenged Lindsell's view of what divinely inspired Scripture looks like. Such proposals do

13. Harold Lindsell, *The Battle for the Bible* (Grand Rapids: Zondervan, 1976), 174–76. Lindsell gives credit to J. M. Cheney for this idea that he received in 1965 via personal communication. Cheney later published his hypothesis in Johnston M. Cheney, *The Life of Christ in Stereo: The Four Gospels Combined as One*, rev. ed. (Portland, OR: Western Baptist Seminary Press, 1969), 189–92, 257–58. This attempt to harmonize is extreme and goes well beyond the extent to which most harmonizers go.

little good to promote the reliability of the Bible. Instead, they have the appearance of being desperate attempts to rescue a Bible believed to be in trouble. Although some have gone to extremes in their harmonization efforts, solutions to the differences that employ harmonizations are often plausible. However, that's not enough to say they represent what actually happened. Just because something is plausible or possible does not mean that it is probable or actual.

I found myself dissatisfied with all of these approaches and thought there must be a better way.

THE JOURNEY THAT LED ME TO FORM THE APPROACH IN THIS BOOK

Since the Gospels tell the story of Jesus's life, they were regarded as biographies by most for a very long time. Then some scholars proposed that they belong to a genre class all their own that their authors invented. However, in the latter half of the twentieth century, several scholars proposed a return to identifying the Gospels as ancient biographies. Richard Burridge's 1992 book *What Are the Gospels?* ended up being the most influential. As a result, there was a large shift in the world of New Testament scholarship so that a very large majority of scholars now think that the Gospels either belong to the genre of ancient biography or have much in common with it.[14]

There is more to the matter than recognizing the biographical nature of the Gospels. We would not assume that someone living in North America 300 years ago wore clothing like North Americans dress today. We should also not assume that the literary conventions used by ancient biographers were the same as those used by modern biographers. Even before Burridge's book, classicists had been writing on ancient biography and how it differed in some respects from modern biography. Ancient biography had different objectives and allowed more flexibility in the way the past was reported than how modern biography is generally written. A question that remained to be answered is how might this affect the way we should read the Gospels. Unfortunately, most scholars seemed

14. In 2019, the twenty-fifth anniversary edition was published by Baylor University Press and contains more than 100 new pages: Richard A. Burridge, *What Are the Gospels? A Comparison with Graeco-Roman Biography*, 25th anniversary ed. (1992; repr., Waco, TX: Baylor University Press, 2018). Ancient biography was a fluid genre. Sean Adams opines that while the Gospels participate in the genre of Greco-Roman biography, they also include "features typical of Jewish composition." See Sean A. Adams, *Greek Genres and Jewish Authors: Negotiating Literary Culture in the Greco-Roman Era* (Waco, TX: Baylor University Press, 2020), 274–75.

to accept the genre of the Gospels as biography and then move along to other matters without diving deeply into the implications of the biographical genre on our reading of the Gospels.[15] Fortunately, however, things have begun to change. Several years ago, New Testament scholar Craig Keener began research to see how the biographical nature of the Gospels plays out. Several of his doctoral students have conducted focused research in this area as well.[16] I have focused on it too.[17]

> A "classicist," also referred to as a "classical scholar," is a scholar proficient in the classics, which refers to the languages, literature, culture, and history of the ancient Greeks and Romans.

The first step I took was to make a list of all the extant biographies written within around 150 years before and after Jesus—about 300 years in all. Biographies were called "*Lives*" at that time (e.g., *Life of Cicero*, *Life of Caesar*). The English word *biography* did not come along until the seventeenth century. I began reading those biographies, starting with Plutarch's *Lives*. Many classicists regard Plutarch to be the greatest biographer in antiquity. He began writing his *Lives* at the end of the first century and continued writing them until shortly after the year AD 120. He wrote more than sixty *Lives*, forty-eight of which have survived. Nine of the forty-eight feature Roman main characters, most of whom knew one another. Those nine even participated in some of the same events. So I read through those nine *Lives* three times, making a list of all the events reported in them. Then I made a list of all the events that appear in two or more of those *Lives*. For example, the assassination of Julius Caesar is mentioned in Plutarch's *Lives* of Caesar, Cicero, Brutus, and Antony. So we can compare how Plutarch reports the same story in all

15. Helen K. Bond, *The First Biography of Jesus: Genre and Meaning in Mark's Gospel* (Grand Rapids: Eerdmans, 2020), 2–4, 35–36.

16. See Craig S. Keener and Edward T. Wright, eds. *Biographies and Jesus: What Does It Mean for the Gospels to Be Biographies?* (Lexington: Emeth, 2016); and Craig S. Keener, *Christobiography: Memory, History, and the Reliability of the Gospels* (Grand Rapids: Eerdmans, 2019).

17. Michael R. Licona, "Viewing the Gospels as Ancient Biographies Resolves Many Perceived Contradictions," in Keener and Wright, *Biographies and Jesus*, 323–28; Licona, *Why Are There Differences in the Gospels?*; Licona, "Compositional Techniques within Plutarch and the Gospel Tradition," in *Christian Origins and the Establishment of the Early Jesus Movement*, ed. Stanley E. Porter and Andrew W. Pitts, Texts and Editions for New Testament Study 12 (Boston: Brill, 2018), 134–48.

four *Lives*. This is a unique opportunity and differs from comparing how the story of Caesar's assassination is told by several different authors. By focusing on Plutarch, I could assess how the same author, very often using the same sources and writing at the same time, reported the same stories. I identified three dozen stories Plutarch told two or more times in the nine *Lives* on which I was focusing. My thinking was I could go through these stories with a fine-tooth comb and observe whether Plutarch "copied and pasted" stories. If there are differences, perhaps I could discover why they are present and see if they may shed some light on the differences in the Gospels.

I recognized that this was a substantial project and would take a lot of time. So prior to proceeding further, I wondered if someone else had already completed with Plutarch what I was planning to do. Surely a classicist had done so! I contacted my friend John Ramsey, who at the time was teaching classics at the University of Illinois in Chicago. I asked him if he was aware of anyone who had already completed such a project with Plutarch. Professor Ramsey referred me to his friend Christopher Pelling, who he said is the foremost authority on Plutarch. Pelling was teaching at Christ Church Oxford at the time and is the former tutor of Richard Burridge, mentioned earlier as the author of the game-changing *What Are the Gospels?* I contacted Professor Pelling. He informed me that a few others had conducted the type of work about which I was inquiring. However, the most comprehensive was a journal article he had written and republished in 2002 as a single chapter in his book *Plutarch and History*.[18] He added that his research involved comparing six *Lives* rather than nine. And it took only a handful of stories into consideration rather than every story that appeared more than once. Nothing had yet been completed that approached the scope of the project I was proposing.

So I embarked on my research. I placed limits on its scope to avoid going down countless rabbit trails and never completing it. I also set limits by proceeding with certain assumptions. I began with the assumption that, at minimum, the Gospels share much in common with the genre of ancient biography, since this is the position of a large majority of New Testament scholars, even evangelical New Testament scholars. The literature I had read on the subject convinced me of the Gospels' biographical genre. After all, if you were going to write about the life of an important

18. Christopher Pelling, *Plutarch and History: Eighteen Studies* (Swansea: Classical Press of Wales, 2002).

person, what genre would you use? Poetry, horror, fiction, or biography? And let's say you're a biographer in the first century, writing for readers living in the first century about a person who had lived in the first century. Would you use the literary conventions in play in the first century or those that would not come into play until more than fifteen hundred years later? The answers to these questions are obvious. While some still claim that the Gospels are a unique genre and belong in a category shared with no other literature, such a position seems odd to me. Every other bit of literature in the Bible fits into a genre that is shared with other literature outside the Bible. Why must the Gospels be the only exception, especially when they share so much in common with ancient biography?

I also assumed that many New Testament scholars over the years have been correct that the authors of the Gospels used a variety of literary devices, such as telescoping, spotlighting, and others. (I will touch on these later.) Although they rarely provided evidence to support their contention that these were standard devices used by the ancients, their proposals seemed quite plausible to me—more plausible than viewing the differences as errors or by engaging in strained harmonization efforts, especially since we use many of these devices today in ordinary communication.

I read literature written by classicists and discovered that they spoke of many of the same literary devices as New Testament scholars, along with a few additional ones. Classicist J. L. Moles commented that a number of these literary devices are "practically universal in ancient historiography."[19] Since Pelling refers to them as "compositional devices," I adopted that term. The scope of my project would be largely limited to examining stories told in two or more of Plutarch's *Lives* that featured characters who lived during the Late Roman Republic: iconic figures such as Julius Caesar, Cicero, Brutus, and Antony. I would identify differences in the details and look for occasions where compositional devices might be in play. If the majority of New Testament scholars and classicists are mistaken about the existence of these devices, then I am too, since I was standing on the shoulders of Christopher Pelling, J. L. Moles, Richard Burridge, Craig Keener, and many other highly regarded scholars when I launched into this expanded research that breaks some new ground. The entire project took around eight years.

During my research, I was quite surprised to observe how often Plutarch

19. J. L. Moles, *Plutarch: The Life of Cicero* (Eastbourne, UK: Aris and Phillips Classical Texts, 1988), 40.

appears to have used the compositional devices identified by classicists. I also read through the Gospels eight times in their original language, Greek, and made a list of all the differences I observed. I then read those stories in view of the compositional devices posited by classicists and was surprised by how often the authors of the Gospels appear to have used them. Oxford University Press published my research in 2017 in a book titled *Why Are There Differences in the Gospels? What We Can Learn from Ancient Biography*.

> Scholars refer to the authors of the Gospels as "Evangelists." The term derives from the Greek word *euangelion*, which means "Good News." To its first-century readers, the *Gospel of Matthew* meant the *Good News as Told by Matthew*. Throughout this book, I will usually refer to an author of a Gospel as *evangelist*.

RESPONSE TO MY FIRST BOOK

My book received praise from Professor Pelling, who called it "an exemplary crossover of classical and New Testament studies." Richard Bauckham called it "an illuminating fresh approach to understanding how the Gospel writers used their sources." Dale Allison referred to it as a "significant volume," while Scot McKnight said it is "the most important book I've ever read on the literary techniques of the Evangelists." All of these are highly respected scholars in their relevant fields. And the esteemed evangelical theologian and churchman J. I. Packer referred to my book as "an accomplished piece of work which it is a pleasure to commend."

However, not everyone has been impressed by the approach I took in that book. One reviewer on the theological left asserted that the book was addressed to "novices in the moderate evangelical camp," "an undergraduate (or church-attending) audience," and that it defended a form of biblical inerrancy.[20] Some on the theological right complained that what I wrote undermines the reliability of the Gospels and accused me of trying to befriend mainstream scholars.[21] But motives often prove difficult to discern. I did not write the book to appease or impress anyone, and the

20. Review by Matthew C. Baldwin in *Review of Biblical Literature*, May 17, 2018.

21. Review by Doug Potter at http://www.isca-apologetics.org/sites/default/files/papers/dpotter/Reivew%20of%20Licona_Why_Differences.pdf (page 8), plus various comments on social media platforms.

book does not address the matter of biblical inerrancy. I conducted the research to discover authentic answers. I confess to being theologically conservative. When my conclusions support theologically conservative views, it is a bonus for me. When they do not, I want to revise or expand my present views to accommodate the conclusions to which I believe my research has led.

I believe my critics are well-intentioned. It is expected that some resistance will occur when a paradigm of the Gospels is proposed that challenges one that has been firmly held for a long time. Accepting a different paradigm should not occur quickly or carelessly. Instead, a new proposal should be scrutinized carefully and assessed to see if it provides any valuable insights.

Shortly after my previous book was published, its publisher, Oxford University Press, asked me to consider writing a version that would be an easier read for nonscholars since the original volume was written for scholars and advanced students. Consequently, the original volume approaches the topic with an attempt to be neutral pertaining to theological matters that are beyond what can be historically assessed, such as whether the Gospels are divinely inspired and free of errors. At first, I declined the idea of writing the less academic version because I had already embarked on my next research project, the historical reliability of the Gospels. However, I began to receive comments from laypeople in the church, even highly educated ones, asking for a more easily understood presentation that also addresses how my proposals fit with the doctrines of divine inspiration and inerrancy. But it was not until I had lectured on Gospel differences to several groups of Christians in Southeast Asia and they too requested an easier-to-understand version that I decided to place my current research project on hold to write this book.

Therefore, the present volume you are reading is written primarily for Christians with a high view of Scripture (i.e., Scripture is divinely inspired and authoritative) and are not necessarily interested in dry academic writing. This book provides fewer examples and devotes more time to explaining items with which classicists, New Testament scholars, and advanced students are already familiar. Six years have passed since the publication of my previous book on Gospel differences. Further research and reflection during those years have led me to fine-tune and expand on some of what I wrote in that book. These updates are included in this book.

The approach I am proposing in this book is not a Rosetta Stone for understanding all Gospel differences. But in this book and in the academic version that preceded it, I propose that many items in the Gospels become clearer when the Gospels are read through a lens that has first-century literary conventions in view. If I am mistaken on some of the explanations I propose in this book, the general proposal can still be correct. You be the judge.

I have taught the contents of this book to graduate students and to thousands of others in conferences and in churches all over the world. Since the responses have been virtually the same regardless of audience and location, I'm venturing to guess they will be similar for readers of this book. For some of you, what you are about to read will immediately turn on a welcomed light that illuminates the Gospels for you as never before! For others, reading this book will be like a roller coaster ride. It will be scary at times and make you uncomfortable, because this book will challenge the way you presently view the Gospels and the Bible. You may even get the impression that the foundation of your faith is being shaken when, in reality, it is *your view of Scripture* that is being challenged. But there will also be times when, like the other readers, what you read illuminates the Gospels for you and you enjoy the ride. No matter who you are, this book will probably change the way you read the Gospels going forward. After reading my earlier book on Gospel differences, some of my students have told me that when they read the Gospels now, it is like reading them for the first time . . . again!

When we observe how the Gospels tell the same story, there are differences. But why are they there, and what do they mean for Bible readers? The purpose of this book is to answer these questions! And you will reap three key rewards from reading it:

1. You will obtain a fresh confidence in the reliability of the Gospels.
2. You will discover new insights in Scripture, both theological and historical.
3. You will develop a refined view of the nature of Scripture.

SUMMARY

The Gospels report what Jesus said and did, often in a manner that has some of the minor details appearing to be at odds with one another. Even ancient church leaders acknowledged this. However, the way they explained the differences differed. And this has been the case from antiquity to the present day. However, we should keep in mind that some errors in minor details do not discredit the general reliability of an account, just as discrepancies in the testimonies of survivors of the *Titanic* do not negate the general reliability of their accounts that the *Titanic* sank. We observed that attempts to harmonize differing accounts is a popular approach, but it can sometimes go too far. I am proposing another approach in this book that can shed light on why there are differences in the Gospels.

QUESTIONS FOR FURTHER THOUGHT (TRY SAYING THAT THREE TIMES RAPIDLY!)

1. Were you aware of differences in the Gospels before now? If so, describe a time when you became or were made aware of a difference between the Gospels and what your thoughts about it were at the time.
2. Does the presence of differences in the Gospels trouble you now? If so, why? If not, why not?
3. Is there a particular Gospel difference that has especially troubled you?
4. Have you witnessed someone trying to resolve a difference in the Gospels that went too far? If so, what impression did that leave on you?

CHAPTER 2

NORMAL VARIATION IN REPORTING AND THE USE OF SOURCES

Imagine that you and three of your colleagues are eating in a restaurant. A couple at the table next to you begins arguing with one another. Over the course of ten minutes, the argument intensifies to a point that the couple begins screaming at one another. The woman then picks up a wine bottle and breaks it on the man's face, creating a huge gash. Paramedics and police arrive shortly thereafter. As the paramedics tend to the man's wound, a police officer handcuffs the woman while her partner asks you and your three colleagues to write your accounts of what happened. He asks that all of you include the words uttered by the couple as best as you can remember. He also asks that each of you write them without consulting with the other three. That way, there will be four independent accounts.

Since all four of you are eyewitnesses and are writing within only a few minutes of the event, the details will be fresh for recall. Imagine how each of those accounts would be similar and how they would differ. The general thoughts would likely be the same; however, each of you would word your account differently. And some of you would mention details overlooked by the others.

When the police officer gathers all four of your accounts and reads them, he will notice the similarities and the differences. He recognizes that the differences fall within the *normal range of variation* typically present when several eyewitnesses provide independent testimony of how they remember the event. Despite the differences, the officer will be able to write a single account of what had transpired that includes most, if not all, of the details. This is known as "harmonizing the accounts."

Normal variation in reporting is present in the Gospels. For example, take some time right now before proceeding further and read carefully through the accounts of Jesus before the Roman governor Pontius Pilate in all four Gospels (Mark 15:1–15 // Matt. 27:1–26 // Luke 23:1–25 // John 18:28–40).[1] The story is the same, and on a very few occasions you will observe a phrase or two where the wording is very similar. For the most part, however, the wording differs to an extent we may expect if four people were independently describing the same event. You will likewise observe that one of the Gospels may report an item overlooked by the others. For example, Luke is the only Gospel to report Pilate sending Jesus to Herod.

Let's now modify our restaurant story. All is the same until after the police officer collects your four accounts. While reading them, he observes verbatim agreement, or nearly so, in the words all four of you used to recall the event and what was said. What do you suppose the police officer would think? Would he recognize that the striking similarities are akin to those normally present when multiple eyewitnesses provide testimony?[2] Or would he suspect the four of you had collaborated?

Another detail must be considered: *the couple was arguing in Spanish.* Fortunately, you and your colleagues are all fluent in Spanish! However, the officer is not. So he asks all of you to recall the event and summarize the conversation *in English.* Now everyone who has some training in another language understands that translation is not a precise science. Languages have differing grammatical structures, and some words have no exact equivalents in other languages. Because of these factors, how a person translates a paragraph today will likely differ somewhat from how they would translate the same paragraph tomorrow. What if the police officer found that all four of your *translated accounts* of the quarreling couple's conversation were almost verbatim? He would not think that the striking similarities between your accounts are akin to those normally present when several eyewitnesses provide independent testimony that had been translated. He would be justified in concluding that the four of you had collaborated to a large extent. He may even suspect that some of you had copied from the other.

---

1. Since a very large consensus of New Testament scholars think Mark's Gospel was written first, I have followed the standard practice of listing Mark prior to Matthew. We will discuss the order of composition in chapter 3.

2. One would not be surprised to observe verbatim agreement in pithy expressions such as "I hate you!" or "You betrayed me!" These differ from longer statements.

Now let's go even further and say that the four of you are brought in by a cold case detective twenty years later. The detective informs you that the man had died as a result of the injury sustained by the wine bottle broken on his face. The detective places the four of you in a room together and asks each of you to do your best to write down *in English* what you remember of the couple's actions and their words, which had occurred in Spanish twenty years earlier. Upon reading your reports, the detective would be certain that collaboration had occurred if near-verbatim similarities persisted in your translated accounts after such a long time.

We have something similar when we compare how Matthew, Mark, and Luke narrate the same story: three authors are narrating the same events and conversations, the large majority of the words being originally spoken in Aramaic but recorded in Greek decades later, and often verbatim with one another, nearly so, or enough to suggest there is some sort of relationship between them. For these reasons and others, New Testament scholars recognize that a *relationship* exists between Matthew, Mark, and Luke. How they are related is a perplexing puzzle, which scholars refer to as the "Synoptic problem." Let's now move beyond this illustration and look at some specific examples in the Synoptic Gospels (i.e., Matthew, Mark, Luke) that strongly suggest that a relationship exists between them.

THREE MAJOR OBSERVATIONS THAT SUGGEST A RELATIONSHIP EXISTS BETWEEN THE SYNOPTIC GOSPELS

For several reasons, nearly every New Testament scholar today thinks there is some relationship between Matthew, Mark, and Luke. In what follows, I provide the three most common reasons they provide for holding this position.

1. Verbal Agreement

As we just discussed, when a number of people independently report the same item, we will observe them using different wording. However, this degree of variance is not what we often observe when Matthew, Mark, and Luke are reporting the same item. Instead, we can observe chunks of text that are nearly verbatim. Therefore, it is not the differences but rather the striking similarities of the wording in the Gospels that often grab a reader's attention. Let's look at a few examples.

MEN OF NINEVEH AND QUEEN OF THE SOUTH (Matt. 12:41–42 // Luke 11:31–32)

Matthew 12:41–42	Luke 11:31–32
The men of Nineveh will stand up with this generation at the judgment and condemn it because they repented at the preaching of Jonah; and behold, something greater than Jonah is here. The Queen of the South will rise up with this generation at the judgment and condemn it, because she came from the ends of the earth to hear the wisdom of Solomon; and behold, something greater than Solomon is here.	The Queen of the South will rise up with the men of this generation at the judgment and condemn them, because she came from the ends of the earth to hear the wisdom of Solomon; and behold, something greater than Solomon is here. The men of Nineveh will stand up with this generation at the judgment and condemn it because they repented at the preaching of Jonah; and behold, something greater than Jonah is here.

The main difference between how Matthew and Luke report this saying is the order. Matthew places the men of Nineveh first, followed by the Queen of the South, whereas Luke presents them in the opposite order. Watch what happens when we flip the order in Luke.

Matthew 12:41–42	Luke 11:31–32 (in reverse order)
The men of Nineveh will stand up with this generation at the judgment and condemn it because they repented at the preaching of Jonah; and behold, something greater than Jonah is here. The Queen of the South will rise up with this generation at the judgment and condemn it, because she came from the ends of the earth to hear the wisdom of Solomon; and behold, something greater than Solomon is here.	The men of Nineveh will stand up with this generation at the judgment and condemn it because they repented at the preaching of Jonah; and behold, something greater than Jonah is here. The Queen of the South will rise up with the men of this generation at the judgment and condemn them, because she came from the ends of the earth to hear the wisdom of Solomon; and behold, something greater than Solomon is here.

Matthew and Luke provide a verbatim recollection of Jesus's words with only two exceptions. Matthew has "this generation," whereas Luke has "the men of this generation." And Matthew uses the pronoun *it* when referring to "this generation," whereas Luke uses the pronoun *them* to refer to "the men of this generation."

We observe another example of virtually verbatim reporting with the words of John the Baptist:

Matthew 3:7-10	**Luke 3:7-9**
Brood of vipers! Who warned you to flee from the coming wrath? Therefore, produce fruit worthy [singular] of repentance. And do not think to say to yourselves, "We have Abraham as our father." For I say to you that God is able from these stones to raise up children for Abraham. And now the axe is laid at the root of the trees. Therefore, every tree not producing good fruit is cut down and thrown into the fire.	Brood of vipers! Who warned you to flee from the coming wrath? Therefore, produce fruit worthy [plural] of repentance. And do not begin to say to yourselves, "We have Abraham as our father." For I say to you that God is able from these stones to raise up children for Abraham. And even now the axe is laid at the root of the trees. Therefore, every tree not producing good fruit is cut down and thrown into the fire.

Only three minor differences stand in the way of verbatim recollection. First, Matthew speaks of "fruit worthy" in the singular, whereas Luke uses the plural. Unfortunately, English readers cannot see this, since the English word *fruit* can refer to a piece of fruit or multiple pieces. Second, Matthew uses the term *think*, whereas Luke uses *begin*. And third, Luke includes the word *even*, which is absent in Matthew. Since Jesus and John the Baptist are speaking to Jewish leaders, the conversations were almost certainly in Aramaic, while Matthew and Luke have reported them decades later in Greek.

Which seems more probable in these two examples? (1) Matthew and Luke independently report testimony remembered by or relayed to them decades later. Either they or their sources translated the stories into Greek and, by mere coincidence, this resulted in the reports being virtually verbatim. Or (2) either Matthew and Luke are drawing on the same source, or one of them is using the other as a source. The answer is obvious. The normal variations present when the same event is recalled by multiple eyewitnesses almost never yield this degree of verbal agreement. Because the events and translated words of Jesus are being recalled by the authors of the Gospels or their sources decades later, we are almost assuredly not reading independent recollections.

2. Puzzling Verbal Agreement

Matthew, Mark, and Luke report John the Baptist saying, "A voice of one crying in the wilderness, 'Prepare the way of the Lord! Make his paths straight!'" (Mark 1:3 // Matt. 3:3 // Luke 3:4). The Baptist is quoting Isaiah 40:3, and Matthew, Mark, and Luke report it with the exact words. What makes this of particular interest is the last statement, "Make his paths straight," because it differs from the way it is reported in both the Hebrew and Greek texts of the Old Testament.

> **Hebrew:** "Make straight in the desert a highway for our God" (NIV).
> **Greek (LXX):** "Make straight the paths of our God."

It is possible that Matthew, Mark, and Luke were using another Greek text of which we are unaware. But it is also possible that one of the Gospels rendered the text as "Make his paths straight" and the other two used that Gospel as their source for the story.

> The ancient Greek translation of the Old Testament is called the Septuagint. Legend states that seventy scholars served as translators, and for this reason, the Septuagint is often represented by the Roman numeral LXX.

This raises some interesting questions. Which is the divinely inspired text of Isaiah: the Hebrew version, the LXX version, the one found in the Gospels, or all three? The authors of the Gospels provide a different text than what we observe in the Old Testament. How might this inform us in discussions concerning the best English translations? Does this suggest that God is most often more concerned with the message behind the words than with the specific words used, as Augustine suggested?[3]

3. Parenthetical Comments

In our everyday conversations, we sometimes interrupt one thought with another and then return to the original thought. Let's say that I tell my students the following: "Today, we are going to discuss Gospel differences and—pay attention because there's going to be a quiz on this—the use of compositional devices by ancient historians." I begin my sentence, which is interrupted by another thought, and then I return to the original one. Now if my students were having a discussion later about what was discussed in class that day, some may make mention of my alerting them of a forthcoming quiz on the covered material. However, it is unlikely

---

3. Augustine, *Serm.* 21.13.

that any of them would include the portion about a quiz precisely in the awkward location where I had said it.

What if we were to observe a parenthetical statement in the same awkward location appearing in more than one Gospel? This occurs in several locations. During his final week, Jesus and his disciples were in Jerusalem. One day, as they were leaving the temple, his disciples commented on the beauty of the temple complex. Jesus replied that a day was coming when the temple would be destroyed and not one of its stones would be left upon another. Later that day, they were on the Mount of Olives and his disciples asked when this would occur. Jesus answered with what is called the Olivet Discourse (Mark 13:14 // Matt. 24:15–16). He tells the disciples that false messiahs will come and mislead many. There will be wars and rumors of wars. There will be earthquakes and famines. Jesus's followers will be persecuted. Then Jesus says the following:

> But when you see the abomination of desolation standing where he ought not to be (let the reader understand), then let those who are in Judea flee to the mountains. (Mark 13:14)

Of particular interest is the clause "let the reader understand." What does it mean, and why is it there? A very large majority of people in antiquity were illiterate, and many of those who were literate could not afford to purchase books. So it was standard practice in the early church for someone to read Scripture during a worship service. The clause "let the reader understand" appears in an awkward position in this text, interrupting the flow and thought. Mark probably included that note for the reader of his Gospel, perhaps to suggest that the reader could pause and expound on the relevant prophetic text in Daniel (Dan. 11:31).[4]

Matthew also includes this clause in precisely the same location in the Olivet Discourse:

4. A different way of understanding the parenthetical statement is that Jesus was telling his disciples to read the text in Daniel for greater understanding pertaining to this being a fulfillment of prophecy. However, this would not have made much sense if most of the disciples were illiterate, as most scholars think. In either sense, the point being made still stands: the same awkward location of the parenthetical statement in both Matthew and Mark is a much cleaner fit with there being a *literary relationship* between Matthew and Mark than with an appeal to normal variation in eyewitness reporting.

> So when you see the abomination of desolation spoken of by the prophet Daniel, standing in the holy place (let the reader understand), then let those who are in Judea flee to the mountains. (Matt. 24:15–16)[5]

It would be quite a coincidence if Matthew and Mark had, independently, placed the same note in their texts at precisely the same awkward position in the sentence. It is more likely that either Matthew or Mark was using the other Gospel as its source at this point or both made use of another source we no longer have. The comment "let the *reader* understand" suggests the source was a document rather than oral tradition. Thus, we have evidence that a literary relationship existed at times between some of the Gospels. There are additional examples of two or three of the Gospels containing the same parenthetical comment.[6]

That a relationship exists between Matthew, Mark, and Luke is acknowledged by virtually all New Testament scholars. Being able to determine the nature of that relationship is far more challenging. Did Matthew use Mark, or did Mark use Matthew? Did Matthew and Luke use an earlier draft of Mark? Did Luke use Matthew or vice versa, or did both use a common source we no longer have? Scholars disagree about how best to answer these questions. Even the present majority position does not adequately account for everything we observe.

I stated previously that the matter of the nature of the relationship between Matthew, Mark, and Luke is a puzzle that scholars refer to as the "Synoptic problem." The term *synoptic* derives from two Greek words: *syn* meaning "with" and *opsis* meaning "to see or view." Therefore, *synopsis* means "to view together." In the field of New Testament studies, scholars and graduate students make use of a book called *Synopsis of the Four Gospels*.[7] This book includes every story in the four Gospels, which is quite helpful where two or more Gospels report the same event because it lays out each version of the story in parallel columns, line by line, enabling readers to make clear comparisons. As readers comb through several

---

5. Luke does not include the parenthetical comment but reports the gist of what we read in Mark and Matthew (Luke 21:20–21).

6. For additional examples, see the story of Jesus healing a paralytic (Matt. 9:6 // Mark 2:10–11 // Luke 5:24), the story of Jesus casting out demons (Mark 5:1–8 // Luke 8:26–29), the description of Judas Iscariot as being one of the Twelve (Matt. 26:14 // Mark 14:10 // Luke 22:3), and the statement of why the Jews had handed Jesus over to Pilate (Matt. 27:15–18 // Mark 15:6–10).

7. Kurt Aland, ed., *Synopsis of the Four Gospels*, 15th ed. (Stuttgart: German Bible Society, 2013).

stories in a synopsis, they observe that Matthew, Mark, and Luke report their stories in a manner that is often strikingly similar to one another, while John's account is often worded much differently. Due to their similarities, the Gospels of Matthew, Mark, and Luke are called the *Synoptic Gospels* (or simply the *Synoptics*).

WHY THIS IS IMPORTANT

Prior to reading this chapter, many of you may have thought the authors of our four Gospels were writing entirely independent of one another. The differences we observe in the Gospels are often the kind and degree of variation we would expect to see if this had occurred. However, spending even a modest amount of time perusing a *Synopsis of the Four Gospels* will reveal that, more often than not, something is going on other than the normal variation found among multiple independent reports of the same event. This observation is important because, as we will discover, the matter of why there are so many close similarities in the Synoptic Gospels is one of the keys to answering the matter of their differences. And the first step to solving this puzzle is to determine which Gospel was written first.[8] This will be the subject of the next chapter.

There is another takeaway. Most Christians believe the Bible is God's divinely inspired Word. The Bible tells us very little about what it means to be divinely inspired or the process(es) involved for something to be regarded as "Scripture." We will examine these matters in later chapters. For now, we have learned that whatever ideas we may have about how we came to have God's Word, it involved the Evangelists (i.e., the authors of the Gospels) using other sources. So divine inspiration was not a matter of the authors listening carefully to the voice of God audibly dictating what to write.

SUMMARY

In this chapter, we saw that the manner in which the Gospels report the same event sometimes reflects the normal variation present when multiple

8. There is more to the Synoptic problem than will be discussed in this book. Our only concerns here will be to show that a relationship between the Synoptic Gospels exists and to ascertain which Gospel was probably composed first. For those interested in pursuing the Synoptic problem further, I recommend the following two introductory books: Mark Goodacre, *The Synoptic Problem: A Way through the Maze* (New York: Continuum, 2001); Robert H. Stein, *Studying the Synoptic Gospels: Origin and Interpretation*, 2nd ed. (Grand Rapids: Baker Academic, 2001).

eyewitnesses report that event. That said, we have given attention to three observations that, when taken together, suggest it is highly likely that a relationship exists between the Synoptic Gospels: verbal agreement, puzzling verbal agreement, and parenthetical comments. Although the Synoptic Gospels likely made use of some common oral traditions, they also likely made use of the same written source(s). Our view of divinely inspired Scripture should include the understanding that the Evangelists used sources rather than transcribed what was divinely dictated to them. What were those source(s), and what is the nature of the relationship among the Gospels? This puzzling matter is referred to as the "Synoptic problem."

QUESTIONS FOR FURTHER THOUGHT

1. God has the ability to give us the Gospels without their authors using sources. However, he did not choose to go that route. Prior to reading this chapter, were you aware that there is a literary relationship between the Synoptic Gospels? If not, how did you view them?
2. The authors of the Gospels often quote from the ancient Greek translation of the Old Testament (LXX), which many times differs in its wording from the corresponding Hebrew text. How does this inform your view of the divine inspiration of Scripture?
3. In some of today's Christian communities, there are disputes over English translations of the Bible. For example, some contend that the King James Version is the only legitimate English translation. In the first century, the LXX was the (relatively speaking) modern Greek translation of the Hebrew Old Testament. When we consider that the LXX often differs from the Hebrew text, it appears that the writers of the New Testament literature did not quibble over the differences between the original Hebrew and its Greek translation. What implications might this have pertaining to viewing modern English translations?

CHAPTER 3

WHO WROTE FIRST?

In our New Testaments, the Gospels appear in the order of Matthew, Mark, Luke, and John. Although we do not know why this particular order has come down to us, it is probably because several leaders in the early church believed it is the order the Gospels were composed. However, this belief was not unanimous. In what follows, we will look at the two major positions of which Gospel was written first.

MATTHEW (AKA MATTHEAN PRIORITY)

Today there are two major arguments offered to contend that Matthew was the first Gospel composed.

Argument 1

The first is the observation just mentioned: some of the early church fathers believed Matthew wrote first. Irenaeus (writing ca. AD 174–189) lists the order of composition as Matthew, then Mark and Luke (although he does not specify that Mark preceded Luke), and then John.[1] Clement of Alexandria (ca. AD 198–203) says the first Gospels written were those that include genealogies: Matthew and Luke. But he does not specify which of the two was written first. These were followed by Mark then John.[2] Tertullian (ca. AD 200–220) says John and Matthew were written first (though he does not specify that John preceded Matthew and lists them in the opposite order elsewhere). These were followed by Luke and Mark.[3] A little later, he states that Matthew, John, and perhaps

1. Irenaeus, *Haer.* (*Against Heresies*) 3.1.1.

2. Clement of Alexandria in Eusebius, *Hist. eccl.* (*Ecclesiastical History*) 6.14.5–7. Both Clement and Irenaeus before him are not as clear as one would like pertaining to the order of composition. However, they both seem to suggest that John was written after the others. The language they use related to John may also suggest, though in a weaker sense, that the order they mention the previous Gospels is the order of their composition.

3. Tertullian, *Marc.* (*Against Marcion*) 4.2 (see also 4.5). Daniel Wallace has presented a case

Mark were written prior to Luke.[4] Thus, Tertullian's order is John and Matthew, then Mark and Luke. Origen (ca. AD 244–249) and Augustine (ca. AD 400–405) specify the order of composition as Matthew, Mark, Luke, and John.[5]

Augustine also appears to be our first source to recognize the existence of a relationship between some of the Gospels. He asserts that the authors of the Gospels were not ignorant of one another's work and that Mark follows Matthew's Gospel closely and summarizes him.[6] The Anti-Marcionite Prologue to Luke[7] states that Matthew and Mark were composed first, although it does not specify that Matthew preceded Mark. These were followed by Luke then by John. And Jerome says Matthew was the first and John the last of the four Gospels to be composed.[8]

Of the seven earliest sources who mention the order the Gospels were composed, four state clearly that Matthew appeared first—Irenaeus, Origen, Augustine, and Jerome—while three do not take a firm position. Clement of Alexandria said it could be Matthew or Luke. Tertullian said it could be Matthew or John. And the Anti-Marcionite Prologue to Luke said it could be Matthew or Mark. And all but Tertullian locate John as the final of the four Gospels to be composed.

Notably, several early church fathers, including the four who clearly said Matthew was written first, reported that Matthew composed his Gospel *in Hebrew*: Papias (who says the *Hebrew dialect*, perhaps referring to Aramaic), Irenaeus, Clement of Alexandria, Origen, Eusebius, Ephrem the Syrian, Jerome, Chrysostom, and Augustine.[9] The oldest version of a

---

that John wrote his Gospel prior to the destruction of the temple in Jerusalem in AD 70 (Daniel B. Wallace, "John 5,2 and the Date of the Fourth Gospel," *Biblica* 71 [1990]: 177–205). While compatible with Tertullian's view that John and Matthew wrote prior to Mark and Luke, Wallace does not require that John wrote first. Moreover, the matter of a relationship between the Gospels primarily involves the Synoptics. There is no consensus among scholars pertaining to whether John was aware of the Synoptic Gospels. Many think John did not make use of them, even if he knew of them.

4. Tertullian, *Marc.* 4.5.

5. Origen cited in Eusebius, *Hist. eccl.* 6.25.4–6; Augustine, *Cons.* 1.2.3.

6. Augustine, *Cons.* 1.2.4; 1.3.6.

7. The date of composition for the Anti-Marcionite Prologues is uncertain. Some date them ca. AD 160–180 while others prefer sometime after the mid-fourth century.

8. Jerome, *Ad Damascus* (AD 383); *De viris illustribus* 9 (AD 392–393).

9. Papias, *Fragments of Papias*, 3:16, Holmes numbering, AD 100–150; Irenaeus, *Adv. Haer.*, 3.1, AD 174–189; Clement of Alexandria (preserved by Eusebius in *Hist. eccl.* 3.24.6); Origen, *Commentary on Matthew*, book 1 (this work is no longer extant but is preserved by Eusebius in *Hist. eccl.* 6.25.3–4.); Eusebius, *Hist. eccl.* 5.10.3, AD 324; Ephrem the Syrian, *Commentary on Tatian's Diatessaron*, ca. AD 330–373 (see *Saint Ephrem's Commentary on Tatian's Diatessaron: An English Translation of Chester Beatty Syriac MS 709 with Introduction and Notes* by Carmel McCarthy, Journal

so-called Gospel of Matthew in Hebrew appeared in the anti-Christian treatise *Eben Bohan* (*The Touchstone*) by the Jewish Rabbi Shem Tov ben Isaac ben Shaprut, composed with revisions in the late fourteenth century. It contends that Jesus is neither God nor Messiah. Today it is known as *Shem Tov's Hebrew Gospel of Matthew*.[10] However, this manuscript is very late, and most scholars remain unconvinced that it represents the Hebrew Gospel of Matthew mentioned by the church fathers.

The view that Matthew's Gospel was composed first is beset by three major challenges. First, there are reasons to think that the Gospel of Matthew in our New Testament was originally written in Greek. Virtually all manuscripts of Matthew are written in Greek, certainly the best ones are. The first to claim Matthew wrote in Hebrew is Papias. Unfortunately, ambiguities in Papias's words have led to numerous ways of interpreting them. Papias states that Matthew wrote his Gospel in the *Hebrew dialect*.[11] Scholars have offered a number of explanations for what this means. Some interpret Papias to be referring to the Hebrew language, while others have in mind the language of the Hebrews, which was primarily Aramaic at that time. Robert Gundry suggests Papias is referring to Matthew's presentation of Jesus as Messiah in a Hebrew manner, which accords with Matthew being thought by many as the most Jewish of the Gospels.[12] Moreover, Papias's statement pertaining to his source is not clear. More on this shortly. Crawling through the weeds here, although interesting to some of us New Testament geeks, would take us off on a rabbit trail that is unnecessary for addressing the question I am seeking to answer in this book: *Why do differences in the Gospels exist?* What can be stated here is that Matthew may have written a Gospel in Hebrew prior to Mark as several church fathers asserted. If he did, that Hebrew Gospel has very likely been lost and was at least somewhat different from the Gospel of Matthew in the New Testament.[13]

---

of Semitic Studies Supplement 2 [Oxford: Oxford University Press on behalf of the University of Manchester, 1993]); Jerome, *Ad Damascus*, AD 383, and *De viris illustr.* 3, 36, AD 392–93 (in *De viris illustr.* 3, Jerome claims that the Hebrew Gospel of Matthew was preserved in the library at Caesarea); Chrysostom, *Hom. Matt.* 1:3, ca. AD 390; and Augustine, *Cons.* 1.2.4.

10. Several English translations with commentary exist. The earliest is George Howard, *The Gospel of Matthew according to a Primitive Hebrew Text* (Macon, GA: Mercer University Press, 1987). It is now available to view online at https://archive.org/details/Hebrew.Gospel.of.MatthewEvenBohanIbn.ShaprutHoward.1987/mode/2up.

11. Gk. *hebraidi dialektō*.

12. Robert H. Gundry, *Matthew: A Commentary on His Handbook for a Mixed Church under Persecution*, 2nd ed. (Grand Rapids: Eerdmans, 1994), 619–20.

13. James Edwards has provided what is to my knowledge the most extensive treatment

Second, the report of the earliest and most important source pertaining to the authorship of Matthew and Mark creates a strong tension with the position that the Gospel of Matthew in the New Testament predates Mark's Gospel. This is a much stronger challenge than the first and will require some explanation. The earliest source that mentions the traditional authorship of any of the Gospels is Papias, who wrote sometime between the late AD 90s and 150. Most of today's scholars locate his writing at ca. AD 130, although some are persuaded that Papias wrote a little earlier, perhaps AD 100–110.[14] As with much of ancient literature, Papias's writings have been lost. Fortunately, portions of them have been preserved in the writings of other ancient authors who quoted from them. The collection of these quotes is referred to as the *Fragments of Papias*.

Some of the fragments are preserved in the writings of the first church historian, Eusebius (ca. AD 324), who quotes Papias and interprets him as saying he is reporting what he had heard from those who had been close associates of Jesus's disciples, even while some of those disciples were alive and teaching.[15] If true, this means that Papias received information from these valuable sources sometime in the latter part of the first century. However, Eusebius may be mistaken when he interprets Papias to be saying he heard these things from close associates of the apostles. The text could easily mean that Papias heard from *both* the apostles *and* their associates.[16] This would agree with Irenaeus, who wrote about 135 years before Eusebius and claimed that Papias had been "a hearer of John" (i.e., Papias had heard John speak, perhaps even being a disciple of John).[17]

---

pertaining to a Hebrew Gospel of Matthew. It is an impressive work that includes every reference in antiquity to the Hebrew Gospel of Matthew. Although I think he occasionally pushes some related matters further than the evidence justifies, the volume remains quite valuable. For example, Edwards convincingly argues that the Hebrew Gospel of Matthew was known to many early church fathers, that it was probably not a translation of our Greek Gospel of Matthew (and vice versa), and that it was quite lengthy, perhaps nearing the length of our Greek Gospel of Matthew. See James R. Edwards, *The Hebrew Gospel and the Development of the Synoptic Tradition* (Grand Rapids: Eerdmans, 2009).

14. Robert W. Yarbrough, "The Date of Papias: A Reassessment," in *Journal of the Evangelical Theological Society* 26, no. 2 (June 1983): 181–91, https://www.etsjets.org/files/JETS-PDFs/26/26-2/26-2-pp181-191_JETS.pdf. See also Richard Bauckham, *The Christian World around the New Testament* (Grand Rapids: Baker Academic, 2017), 143n2.

15. Papias, *Frag.* 3.3–4, in Eusebius, *Hist. eccl.* 3.39.3–4.

16. Papias's words are ambiguous enough in several cases that many scholars have debated how to understand him properly. At present, I lean toward interpreting Papias as claiming that he received information directly from some of the apostles. However, I have changed my mind on the matter several times over the years!

17. Henry George Liddell et al., *Greek-English Lexicon* (Oxford: Clarendon, 1996), 53. Craig A. Evans writes, "We should not accept Eusebius' version of the Elder/Papias tradition over Irenaeus,

John S. Kloppenborg Verbin regards Papias's statement about a Hebrew Matthew as "legendary at best."[18] However, good cases have been made that this statement of Papias and others he made are more reliable than some scholars are willing to grant.[19]

Scholars debate on when Papias composed his work, whether he received information directly from one or more of the apostles or from those who knew them, whether the apostle he had in mind was John the son of Zebedee or a minor disciple also named John who had traveled with Jesus, and what Papias meant by stating Matthew had written in the Hebrew dialect. However, one matter is clear: Papias reports that Mark wrote what he remembered Peter saying Jesus had said and done:

> And the elder used to say this: "Mark, having become Peter's interpreter, wrote down accurately everything he remembered, though not in order, of the things either said or done by Christ. For he neither heard the Lord nor followed him, but afterward, as I said, followed Peter, who prepared his teachings as *chreiai*[20] but had no intention of giving an ordered account

---

the older witness." Craig A. Evans, *Jesus and the Manuscripts: What We Can Learn from the Oldest Texts* (Peabody, MA: Hendrickson Academic, 2020), 5. Evans provides additional reasons for rejecting Eusebius's interpretation of Papias (5–6). In contrast, Stephen Carlson provides reasons for preferring Eusebius' interpretation of Papias over that of Irenaeus. See Stephen C. Carlson, *Papias of Hierapolis* Exposition of Dominical Oracles*: The Fragments, Testimonia, and Reception of a Second-Century Commentator* (Oxford: Oxford University Press, 2021), 33–34.

In his earlier written *Chronicle*, Eusebius had a positive view of Papias and even regarded him as a hearer of John. See Carlson, *Papias of Hierapolis* Exposition of Dominical Oracles, 33. But that view had changed by the time he wrote *Church History* in which he says Papias did not know John but rather had received information from friends of the apostles. He also says Papias was a man of "very little intelligence" (*Church History* 3.39), an insult that was likely motivated from Eusebius's holding an eschatological view that differed from Papias's. It is common for modern critics of Papias to appeal to his rendition of the death of Judas, which is reported by Apollinaris of Laodicea (4th cent.). However, Carlson convincingly argues that much of the relevant content in this text of Apollinaris originates with his fourth-century sources rather than from Papias (40–56).

18. John S. Kloppenborg Verbin, *Excavating Q: The History and Setting of the Sayings Gospel* (Minneapolis: Fortress, 2000), 72–80.

19. See Richard Bauckham, *Jesus and the Eyewitnesses: The Gospels as Eyewitness Testimony*, 2nd ed. (Grand Rapids: Eerdmans, 2017), 12–38; Bauckham, *The Christian World around the New Testament*, 143–64; Stephen C. Carlson, Papias of Hierapolis Exposition of Dominical Oracles, 15–109; Craig A. Evans, *Jesus and the Manuscripts*, 2–11; Charles E. Hill, "The Fragments of Papias" in *The Writings of the Apostolic Fathers*, Paul Foster, ed. (New York: T&T Clark, 2007), 42–51.

20. "Who prepared his teachings as *chreiai*" can just as easily be translated as "who adapted his teachings as needed." *Chreiai* are short sayings and anecdotes useful for teaching others, such as the

of the Lord's sayings. Consequently Mark did nothing wrong in writing down some things as he remembered them, for he made it his one concern not to omit anything that he heard or to make any false statement in them."[21]

Papias is our earliest and best source pertaining to the authorship of the Gospels. If Papias is correct that Mark wrote what he remembered Peter saying about Jesus, then Mark was not using Matthew as his primary source. This creates a serious tension with those reports that Matthew wrote in Hebrew, *if those reports are referring to the Gospel of Matthew in the New Testament*. Here is the problem: if our present version of Matthew is a later Greek translation of an earlier Hebrew version, the striking verbal similarities that frequently occur between Matthew and Mark would require that Mark made substantial use of Matthew.[22] But Papias asserts that Mark wrote what he remembered Peter saying. Therefore, the position that Matthew's Gospel was written first and that Mark made use of it stands against Papias's report, our earliest by far, that Peter, not Matthew, was Mark's primary source for his Gospel.

Of course, this only holds if it is being claimed that our Greek Gospel of Matthew is a translation of the Hebrew Gospel of Matthew. If they are the same Gospel and Matthew wrote first, then Mark used Matthew as his primary source and Papias is mistaken when he claimed Mark wrote what he remembered Peter saying. However, Matthew could have written two Gospels, the first in Hebrew, which has been lost, and then an entirely new Gospel in Greek, which is contained in the New Testament. If a Hebrew Gospel of Matthew existed, it has probably and unfortunately been lost. For our present task, we can only consider the Gospel of Matthew in the New Testament, which was composed in Greek.[23]

---

story of Jesus being asked whether to pay the poll tax: "Pay to Caesar the things that are Caesar's and to God the things that are God's" (Matt. 22:21). *Chreiai* appear in abundance in the Gospels.

21. Papias, *Frag.* 3:15. Eusebius said Clement of Alexandria reported in the sixth book of the *Hypotyposes*, which has since been lost, that at the consistent requests of some believers, Mark provided a written record of Peter's teachings and that Peter endorsed the work (Eusebius, *Hist. eccl.* 2.15). Although this report should not be ignored, reports by Clement of Alexandria (not to be confused with the earlier Clement of Rome) must be assessed with caution since he is one of the most unreliable early church fathers.

22. This is the view of Augustine, who claimed that Mark summarized Matthew's Hebrew Gospel (Augustine, *Cons.* 1.2.4).

23. Some have posited that we may accept Papias's claim about Mark writing what he remembered Peter saying and reject his claim pertaining to Matthew being written in Hebrew. I am not inclined to reject what Papias says about Matthew, especially when so many church fathers believed that Matthew wrote his Hebrew Gospel first. Some have gone so far as to assert both claims of

The third major challenge to the claim that Matthew was written first is evidence that Mark wrote first and (our present version of) Matthew used Mark as his primary source. We will examine this evidence shortly.

Argument 2

A second argument for Matthean Priority appeals to *redundancies in Mark*. The scenario has Matthew composing his Gospel first, Luke using Matthew as a source, and then Mark using Matthew and Luke as sources. This solution was first proposed in the eighteenth century by Johann Griesbach and is commonly referred to as the "Griesbach Hypothesis." The initial support for Griesbach's theory waned, but William Farmer revived it in the middle of the twentieth century.[24] For support, adherents appeal to incidents where Mark reports a story that includes elements found in Matthew and Luke when reporting the same story but which end up being redundant. Consider the following example pertaining to when Jesus healed some people in Capernaum:

> Matt. 8:16: "that evening"
> Luke 4:40: "as the sun was setting"
> Mark 1:32: "that evening at sundown"

It appears that Mark may have combined the wording of Matthew and Luke. Though interesting, Markan redundancies are not nearly as compelling as one might initially think. For of the 213 Markan redundancies, only 17 (or 8 percent) include elements from Matthew and Luke as in the above example.[25] On six occasions, Matthew and Luke also have the redundant remark found in Mark, showing Mark did not create that particular redundancy—unless Matthew and/or Luke were using Mark! On thirty-nine occasions, Matthew and Luke lack the same single portion of Mark's redundant expression, and Matthew and Luke lack both portions of it on another thirty-seven occasions. There are additional observations, but this is enough to suggest that Markan redundancies are more plausibly

---

Papias are mistaken. However, this seems like a hasty dismissal. Papias is an early source who has a reasonably good claim to having received the information from a credible source.

24. William Farmer, *The Synoptic Problem: A Critical Analysis* (New York: Macmillan, 1964).

25. David Wenham and Steve Walton, *Exploring the New Testament: A Guide to the Gospels and Acts*, 2nd ed., vol. 1 (Downers Grove, IL: IVP Academic, 2011), 71, 73; Robert H. Stein, *Studying the Synoptic Gospels: Origin and Interpretation*, 2nd ed. (Grand Rapids: Baker Academic, 2001), 65–67.

attributed to Mark's writing style than his familiarity with Matthew and Luke.[26]

The position that Matthew wrote first has several weaknesses—at least the position that Matthew wrote the Greek Gospel prior to Mark. Therefore, few New Testament scholars today think Matthew's Gospel was written first.

MARK (AKA MARKAN PRIORITY)

In the eighteenth century, a German theologian named Gottlob Storr contended that Mark was the first Gospel composed.[27] There are good reasons to think Storr is correct. Let's consider some of the data in favor of Markan Priority. The first identifies Mark as the "middle term." There are two key observations here.

The first observation pertains to verbal agreement. All three Synoptics tell the same story on several occasions. Although the wording between them is similar, the wording between two of the three is even closer. Consider Jesus calling Matthew (or Levi) to follow him:

Matthew 9:9	**Mark 2:14**	**Luke 5:27**
And passing by from there,	And passing by	And
Jesus saw	he saw	he beheld
a man	Levi son of Alphaeus	a tax collector named Levi
sitting at the tax booth,	sitting at the tax booth,	sitting at the tax booth,
called Matthew,		
And he says to him,	And he says to him,	And he said to him,
"Follow me."	"Follow me."	"Follow me."
And	And	And
		having left everything
having arisen,	having arisen,	having arisen,
he followed him.	he followed him.	he followed him.

26. See Stein, *Studying the Synoptic Gospels*, 66, who draws from Christopher M. Tuckett, *The Revival of the Griesbach Hypothesis: An Analysis and Appraisal*, Society for New Testament Studies 44 (Cambridge: Cambridge University Press, 1983), 20.

27. Gottlob C. Storr, *Über den Zweck der evangelischen Geschichte und der Briefe Johannis* (Tübingen: Herrbrandt, 1786).

So that you may see the similarities and differences clearly, I have translated all three texts as closely as possible to the Greek. You will notice that the wording is quite similar in all three. However, the wording in Matthew and Mark are even closer. There are many instances, such as this one, where Matthew and Mark are closer, and many others where Mark and Luke are closer. Since Mark appears in both situations, Mark is referred to as the middle term and suggests that Matthew and Luke may have used Mark.

The second key observation supporting Mark as the middle term concerns the order of events. Authors have the right to narrate events however they desire. They can order them by theme, such as arranging a collection of stories featuring meals. They also can be narrated in a chronological order. Of course, we expect that many of the events of Jesus's life will appear in the same order: his birth, baptism, ministry, the Last Supper, his arrest, crucifixion, and resurrection. This is a natural order, since we would not expect for Jesus's baptism to precede his birth or for his resurrection to precede his crucifixion.

That said, multiple events for which there is no natural or required order often appear in the same order in all three Synoptic Gospels. Consider the following stories that appear in the same succession, with only three exceptions where a particular Gospel does not report it: (1) Peter's confession that Jesus is the Messiah, (2) Jesus predicts his impending execution and resurrection, (3) Jesus teaches on being his disciple, (4) Jesus's transfiguration, (5) the coming of Elijah (absent in Luke), (6) Jesus heals a boy possessed by a demon, (7) Jesus predicts his impending execution a second time, (8) Jesus's thoughts pertaining to the temple tax (only in Matthew), (9) the disciples dispute with one another over which of them is the greatest, (10) an anonymous exorcist (absent in Matthew), and (11) how to deal with one's sin (Luke locates it elsewhere). These eleven events do not require any particular chronological order. So is the order in which most of them appear similar because it reflects the order in which they occurred and were recalled years later? Or is it because some of the Evangelists were using the same source? Most scholars hold that the latter is the correct answer for a few reasons. First, several of the stories in that long narration of events also have strong verbal agreement. However, a more important observation is that when Matthew presents a different order of events than Mark, Luke usually follows the order we find in Mark. And when Luke diverges from Mark's order, Matthew usually follows Mark. Once again, Mark is the middle term. This suggests Matthew and Luke made use of Mark.

A second argument for Markan Priority is Mark's crude style that sometimes appears in his Gospel. For example, Mark reports that the Spirit "drove out" Jesus into the wilderness immediately after he was baptized (Mark 1:12). The Greek word Mark uses for "drove out" is *ekballō*, and it appears sixteen times in Mark.[28] In every instance, it refers to a violent act. In fact, in ten of the sixteen occurrences, the term is used in reference to casting out demons. When Matthew and Luke report the same story of the Holy Spirit's action to get Jesus in the wilderness, they use different terms. Matthew 4:1 has "led up" (*anagō*), while Luke 4:1 has "led" (*agō*), both of which are much softer terms than *ekballō*. Which, then, seems more likely: (1) because Mark is using Matthew and perhaps Luke as a source, he changed what Matthew wrote, *anagō*, to a somewhat crude term, *ekballō*, or (2) Matthew and Luke softened Mark's word choice?

Let's look at another example. In Mark 4:22, Jesus says, "For nothing is hidden except that it be revealed." We have a sense of what Jesus is saying, despite the fact that the grammar is quite awkward in both the English translation and the original Greek. When we read the same statement in Matthew 10:26, Luke 8:17, and 12:2, it says, "For nothing is hidden that will not be revealed." Now those verses sound correct because they have good grammar. Once again, we ask which seems more likely: (1) Mark has corrupted the good grammar of Matthew and Luke, or (2) Matthew and Luke have improved Mark's grammar? Most scholars are inclined to prefer the second option in both of the above examples.

A third argument for Markan Priority concerns the presence of *awkward content unique to Mark*. In Mark 7:32–37, Jesus heals a man who is deaf and dumb by putting his fingers into the man's ears and then spitting and touching the man's tongue with his saliva. In Mark 8:22–25, Jesus spits on the eyes of a blind man and places his hands on his eyes. However, the attempt only leaves the man partially healed. So Jesus again places his hands on the man's eyes before he can see clearly. Jesus's use of his own saliva to heal and the need for a second attempt to heal a person are omitted by Matthew and Luke.[29] Did Matthew and Luke omit the stories because they regarded them as possessing an embarrassing element? This seems more probable than Mark adding the embarrassing element.

---

28. Mark 1:12, 34, 39, 43; 3:15, 22, 23; 5:40; 6:13; 7:26; 9:18, 28, 38, 47; 11:15; 12:8. In addition, though Mark 16:9–20 is spurious, *ekballō* also appears in 16:9, 17, both of which refer to casting out demons.

29. John will later report Jesus's use of saliva when healing a man born blind (John 9:1–7). And Jesus's first attempt is successful.

Fourth, *Mark provides problematic content absent from Matthew and Luke*. Mark 2:25–26 reports that Abiathar was the high priest when David and his men ate the consecrated bread. Matthew 12:4 and Luke 6:4 report the same event but do not mention the name of the high priest. Why the omission? Did they not regard it as being important, or was there another reason? According to 1 Samuel 21:1–6, Ahimelech was the high priest when David and his men ate the consecrated bread, and 22:20 says that Abiathar was Ahimelech's son. Some have attempted to harmonize Mark's statement with 1 Samuel. At most those attempts may be said to be *possibly correct*. Yet even if a solution involving harmonization turns out being correct, strong surface tension can still be acknowledged. With that in mind, which seems more likely: (1) Mark created the tension by adding the name of the high priest, or (2) Matthew and Luke were aware of the tension and, to avoid confusion, chose to mention what David and his men did without naming the high priest?

CHALLENGES TO MARKAN PRIORITY

The greatest challenge to Markan Priority is that most, or perhaps all, of the seven church fathers who commented on the matter held that Matthew wrote prior to Mark. Such a nearly unanimous opinion should not be ignored or minimized. One is often justified in saying that those who wrote anywhere from a decade to three hundred years after the final Gospel may know better than the modern scholars wrestling with these matters two thousand years later. Nonetheless, we observed some fairly strong challenges to the claim that the Gospel of Matthew in the New Testament was written first. (1) The early church fathers did not all agree on the order of composition of the other Gospels. (2) If Matthew wrote his Gospel in Hebrew, we no longer have it and can only deal with our Matthew, which is based on a Greek text. (3) The striking verbal similarities between Greek Matthew and Mark practically require that one used the other as its primary source. Accordingly, if Greek Matthew came first, Mark used it as its primary source. And this would stand in tension with our earliest source, Papias, who claimed that Mark wrote what he remembered Peter had said.

Another significant challenge to Markan Priority are the instances where all three Synoptics show close verbal similarities, but Mark is not the middle term. This is when Matthew and Luke are closer to one another in their wording than either are to Mark. Scholars refer to this as *minor agreements between Matthew and Luke against Mark.*[30] Admittedly, this issue gets quite technical. And I want to avoid spending too much time on a topic that, though interesting to some of us New Testament geeks, would take us on a distracting detour from the main point of this book. I do not have the space to touch on every element to the Synoptic problem here. It is a complex matter for which New Testament scholar Mark Goodacre writes, "In the Synoptic Problem one has, without doubt, one of the most fascinating literary puzzles in world history."[31] For our purposes, however, all we need to understand is that the case for Markan Priority is stronger than the case for Matthean Priority, at least if we have in mind the Gospel of Matthew in the New Testament. Although other theories cannot be ruled out, Markan Priority is more plausible than Matthean Priority.

WHAT ABOUT JOHN'S GOSPEL?

Thus far, we have spent our time discussing the Synoptic Gospels because they are so similar. But what about the Gospel of John? Those who spend their days immersed in the Gospels as a career end up observing things that are not so apparent to others. And something becomes quite clear to them: the Gospel of John is often very different than the Synoptic Gospels. But why is it different? In his very large and historically informed commentary on John's Gospel, Craig Keener writes that "all scholars acknowledge some adaptation and conformity with Johannine idiom."[32] In other words, Gospels scholars who have specialized in the study of John's Gospel acknowledge that John has, in essence, restated Jesus's teachings in his own words. Jesus's very words (*ipsissima verba*) may not be preserved in John, but his very voice—in other words, the meaning (*ipsissima vox*)—is.[33]

If you would like to experience first-hand a taste of how the majority of Johannine specialists came to have this opinion, here is an easy exercise

---

30. Craig Evans offers the fascinating and quite plausible proposal that the minor agreements between Matthew and Luke against Mark resulted from Matthew and Luke using Mark's notes, which he refers to as "proto-Mark," rather than his completed Gospel as their primary source. See Evans, *Jesus and the Manuscripts*, 24–25.

31. Goodacre, *The Synoptic Problem*, 30.

32. Craig S. Keener, *The Gospel of John: A Commentary*, 2 vols. (Peabody, MA: Hendrickson, 2003), 1:52.

33. Craig Blomberg writes, "We need not hesitate to acknowledge the distinctive style of Jesus's speech in the Fourth Gospel or to attribute it largely to John himself." See Craig L. Blomberg, *Jesus the Purifier: John's Gospel and the Fourth Quest for the Historical Jesus* (Grand Rapids: Baker Academic, 2023), 213; cf. 220.

you can complete: read through Matthew five times, then read Mark five times, and then read Luke five times. You will notice that Jesus sounds very similar in all of them. Then read John's Gospel five times. Finally, read 1 John five times. You will observe that, although Jesus's message in John's Gospel is similar to what we read in the Synoptic Gospels, the way Jesus *sounds* in John is often different than the way he sounds in the other Gospels. You will also observe that the way *Jesus sounds* in John's Gospel is very similar to how *John sounds* in 1 John. The grammar, vocabulary, and overall style of writing in John and 1 John are astonishingly similar. This second observation could have resulted from John adjusting his style to be like that of his master after spending a lot of time with him.[34] This would be similar to how some married couples adapt their laughs and expressions to one another over time. The other option is that John often paraphrases Jesus using his own style and words. This is the option held by most Johannine specialists.

Additional factors point to how John differs from the Synoptic Gospels. Consider the following reported by Matthew:

> Jesus said all of these things in parables to the crowds. And he did not speak to them without a parable, so that what was spoken by the prophet may be fulfilled, saying, "I will open my mouth in parables. I will proclaim what has been hidden from the foundation of the world." (Matt. 13:34–35; cf. Mark 4:33–34)

Matthew is here speaking hyperbolically since he reports Jesus teaching without the use of parables elsewhere, the Sermon on the Mount being a prime example. Nevertheless, his point is that Jesus very often spoke in parables and, in fact, does so in fulfillment of prophesy. It is of interest, then, that in John *none of Jesus's teachings appear in parables*.[35]

So how far did John go when restating Jesus's words? It is impossible to know. However, the "I am" statements in John are of prime interest in the matter. John's Gospel attributes several statements to Jesus where he says something about his identity while using "I am" (*egō eimi*). Here are a few

34. I mention John here as the traditional author while being aware that most modern scholars do not think that John the son of Zebedee is the author. However, most Johannine specialists think either one of Jesus's minor disciples wrote the Gospel or that the author's primary source was one of Jesus's minor disciples and perhaps even John the son of Zebedee.

35. In addition, John does not include any stories of Jesus casting out demons, whereas the Synoptic Gospels are full of them.

examples: “I am the bread of life” (John 6:35; cf. 6:41, 48, 51); “I am the light of the world” (8:12); “I am the one who bears witness about myself” (8:18); “Before Abraham came to be, I am” (8:58); “I am the door for the sheep” (10:7; cf. 10:9); “I am the good shepherd” (10:11, 14); “I am the resurrection and the life” (11:25); “I am the way and the truth and the life” (14:6); “I am the true vine” (15:1; cf. 15:5).[36] In contrast, the Synoptic Gospels contain only four statements attributed to Jesus where he says “I am” (*egō eimi*) in reference to himself.[37] However, in none of them is it clear that he is using it in a sense similar to how John uses it. That said, in the Synoptics we observe statements and deeds of Jesus that communicate the same messages as do the “I am” statements in John.[38] Consider the following:

> I am the way and the truth and the life. No one comes to the Father except through me. (John 14:6)

Now look at the following statements of Jesus in Matthew that essentially communicate the same message:

> All things have been handed over [to me] by my Father. And no one knows the Son except the Father. Nor does anyone know the Father except the Son and to whomever the Son desires to reveal him. Come to me, all those who are laboring and have been loaded down, and I will give you rest. Take my yoke upon you and learn from me, for I am gentle and humble in heart, and you will find rest for your souls. For my yoke is easy and my burden is light. (Matt. 11:27–30; cf. Luke 10:22)

The statement of Jesus in Matthew 11:27 communicates much of the same message that we read in John 14:6. Moreover, when readers notice that the tone of Jesus’s words in Matthew 11:28–30 sounds similar to how Jesus

---

36. Other “I am” (*egō eimi*) statements in John are 4:26; 8:24, 28; 13:19; 18:5.

37. Mark 6:50 // Matt. 14:27 // John 6:20; Mark 13:6 // Matt. 24:5 // Luke 21:8; Mark 14:62 // Luke 22:70; Luke 24:39. Elsewhere in the Synoptics, Jesus uses “I am” (*egō eimi*) when quoting God’s statement to Moses: Matt. 22:32 (cf. Mark 12:26 where only “I” [*egō*] appears). And on three occasions others use “I am” (*egō eimi*) when referring to themselves: Jesus’s disciples (Matt. 26:22, 25), Gabriel (Luke 1:19), and a man born blind (John 9:9).

38. Paul N. Anderson, *Riddles of the Fourth Gospel: An Introduction to John* (Minneapolis: Fortress, 2011), 59: “All of the Johannine I-am metaphors are present in the teachings of the Synoptic Jesus, so one cannot rule out the possibility of Johannine paraphrasing of actual words of Jesus.”

sounds in John, it is easy to understand why New Testament scholars have often referred to this text in Matthew as the "Johannine thunderbolt"!

Related to another of Jesus's "I am" (*egō eimi*) statements, Craig Blomberg opines,

> Did Jesus ever speak the words "I am the good shepherd" (John 10:11)? He might have. The Lukan parable of the lost sheep likens God to a shepherd (Luke 15:3–7), and Luke summarizes Jesus's message as "the Son of man came to seek, and to save the lost" (Luke 19:10). Both passages are frequently accepted as authentic, at which point the historical Jesus is implicitly claiming to be God's agent as shepherd to recover the lost. Even if Jesus never spoke the closest Aramaic equivalent to "I am the good shepherd," John would not have been out of line in attributing that claim to him.[39]

The "I am" statement of Jesus for which the authenticity is most debated is found in John 8:58, "Before Abraham came to be, I am!" It is crystal clear that Jesus is here making the claim to being Yahweh, who at the burning bush in Exodus 3:14 answered Moses's request to know his name: "I am that I am."[40] With the possible exception of Mark 6:50 and parallel texts, such a statement appears nowhere in the Synoptic Gospels. And some have used this observation to claim that an evolution of Jesus's identity is present in the Gospels. But those making this assertion will be proven wrong in the next chapter where I will demonstrate that the view of Jesus as divine in John is clearly present throughout Mark's Gospel, the first composed of the four Gospels.

Of course, the Synoptic Gospels do not preserve everything Jesus said, and John preserves many traditions of Jesus not included in the Synoptics. So we should by no means rule out the possibility that Jesus uttered this or any of the other "I am" statements in John. However, we must likewise notice that in all four Gospels Jesus is often cryptic in public pertaining to his claim to be the Messiah. In Matthew 16:16–20 and Luke 9:20–21, Jesus charges his disciples that they should tell no one that he is the Messiah. In Luke 4:41, Jesus does not allow the demons to speak because they know he is the Messiah. Even in John 10:23–25, Jesus is walking in the temple when some Jews gather around him and say, "How long will

39. Blomberg, *Jesus the Purifier*, 380.

40. Jesus makes a similar "I am" (*egō eimi*) statement in John 18:5. Given the response of those who came to arrest Jesus in 18:6, John clearly has them understanding Jesus to be making a claim to deity.

you keep us in suspense? If you are the Messiah, tell us plainly." Now if Jesus was hesitant to announce publicly and plainly that he is the Messiah, we would not expect for him to be claiming to be God publicly and as plainly as we observe John reporting him saying, "Before Abraham was, I am!" Of course, this could be a rare exception to the rule. However, if Jesus did not make such explicit claims in public, what might be going on in John's Gospel?

The early church fathers were aware that John was a Gospel of a different type than the Synoptics. Clement of Alexandria and Origen both referred to John as a "spiritual Gospel."[41] In fact, Origen noted several narratives in John having parallels in the Synoptics and elsewhere that he regarded as impossible to harmonize in a historical sense. So he contended that their truth must be sought for not in the letter but in the message, which must be spiritually interpreted.[42] Darrell Bock suggests, "What John is oftentimes doing is making explicit things that were implicit in what Jesus was saying as we get them in the Synoptics."[43]

So there are some good reasons for thinking John adapted Jesus's teachings. What is left is to determine the extent to which those adaptations went. And this is what perplexes scholars. N. T. Wright's humorous comment accurately summarizes the thoughts of many Johannine scholars: "I feel about John like I feel about my wife; I love her very much, but I wouldn't claim to understand her."[44]

---

41. Or *pneumatikon . . . euangelion* (from Eusebius, *Hist. eccl.* 6.14.7, who is aware of Clement's *Hypotyposeis*, which is no longer extant). Either quoting from Clement or summarizing him, Eusebius writes, "But John, the last of all, perceiving *that the bodily things* [*tá sōmatika*] in the Gospels had been made clear, having been urged by his acquaintances, and inspired by the Spirit [*theophorēthenta*], composed a *spiritual Gospel* [*pneumatikon euangelion*]." Origen, *Commentary on the Gospel according to John, Books 1–10*, 80:42–43, book 10, par. 40 (Heine). For the Greek text, see Origen, *Origenous ta euriskomena panta = Origenis opera omnia, patrologiae cursus completus, series graeca*, t. 13 (Paris: Migne, 1862). Those interested may access this Greek and Latin text at https://bit.ly/2o9mlRS and scroll to page 36, 9.40 and 37, 10.45.

42. Origen, *Commentary on the Gospel according to John*, 10. The entirety of book 10 focuses on the spiritual interpretation of Scripture.

43. Darrell L. Bock, "Different Depictions of Christ / Highlight," Mike Licona (Youtube channel), June 3, 2021, https://youtu.be/u0O7GzyAxyo?t=393 (begins at 6:33). See also Christopher Skinner, "The Gospel according to John," in *The Cambridge Companion to the Gospels*, ed. Stephen C. Barton and Todd Brewer, 2nd ed. (New York: Cambridge University Press, 2021), 199. Blomberg (*Jesus the Purifier*) offers the following caution in reference to understanding Jesus's "I am" sayings in John as the very words of Jesus: "When we realize that passages like [John] 8:25 and 10:25 show a lack of understanding on the part of Jesus's closest followers, and that even when they say that he is finally speaking clearly (16:29–30) it would seem that they still don't fully grasp matters (vv. 31–33), we had better exercise caution in our descriptions of how explicit Jesus's self-revelation was" (216).

44. N. T. Wright, *Following Jesus: Biblical Reflections on Discipleship*, 2nd ed. (Grand Rapids: Eerdmans, 2014), 35.

F. F. Bruce refers to how John retells the words of Jesus as "an expanded paraphrase," "a translation of the freest kind," "a transposition into another key," "all this and much more the Holy Spirit accomplished in our Evangelist. . . . It is through the Spirit's operation that, in William Temple's words, 'the mind of Jesus himself was with the Fourth Gospel disclosed'; and it is through the illumination granted by the same Spirit that one may still recognize in this Gospel the authentic voice of Jesus."[45]

Paul Anderson has devoted his academic career to studying John's Gospel. He is among the very foremost of today's Johannine specialists and leads the *John, Jesus, and History* section at the annual meeting of the Society of Biblical Literature. Since the inception of this section in 2001, scholars have contributed papers pertaining to how John's Gospel relates to history. As of the time I am writing this (Summer 2023), three volumes containing the most outstanding of those papers have been published and a fourth is presently in the works.[46] Anderson once told me that he regards much in the Gospel of John to be a "theological paraphrase" of Jesus's teachings after John had a few decades of reflecting on them. And in one of his books, he writes,

> As an independent tradition, the Johannine witness works way alongside other traditions, but it tells the story of Jesus with its own voice and distinctive emphases. It represents a dialectical reflection of a theologian who also appears to have encountered Jesus of Nazareth and who develops his understanding of the significance of his mission over several decades of Christian history and experience.[47]

Another Johannine scholar, Craig Keener, writes,

> The Fourth Gospel makes no effort to disguise the Johannine style of its discourses; most Johannine scholars see these discourses as including homiletic elaboration on Jesus's teaching, interpretation that the author would undoubtedly claim was guided by the promised Spirit of truth.[48]

---

45. F. F. Bruce, *The Gospel and Epistles of John: Introduction, Exposition, and Notes* (Grand Rapids: Eerdmans, 1983), 16–17.

46. See Paul N. Anderson, Felix Just, SJ, and Tom Thatcher, *John, Jesus and History*, vol. 1, *Critical Appraisals of Critical Views* (Atlanta: Society of Biblical Literature, 2007); vol. 2, *Aspects of History in the Fourth Gospel* (Atlanta: Society of Biblical Literature, 2009); and vol. 3, *Glimpses of Jesus through the Johannine Lens* (Atlanta: Society of Biblical Literature, 2016).

47. Anderson, *The Riddles of the Fourth Gospel*, 152.

48. Craig S. Keener, *Christobiography: Memory, History, and the Reliability of the Gospels* (Grand

WHY THIS IS IMPORTANT

At this point, I suspect a number of you are thinking, "What relationship does the content of this chapter have with the matter of differences among the Gospels?" It has a lot of relevance. The normal variation found among eyewitnesses reporting the same event is something we can observe at times among the Gospels (e.g., as mentioned above at the beginning of chapter 2, the extent of differences combined with a lack of verbal similarities between all four Gospels when they tell of Jesus's appearance before Pilate). That said, the striking verbal similarities between Matthew, Mark, and Luke that appear with a much greater frequency justify us being confident that a relationship exists between them—that is, they often drew from the same source(s). And it is clear that, at least sometimes and probably quite often, it was a written source. *Therefore, normal variation among eyewitness testimonies should not be the default approach to understanding why such similarities are present in the Synoptic Gospels.* In those instances, harmonization efforts should not be our go-to action because they have a very good chance of leading us astray. Recognizing, instead, that Matthew and Luke regularly use Mark's Gospel as their primary source will yield beautiful and tasty fruit when studying the Gospels in light of their differences, which we will discuss in the chapters that follow. We will be able to observe how Matthew and Luke use Mark. Do they alter what Mark says? If so, to what extent, and why might they have done so?

It should not surprise us that Matthew and Luke probably used Mark as their primary source and supplemented it. Such a practice was common among authors of ancient historical literature. Christopher Pelling, the foremost authority on Plutarch, has argued that Plutarch's *Lives* featuring those characters of the late Roman Republic are largely based on the contemporary history of Rome written by Asinius Pollio. Pelling holds that Plutarch's wide reading of sources apart from Pollio is reflected in, at most, 25 percent of his overall narrative. He adds that this practice "is not unique to Plutarch, nor to biography," but is shared by other historians such as Cassius Dio, Livy, Dionysius of Halicarnassus, and even Tacitus.[49] We will soon be spending more time with Plutarch. For now, I will merely

Rapids: Eerdmans, 2019), 15. Elsewhere he writes, "If any extant first-century Gospel stretches the range of imperial-period biography beyond the contours traced in earlier chapters, it would be John" (364).

49. Pelling, *Plutarch and History: Eighteen Studies* (Swansea: Classical Press of Wales, 2002),

point out that most classicists regard Plutarch to be the greatest ancient biographer and Livy, Sallust, and Tacitus as some of the greatest Roman historians. Since it was a common practice of ancient biographers and historians to begin with a primary source and supplement it with other sources, we should not be surprised when we observe Matthew and Luke making robust use of Mark as their primary source.[50]

There is a nice theological payoff for our labors in this chapter: we discover some things about the nature of the divine inspiration of Scripture. The Bible tells us precious little about what it means for Scripture to be "divinely inspired" or what such a process may have looked like. We will be discussing this in much greater detail in chapter 11. However, I want to touch on the matter briefly here, since some readers may be feeling a bit of anxiety, wondering how what we have just observed is compatible with Scripture being divinely inspired.

In this chapter, we have learned that the divine inspiration of the Gospels included the Evangelists using sources and did not involve divine dictation. Since the Gospels reveal different education levels, writing styles, and the personalities of their authors, divine dictation seems unlikely. Moreover, we would have to imagine the Holy Spirit reviewing Mark's Gospel, noticing his occasional crude style, and saying, "You know, I can do better than that. Let's say it this way in Matthew and in Luke. . . ." Whatever we say about the nature of the divine inspiration of the Bible, it should acknowledge that the end product possesses a distinctly human element that is sometimes imperfect.

Some may find discussions on the Synoptic problem, which Gospel was written first, and how some of the Evangelists used sources to be unnerving. Why? Many of us believe Scripture is divinely inspired—*God-breathed* (2 Tim. 3:16). What impression does this create in our minds? Something similar to divine dictation. Although few of us were taught that inspiration involved God dictating to the biblical writers what to write, the fuzzy concept in our minds of what the divine inspiration of Scripture involved comes very close to it and is, in fact, practically indistinguishable from divine dictation. Unsurprisingly, then, a tension arises when we observe something that challenges this impression. The observations we have discussed thus far are not new. Although they do not challenge the divine inspiration of Scripture, they do challenge some understandings of it.

1–44, esp. 19–20; Christopher Pelling, trans., *Plutarch: Caesar* (Oxford: Oxford University Press, 2011), 39–40.

50. Craig S. Keener, *The Historical Jesus of the Gospels* (Grand Rapids: Eerdmans, 2009), 74.

B. B. Warfield was a conservative Christian scholar who held the Charles Hodge Chair at Princeton Theological Seminary as principal until his death in 1921. One of Warfield's colleagues at the Seminary was J. Gresham Machen, professor of New Testament, who would later resign from his teaching position in order to help form Westminster Theological Seminary as an evangelical alternative to Princeton. Machen said that the old and great Princeton "died when Warfield was carried out."[51] Warfield was a strong proponent of the doctrines of the divine inspiration and the inerrancy of Scripture. It is of interest, then, to observe what he wrote about inspiration. He asserted that the process of inspiration was, in essence,

> to bring the right men to the right places at the right times, with the right endowments, impulses, acquirements, to write just the books which were designed for them. When "inspiration," technically so called, is superinduced on lines of preparation like these, it takes on quite a different aspect from that which it bears when it is thought of as an isolated action of the Divine Spirit operating out of all relation to historical processes. . . . If God wished to give His people a series of letters like Paul's, He prepared a Paul to write them, and the Paul He brought to the task was a Paul who spontaneously would write just such letters.[52]

For Warfield, Scripture was not divinely inspired because God had dictated to the human authors each and every word he desired for them to write. Such would have been similar to Islamic tradition that claims the archangel Gabriel dictated the words of the *Quran* to Muhammad, who then dictated them to others who either wrote them down or committed them to memory and eventually to writing. In contrast, God worked through circumstances that prepared the human authors. These circumstances sometimes began prior to the births of the biblical authors and resulted in them freely writing what they did.

Because our observations of Scripture suggest that it did not result from God dictating each and every word written by the human authors, the divine inspiration of Scripture is not necessarily challenged when we observe the authors of the Gospels using sources. But they do challenge some concepts of divine inspiration. This brings me to a principle by

---

51. Mark Noll, *The Princeton Theology* (Grand Rapids: Baker, 1983), 298.

52. Benjamin B. Warfield, "Inspiration," in *The International Standard Bible Encyclopaedia*, ed. James Orr, 5 vols. (Chicago: Howard-Severance, 1915), 3:1480.

which I am guided: *our view of Scripture should be consistent with what we observe in Scripture.* This principle is not profound, but it is essential and based on common sense.

Observing how Matthew and Luke use Mark will also help us ascertain why many differences in the Gospels are present. Before we go there, we will find it helpful to return to discussing the genre of the Gospels, because genre contributes heavily to forming the lens through which we view and interpret texts. Those who believe the Gospels are novels will interpret them differently than those who regard them as biographies reporting historical events. Approaching the Gospels with an expectation that they are reporting events with the precision of a transcript from a legal deposition will lead to disappointment. Furthermore, reading the Gospels without a proper understanding of their genre could lead to flawed interpretations of those texts.

SUMMARY

In this chapter we observed strong reasons for concluding Mark was the first Gospel composed and that Matthew and Luke made use of Mark as their primary source. John's Gospel is of a somewhat different nature than the Synoptic Gospels. It is often more of a free paraphrase. This chapter suggested that harmonization efforts, such as appealing to the normal variations between eyewitness reports, should not be the default approach toward resolving differences in the Gospels. Finally, it challenged us to rethink what we mean by *divine inspiration* and to understand the *divine inspiration* of Scripture in a way consistent with what we observe in Scripture.

QUESTIONS FOR FURTHER THOUGHT

1. What is the most interesting thing you learned from this chapter?
2. What are your thoughts about a Hebrew Gospel of Matthew?
3. Does it bother you that the early church fathers were not always in agreement? Why or why not?
4. Let's assume Papias is correct that Mark wrote what he remembered Peter saying. Can you think of some reasons why Matthew and Luke would have used Mark as the primary source behind their Gospels?

CHAPTER 4

THE GOSPELS AS BIOGRAPHY

Since the Gospels focus on the life of Jesus, they are some sort of biography. For reasons unknown to us today, Jews wrote very few biographies during that era. We only know of four, all of which were written in the first century: three by Philo (*Life of Moses*, *Life of Abraham*, and *Life of Joseph*) and one by Josephus (his autobiography, *The Life*). According to the late Jewish scholar Louis Feldman, after Josephus "we do not find biographies written by Jews until modern times."[1] Although we are left only to speculate as to why Jewish historians of the past lacked an interest in writing biographies, the fact remains that, aside from the Gospels, only four biographies appear to have been written by Jews in antiquity, all in the first century, while nearly one hundred extant biographies were written by Greeks and Romans within 150 years on each side of Jesus's life, a span of 300 years.

Similar to modern biography, Greek and Roman biographers were often interested exclusively in the life of the main character. Josephus's *Life* and Philo's *Moses* follow this convention. However, Philo's *Abraham* and *Joseph* veer from it, demonstrating keen interest in the lives of others, such as Enosh, Enoch, and Noah. Furthermore, while Philo's *Moses* and Josephus's *Life* follow Greek and Roman biographers in their practice of avoiding allegory, Philo's *Abraham* and *Joseph* frequently use allegory to explain the underlying meaning of a biblical story.[2] It is noteworthy, then, that even two of the four ancient biographies written by Jews more closely resemble those biographies written by Greeks and Romans in some important characteristics than the other two.

1. Louis H. Feldman, *Philo's Portrayal of Moses in the Context of Ancient Judaism* (Notre Dame, IN: University of Notre Dame Press, 2007), 23.

2. Feldman, *Philo's Portrayal of Moses*, 25.

The average length of biographies written by Greeks and Romans was between 10,000 and 25,000 words. Philo's *Abraham* and *Joseph* are within the average at around 13,300 and 12,800 words respectively, while *Moses* is a little longer at close to 31,000 words. However, the autobiography of Josephus is nearly 89,000 words. That is definitely out of the ordinary. Josephus certainly knew a lot about his main character and wanted others to know about him! Since Greeks and Romans are responsible for writing nearly all of the biographies in that era, and half of the precious few biographies written by Jews in the same period conform closely to the conventions followed by Greeks and Romans for writing biography, scholars speak of the genre of *Greco-Roman biography*.[3] Of course, placing the Gospels within this genre does not negate the fact that they draw heavily on the Jewish Scriptures and understand the events they report to be a fulfillment of these Scriptures.[4] That said, going forward I will usually refer to this genre simply as *ancient biography*.

The four Gospels in the New Testament share much in common with the genre of ancient biography. They focus on a single character: Jesus. In contrast, the book of Acts has strong affiliations with the genre of history, since it narrates events in the church that occurred during its first three decades and does not focus on just one character.[5] The Gospels range between 11,000 and 20,000 Greek words, well within the average length

---

3. For an in-depth discussion on the qualities of Greco-Roman biography, see Richard A. Burridge, *What Are the Gospels? A Comparison with Graeco-Roman Biography*, 25th anniversary ed. (1992; repr., Waco, TX: Baylor University Press, 2018). Burridge's treatment is largely responsible for convincing a majority of New Testament scholars to think of the Gospels as belonging to the genre of Greco-Roman biography. Scholars now tend to divide the biographical genre into subcategories. Moreover, some scholars prefer to think of Luke as history rather than biography, since Luke's Gospel shares some qualities of being a history. I regard Luke as a biography, since it focuses on a single character, whereas a history does not. Plutarch's *Life of Caesar* and Tacitus's *Agricola* also possess some qualities that are closer to history than biography and may be said to be hybrids between the two genres. Nevertheless, their size and focus on a single person firmly establish their place within the genre of biography. Burridge observes that Greco-Roman biography was a fluid genre and often blended with other genres (62–67).

4. See Loveday Alexander, "What Is a Gospel?" in *The Cambridge Companion to the Gospels*, Second Ed., Stephen C. Barton and Todd Brewer, eds. (New York: Cambridge University Press, 2021), 27.

5. Some scholars regard Luke's Gospel to be of the same genre as Acts (history), since that Gospel possesses some of the characteristics of the genre of history. I do not share that opinion. Plutarch's *Life of Caesar* likewise possesses characteristics of history (see Pelling, Caesar [21, 22, 25–35]). Notwithstanding, since *Caesar* focuses on the life of a single character, I am not aware of any classicist who regards Plutarch's *Caesar* as belonging to a genre other than biography. Something similar may be said of Luke's Gospel. Despite it possessing some qualities typical of a history, Luke's Gospel clearly focuses on the life of a single character: Jesus.

for an ancient biography.[6] Although the Gospels contain some allegorical elements, such as Jesus's parables, the stories about Jesus are not allegories. On some occasions, the authors explain the underlying meaning of something that Jesus said or did. For example, in John 2:18–22, the author explains what Jesus meant when he said, "Destroy this temple and I will raise it in three days" (v. 19): "When he was raised from the dead, his disciples remembered that he said this. Therefore, they believed the Scripture and the word that Jesus had spoken" (v. 22). However, John is merely providing a brief commentary before moving along with his narrative (see also Mark 7:19).

It was quite common for ancient biographies to spend only a small amount of time mentioning the familial line of the main character (often referred to as the biographee) and then leap forward to the inauguration of his public career.[7] This is what we observe in the Gospels. Matthew and Luke provide genealogies and infancy narratives, which inform us that Jesus is the Messiah, while Mark tells us Jesus is the Lord for whom John the Baptist has prepared a way. John says that Jesus is the Logos who was with God in the beginning, who is God, and who has come in the flesh to be with us. Luke is the only canonical Gospel providing readers with a story of Jesus in his childhood (Luke 2:41–51).[8] All four Gospels then jump to the inauguration of Jesus's public ministry: his baptism. So if you have ever wondered why the Gospels did not report more about Jesus's childhood, you now know that omitting stories of the biographee's childhood was typical of the genre of ancient biography.

OBJECTIONS TO THE GOSPELS AS ANCIENT BIOGRAPHY

Some have resisted the idea that the Gospels are ancient biographies, asserting that the Gospels are *sui generis*, that is, a unique genre, belonging to a class of their own. This seems odd to me. Every other bit of literature in the Bible fits into a genre that is shared with literature outside the Bible. Why must the Gospels be the only exception, especially when they share so much in common with ancient biography? Moreover, even if one

6. Greek words in Mark: 11,304; John: 15,635; Matthew: 18,346; Luke: 19,482.

7. I have used the masculine pronoun *his* rather than the inclusive *his or her* or *their* because one would be hard-pressed to find an ancient biography in that period whose main character is a woman.

8. The *Infancy Gospel of Thomas* provides a few stories of Jesus's childhood. However, I am not aware of any scholar who thinks the apostle Thomas wrote this gospel or that the stories in it are authentic recollections of Jesus.

is hesitant to recognize that the Gospels are biographies, it is undeniable that they are closely affiliated with that genre. In other words, they participate in the genre of ancient biography.

Others resist by contending that, with the possible exception of Luke, who was Greek, the Evangelists were unlikely to have been familiar with the genre of Greco-Roman biography, much less been influenced by it. Would Matthew, a Jewish tax collector, or John the son of Zebedee, a Jewish fisherman, have read or even known of earlier Greco-Roman biographies, much less have known how to write one? At first glance, this appears to be a reasonable line of thought. However, it is entirely irrelevant.

As alluded to above, plenty of data suggest the Gospels are closely related to the genre of Greco-Roman biography. Given that data, if Matthew and John were not familiar with that genre, this could suggest that they did not compose those Gospels rather than suggesting those Gospels do not belong to Greco-Roman biography. Moreover, a huge gap exists between the extent of literacy that would have been required to be a tax collector and what is required to produce a biography as sophisticated as Matthew's Gospel. An even greater gap probably existed between the literacy required of a fisherman, if literacy was even necessary in that occupation, and that of one who could write John's Gospel. The traditional authors of the Gospels would very likely have needed help for writing their accounts of Jesus.

Scholars refer to a clerk who provided services such as copying, taking dictation, and editing as an *amanuensis* and the friendlier term *secretary*. During the final days of the Roman Republic, Cicero was one of its finest statesmen. His training in philosophy, rhetoric, and law assisted him in becoming one of Rome's most powerful men. Although known for his great writing and speeches, most modern readers are unaware that Cicero had a secretary named Tiro. While Tiro was once recovering from an illness, Cicero sent him some letters that have been preserved to this day in copies. In one letter, Cicero tells Tiro,

> Your services to me are beyond count—in my home and out of it, in Rome and abroad, in private affairs and public, in my studies and literary work.[9]

9. Cicero, *Fam.* (*Letters to Friends*) 16.4.3. *Cicero: Letters to Friends, Volume II*, ed. and trans. D. R. Shackleton Bailey LCL 206 (Cambridge: Harvard University Press, 2001), 29. See Richards, *Paul and First-Century Letter Writing*, 75.

That Tiro was very much responsible for aiding Cicero in his writing and in the public reading of what he had written becomes even clearer in another letter Cicero wrote to him:

> Pompey is staying with me as I write, enjoying himself in cheerful mood. He wanted to hear my compositions, but I told him that in your absence my tongue of authorship is tied completely.[10]

> *Pompey* is properly pronounced "POM-Pee," not "Pom-PAY" as one commonly hears. The latter is the name of the Italian city destroyed when Mount Vesuvius erupted in AD 79 and is spelled *Pompeii*.

Although highly educated and proficient in writing and public speaking, Cicero made robust use of his secretary Tiro to improve his content and its presentation.

The apostle Paul also made use of a secretary when writing at least some of his letters. At the end of 1 Corinthians, Colossians, and 2 Thessalonians, Paul uses the same words in all three to say that he wrote the greeting: "I, Paul, write this greeting with my own hand" (1 Cor. 16:21 // Col. 4:18 // 2 Thess. 3:17; see also Gal. 6:11). This suggests that a secretary had written the rest of the letter. But to what extent did secretaries participate in the composition of Paul's letters? Were Paul's secretaries merely transcribers, or did they play the greater role of contributors or even composers?

My friend Randy Richards is an expert on the matter of ancient letter-writing. His book *Paul and First-Century Letter Writing: Secretaries, Composition and Collection* broke new ground.[11] Richards says that shorthand writing was probably invented in the first century BC. John Ramsey

---

10. Cicero, *Fam.* 16.10.2. *Cicero: Letters to Friends, Volume I*, ed. and trans. D. R. Shackleton Bailey, LCL 205 (Cambridge: Harvard University Press, 2001), 226–27. See Richards, *Paul and First-Century Letter Writing*, 75–76. The text as transmitted in the manuscripts reads "Pompeius" (the general and political figure Pompey, thrice consul), for which D. R. Shackleton Bailey in the Loeb edition (2001) prints the conjecture "Pomponius," making Cicero refer to his close friend Atticus (T. Pomponius Atticus). Since "Pompeius" is supported by the manuscripts, I have substituted "Pomponius" in Bailey's translation with "Pompey." Whichever reading is adopted has no bearing on the point Cicero is making, namely, that Tiro's role in Cicero's literary endeavors amounts to much more than merely taking dictation.

11. E. Randolph Richards, *Paul and First-Century Letter Writing: Secretaries, Composition and Collection* (Downers Grove, IL: InterVarsity Press, 2004).

reveals that by the late 50s AD "examples begin to multiply of public addresses (*contiones*) that were committed to writing at the time of delivery and circulated soon afterwards." This informs us that a system of shorthand had probably been developed by that time.[12] And this is when Paul wrote. Those most skilled would likely have been in Rome serving its politicians. However, there were probably secretaries skilled in shorthand who worked outside of the city of Rome. Whether Paul had access to one is unknown. So it is difficult to know the extent of the role played by the secretaries Paul utilized when writing at least some of his letters. That said, had a secretary played a significant role in the composition of one of Paul's letters, he very likely would have sent that letter only after he had given it his final approval.

Even if Paul's secretaries wrote precisely what Paul dictated to them, it is probable that his secretary did more on at least one occasion. The crown jewel of Paul's letters is Romans. Its literary quality far surpasses that of his other letters. So it is very likely that the editorial hand of Paul's secretary for that letter played a significant role in its composition. His name is Tertius, and he mentions his involvement in Romans 16:22: "I, Tertius, who wrote this letter, greet you in the Lord."

Cicero and Paul were highly educated. Still, they made use of a secretary for the composition of the literature they wrote. At least sometimes, the role of their secretary was greater than merely taking dictation from them. It seems reasonable, then, to expect that Matthew, Mark, John, and perhaps even Luke would also have used secretaries when composing their Gospels. Those secretaries likely had at least an equal, if not an even greater, role in the composition of those Gospels than Paul's secretaries had in the composition of his letters since Matthew, Mark, and John were almost certainly less educated than Paul, the Gospels are substantially longer than a letter, and they were written with unique thematic focuses that have been recognized since the days of the early church. Given the degree of literacy required to write the Gospels, the secretaries who assisted the authors in their composition must have been quite familiar with the literary conventions in play at the time. Therefore, the matter of whether Matthew, Mark, and John, as Jews, would have been familiar with a Greco-Roman genre is irrelevant since all that would have been necessary is that their secretaries were.

---

12. From the forthcoming commentary on the Latin historian Asconius Pedianus by John Ramsey (Oxford University Press), note 42C-c.

This observation also answers a popular argument offered by some skeptics. They assert that the traditional authorship of Matthew and John cannot be correct since John and probably Matthew would have been illiterate and, therefore, incapable of composing biographies of Jesus. This argument falls flat on its face when we consider that the authors of Matthew and John probably made use of secretaries.[13]

BIOGRAPHIES AS PORTRAITS

We would be mistaken if we assumed that ancient biography had the same objectives and standards as modern biography. Modern biography is attentive to the psychological makeup of the main character, the biographee. What causes—environment, family structure, education, emotional, social, cultural—shaped the biographee to become who he or she was? The ancients had no such interest because they believed that people were born with the character they would exhibit as adults. Ancient biographers sought to narrate sayings and deeds of the biographee that illuminated his character.

Plutarch, often regarded as the greatest ancient biographer, wrote some of his most important biographies less than twenty years after John's Gospel was composed. The most frequently quoted portion of Plutarch's writings appears in chapter one of his *Life of Alexander*:

> For it is not Histories that I am writing, but Lives; and in the most illustrious deeds there is not always a manifestation of virtue or vice, nay, a slight thing like a phrase or a jest often makes a greater revelation of character than battles where thousands fall, or the greatest armaments, or sieges of cities. Accordingly, just as painters get the likenesses in their portraits from the face and the expression of the eyes, wherein the character shows itself, but make very little account of the other parts of the body, so I must be permitted to devote myself rather to the signs of the soul in men, and by means of these to portray the life of each, leaving to others the description of their great contests.[14]

The tone of Plutarch's words suggests he was following an existing objective of biography rather than amending or inventing it. He makes similar

---

13. I am not contending at this point that the traditional authorship of Matthew and John are correct. I am saying that the argument from illiteracy against their traditional authorship holds no weight.

14. Plut. *Alex.* 1.2–3 (Perrin, LCL).

statements elsewhere.[15] Plutarch compares a *Life* (i.e., a biography) to a portrait. When we think of a portrait being created, whether drawn, painted, or sculpted, we have in mind the subject, referred to as the "sitter," remaining in the same position for hours while the artist meticulously does his or her work. The process no doubt involved such a practice. But creating a portrait involved more.

Even as late as the seventeenth and eighteenth centuries, portrait painters would often employ certain symbolism to communicate aspects of the person featured in the portrait. Art historian Jean Sorabella observes that a hand in a book confers an air of learned nonchalance when a person was sitting. But if the person was standing with a left hand on the hip and the right hand fingering the pages of a book, the sitter was prone to action and bravado. A hand on a hip frequently appears in portraits of rulers and would-be rulers, as in Van Dyck's portrait of James Stuart (ca. 1635). A full-length portrait increased the sitter's air of power and self-possession, while a magnificent costume highlighted the sitter's wealth and taste for fashion. Items from the sitter's profession were often included in a portrait, such as the inclusion of a Bible in a portrait of a pastor.[16]

Portraits attempted to capture the essence and life of a person in a very small space and did not have the objective of representing precise details as one might see in a photograph. Plutarch informs us that the objective of ancient biography is to provide readers with a *literary portrait* of the main character. Although we should not press the portrait analogy too far, we should not conceive of ancient biography as the attempt to provide readers with precise reporting and historical descriptions nearing photographic accuracy. Imposing modern expectations on ancient texts and authors is anachronistic since it assumes a standard not aligned with their objectives. Although this may be new to many reading this book, it has been common knowledge among Gospels scholars for some time. A few decades ago, evangelical New Testament scholar Robert Guelich wrote the following in an article published by the *Journal of the Evangelical Theological Society*:

15. See Plut. *Nic.* 1.5, *Pomp.* 8.7, *Cim.* 2.3–5, and *Cat. Min.* 37.1–5.

16. I am indebted to Tiffany Bergeron, my colleague at Houston Christian University, for these insights in emails dated October 13 and 15, 2017, in which she also referred me to the following article: Jean Sorabella, "Portraiture in Renaissance and Baroque Europe," in *Heilbrunn Timeline of Art History* (New York: The Metropolitan Museum of Art, 2000–), https://www.metmuseum.org/toah/hd/port/hd_port.htm (August 2007).

> Without doubt, therefore, a consensus about the nature and content of the gospels has emerged among evangelical scholars. This consensus has grown out of the Biblical evidence and the unavoidable conclusions of critical scholarship. But the consensus is shared primarily by those who have worked extensively in the gospels themselves. The evangelical scene at large—including lay people, pastors, colleagues in other theological disciplines, and even some in Biblical studies—still operates on the basis of the gospels' being essentially verbal snapshots whose red-letter editions highlight the very words of Jesus. This difference in perspective regarding the gospels among evangelicals has led and will continue to lead to serious tension, since the standards of precision and the criteria of reliability applying to snapshots do not necessarily apply to portraits and vice versa. One way to relieve the tension is to deal with the issue by continuing to produce solid exegetical studies in the gospels, studies employing critical tools. Ultimately, however, one must address the direct implication of the gospels taken as theological portraits.[17]

Since revealing a biographee's character was an objective of ancient biographers, we may anticipate that the Evangelists follow this objective in their biographies of Jesus. Reading the Gospels in view of their biographical nature provides a valuable insight that is often overlooked in the matter of Christology, that is, how the New Testament literature presents Jesus. Some critics have argued that we can view an evolving Christology in the Gospels. These critics have contended that we do not observe a divine Jesus in the first two Gospels composed: Mark and Matthew. It is not until Luke's Gospel that we find Jesus as the divine Son of God, and only John presents Jesus as being God.

However, reading the Gospels in view of their biographical genre sheds great light on Mark's Christology and refutes the above view. Mark begins his Gospel as follows (1:1–3):

> The beginning of the gospel of Jesus Christ [the Son of God].[18] Just as it is written in Isaiah the prophet,

17. Robert A. Guelich, "The Gospels: Portraits of Jesus and His Ministry," *Journal of the Evangelical Theological Society* 24, no. 2 (June 1981): 117–25. I am indebted to Jonathan Hanna for alerting me to this article.

18. Scholars are divided on whether "the Son of God" was original or added later. Therefore, it has been enclosed in brackets.

> Behold, I am sending my messenger before your face
> Who will prepare your way.
> The voice of one crying in the wilderness
> Prepare the way of the Lord.
> Make his paths straight.

Mark is quoting from Malachi 3:1 and Isaiah 40:3. First-time readers might anticipate that Mark is going to write of Jesus preparing the way for God. However, Mark immediately proceeds to inform his readers that God has sent John the Baptist to prepare the way for Jesus, who is called "the Lord." In its original context of Isaiah 40:3, "the Lord" refers to God. And Mark has applied this text to Jesus. Thus, it appears that in the very first sentences of his biography of Jesus, Mark may be portraying Jesus as God, although Mark might be thinking of Jesus as God's emissary without requiring his divinity. Yet there is much more for us to consider.

In chapter 2, Mark tells the story of Jesus healing a paralytic and forgiving his sins, to which the experts in the Jewish law who are present (called "scribes") respond by thinking that Jesus has blasphemed, contending that only God can forgive sins (2:5–11). In Mark 3:22–27, scribes assert that Jesus is able to exorcise demons because he is possessed by Satan. But Jesus answers that Satan does not work against himself. Instead, Jesus claims that his exorcisms demonstrate that he has bound Satan and is now plundering his kingdom of souls. What a bold claim! For what mere human can bind Satan? In Mark 4:37–39, Jesus commands the wind and the waves to be still and they obey, which is an act attributed to God in the Old Testament (Pss. 89:9; 107:28–29; Eccl. 8:8). In Mark 5:22–24, 35–43, Jesus raises someone from the dead, which Ecclesiastes 8:8 asserts is something only God can do. Although the Bible contains a few other instances when the dead are raised, God is doing the raising in answer to the prayer of his servant (1 Kings 17:17–24; 2 Kings 4:17–37; Acts 9:36–42; a possible exception is Acts 20:9–12). But Jesus raised the dead without appealing to God. In Mark 6:45–51 Jesus walks on water, which Job 9:8 states is something only God can do. In Mark 9:14–29 Jesus casts out a demon after his disciples were unable to do so. Later that day his disciples ask him why they were unable to cast out the demon, and Jesus tells them, "This kind is not able to be cast out except by prayer." However, Jesus could do it without prayer. In Mark 12:35–37, the Messiah is David's Lord. In Mark 12:1–12 and 13:32, Jesus claims to be God's Son in a sense that is greater than prophets and angels. In Mark 13:24–27 and 14:61–64, God will give Jesus all authority to judge the world and be worshiped and served in a manner that belongs to God alone (see Deut. 6:13; 10:20; Dan. 7:13–14).[19]

> Richard Hays has noted that readers may hear echoes of the Old Testament when reading Mark's account of Jesus walking on water. Job 9:8 speaks of God who "trampled the waves of the sea" (ESV). The LXX is even clearer here: God "walks upon the sea as upon dry ground." Moreover, Mark's statement that Jesus "desired to pass by them" (6:48) suggests he may have yet another verse in mind, one that appears only three verses later and speaks of God "passing by me" (Job 9:11 LXX). Hays says that Jesus's response to his fearful disciples, "It is I [*egō eimi*; lit. "I am"]. Do not be afraid," further highlights Jesus's claim to divinity in this story.[20]

When Mark is read in view of its biographical genre, it is very clear that he narrates numerous teachings and deeds of Jesus in order to illuminate his character: Jesus is God in some real sense.[21]

WHY THIS IS IMPORTANT

Because the Gospels are God's Word, we want to understand them as their authors intended. Reading them in view of their biographical nature can reveal some things that previously eluded us—for example, the super-high Christology in Mark.[22] Helen Bond writes, "Indeed, the fact that we are dealing with *bioi* [i.e., ancient biography] should be the starting point for all gospel discussion. It is only when we understand something of ancient *bioi* that we can start to understand what the evangelists wanted to communicate, and why they chose this specific literary genre to do it."[23] Moreover, recognizing that secretaries probably played a robust part in the

19. Important references also appear in the Pseudepigrapha: 1 Enoch 38:1–6; 40:4; 45:3; 46:1–3; 48:5; 49:2, 4; 51:1–3; 61:8; 62:5–6, 9, 11; 69:27–29; 4 Ezra 13:8–12, 37–38; 14:3.

20. See Richard B. Hays, *Reading Backwards: Figural Christology and the Fourfold Gospel Witness* (Waco: Baylor University Press, 2014), 24–25, especially 26.

21. It is worth noting that Paul may have written before any of the Gospels, and his view of Jesus is every bit as high as we find in John's Gospel.

22. A "high Christology" or high view of Jesus regards him as being divine in some sense. In contrast, a "low Christology" rejects the view that Jesus is divine in any sense. The Gospel of Mark has what I am referring to as a "super-high Christology" because its portrait of Jesus is that he is in some sense God.

23. Bond, *The First Biography of Jesus*, 4–5.

composition of the Gospels effectively addresses the objection that since most of the authors of the Gospels were Jews, they would not have been familiar with the genre of Greco-Roman biography, much less write in that genre. It also answers a common objection to the traditional authorship of some of the Gospels. At this point, you may not see the relevance of this matter toward addressing differences in the Gospels. Stay with me. It will all make sense as we progress.

SUMMARY

The Gospels possess qualities that suggest they either belong to the genre of ancient biography or, at minimum, participate in that genre. The objective of writing a biography in antiquity was to create a literary portrait of the main character. In doing so, ancient biographers were allowed a bit of freedom in the manner they reported an event. Biographers normally had little interest in their main character's life prior to the launching of their adult vocation. We should not think of the composition of the Gospels as their authors sitting alone and putting reed to papyrus. Secretaries probably played a robust role in their composition, just as they did with other literature, such as some of Paul's letters, which are far shorter than the Gospels.

Reading the Gospels in view of the objective and nature of ancient biography provides interpretive insights. Because the biographer was given a bit of freedom when reporting events, we should not think an author is providing us with "verbal snapshots" that replicate details precisely as they were at the moment being described. Moreover, sometimes the interpretive insights gained from viewing the Gospels as ancient biographies are profound, such as the illumination of Mark's very high Christology.

QUESTIONS FOR FURTHER THOUGHT

1. What is the most interesting thing you learned in this chapter?
2. Let us suppose that an artist has completed a full-length portrait of a general and included battles occurring in the background. That portrait may be said to be accurate in view of the conventions of portrait painting, although it may not be entirely accurate in the sense of a mirrorlike reflection or of a photograph. Do you think this analogy is appropriate for ancient literature, including the Gospels? Why or why not?

3. Very few biographies in antiquity were written by Jews and the Gospels possess several qualities that, at minimum, suggest that they participate in the genre of Greco-Roman biography. How might these observations impact how we read the Gospels?
4. Have you previously considered the possibility of biblical authors using secretaries? What are your thoughts about the role of a secretary in the composition of a Gospel?

CHAPTER 5

TRUTH-TELLING IN ANCIENT BIOGRAPHY

Ancient biographies differed from ancient novels. The latter usually narrated fictitious events that were located in the distant past, and they were typically romances in which two lovers had to face and overcome obstacles. Their characters were almost exclusively fictitious. On rare occasions when an ancient novel included a historical character, that character had not lived as recently as within a century of the time of writing.[1]

None of the Gospels are romances. Not a scrap of evidence supports the novel claim that Jesus and Mary Magdalene were romantically involved. I know of no credible scholar who thinks such a relationship existed between them. All of the Gospels mention historical people who had lived within a century of when the Gospels were written, and most of them had lived within only a few decades. The Roman emperors Augustus and Tiberius, Herod the Great and three of his sons (Archelaus, Antipas, and Phillip), John the Baptist, the Jewish high priests Annas and Caiaphas, the Roman prefect Pontius Pilate, Jesus and his brother James are all historical characters. Mark's Gospel was probably written within only fifteen to thirty-five years of when Pilate was prefect of Judea.[2] The person mentioned in the Gospels who is furthest removed from their composition is Herod the Great. John's Gospel was probably composed last, just under a century after Herod's death.[3]

1. Keener, *The Historical Jesus*, 77.

2. Pilate was removed from his office and summoned to Rome in AD 36 or 37. Mark probably wrote sometime between AD 50 to 70, with the majority of today's scholars dating Mark at some time between AD 65 to 70. See "The Modern-Day Scholarly Opinion of the Dating of Mark's Gospel," an unpublished MA thesis by Joshua Pelletier that I supervised at Houston Christian University. Pelletier surveyed more than 200 critical New Testament scholars writing in English between 1965–2016 and who commented on when Mark composed his Gospel. As I write this in 2023, he is presently expanding his sampling in doctoral research.

3. However, John does not mention Herod the Great and begins narrating events that occurred

Ancient biographies had the underlying objective of reporting historical events about a historical person. This is a general rule and should not be pressed too far because not all biographers and historians in antiquity had the same commitment to accuracy. The Roman historian Tacitus is regarded as being a fairly accurate historian. In contrast, the Greek historian Aristobulus of Cassandreia wrote about the *Battle of Hydaspes* between Alexander the Great and King Porus. In it, Aristobulus invented a scene that depicted Alexander single-handedly killing an elephant. When Alexander read it during a voyage, he discarded the book and said Aristobulus should be treated in a similar manner.[4] Helen Bond observes that while Plutarch and Suetonius "were clearly interested in historical research and reliability," others such as Xenophon and Philostratus were not.[5] Accordingly, after identifying the Gospels as either belonging to or having a close affinity to the genre of ancient biography, it cannot be merely assumed that each of the Evangelists had Tacitus's level of commitment to accurate reporting.

We moderns value precise accuracy in reporting. Great precision was required to go to the moon and return. Great precision is necessary for many of the items to work that we now take for granted in our daily lives, such as personal computers and mobile phones. We demand nothing but precision from the surgeons who remove cataracts from our eyes, repair discs in our backs and necks, extract cancerous tumors, and perform organ transplants. Precision in one's testimony pertaining to an event witnessed and the words that were spoken is required in a court of law. So it is only natural that when historians tell us about the past, we often want to know precisely how those past events transpired, especially when the events carry great importance to our lives. This is not to say that we want to know every detail. But it is to say that we desire that what is reported mirrors to a great degree what we the readers would have seen and heard had we been there.

Historiography can be defined as the presentation of past events in narrative format. Tacitus's *Annals of Rome* (early second century) describes events in the Roman Empire from AD 14 to 68. *Schindler's List* is a movie that dramatizes Oskar Schindler's actions to save Jews during

---

thirty-one to thirty-four years after Herod's death. Luke is probably the last Gospel to mention Herod the Great (Luke 1:5).

4. Lucian, *Hist. conscr.* (*How to Write History*), vol. 6 of *Lucian*, trans. K. Kilburn, LCL 430 (Cambridge: Harvard University Press, 2006), 12.

5. Bond, *The First Biography of Jesus*, 67.

WWII. Whether presented in the format of a book or movie, both are historiography.

Movie producers understand that, even when a story is "based on true events," they are free to take some artistic license. Many times license is taken to bring about greater continuity to the narrative, to increase drama, to illustrate a point more clearly, merely to simplify, or even because the author or producer desires to tell the story in that manner and is willing to set aside a priority on accuracy. Sometimes two or more characters are conflated into a single person. Words or actions performed by a certain person are attributed to another in order to avoid having to introduce a new character. Events are sometimes narrated to have occurred over a shorter period of time. Focus is placed on a single character to the extent that readers get the impression the character in focus is the only one acting rather than being one of several. These are only a few of the liberties taken by modern historiographers. Here is a nice example provided by Darrell Bock:

> One film, *Hacksaw Ridge*, portrays the life of Desmond Doss, a war hero who chose never to wield a weapon in battle for religious reasons. In the movie, Desmond enlists in the army in support of the WWII effort even though he does not believe in killing and will not bear arms in battle. In real life, he was drafted, as an article shows from the *Washington Post* on March 25, 2006. Obviously this is a difference. A colleague disturbed by the movie's change pointed out this detail to me and asked what I thought of the move. When I checked this out, what I found was intriguing. Desmond had been drafted but was offered a conscientious objector status that would have allowed him out of the draft and out of the Army. He refused to take it arguing he wanted to be a medic and serve in a way that could contribute to the war effort in light of his convictions. The Army took him in on this basis. So now the question remains, in the movie's summarizing did portraying him as enlisting, that is, choosing to serve, actually fit well what he did? I might contend this is an adequate summarizing of what took place, reflecting the state of choosing to serve. The example shows the potential ambiguity of a "creative" detail when considered in light of literary tendencies to summarize.[6]

6. Darrell L. Bock, "Greco-Roman and Jewish Historiography as Backdrop for the Gospels," in *Fountains of Wisdom: In Conversation with James H. Charlesworth*. ed. Gerbern S. Oegema, Henry W. Morisada Rietz, Loren Stuckenbruck (London: T & T Clark, 2022), 243.

The first book written by my late friend Nabeel Qureshi was a *New York Times* bestseller: *Seeking Allah, Finding Jesus*. It is an autobiography of his journey from Islam to Christianity. Here is what Nabeel wrote in the introduction:

> By its very nature, a narrative biography must take certain liberties with the story it shares. Please do not expect camera-like accuracy. That is not the intent of this book, and to meet such a standard, it would have to be a twenty-two-year-long video, most of which would bore even my mother to tears.
>
> The words I have in quotations are rough approximations. A few of the conversations represent multiple meetings condensed into one. In some instances, stories are displaced in the timeline to fit the topical categorization. In other instances, people who were present in the conversation were left out of the narrative for the sake of clarity. All of these devices are normal for narrative biographies. . . . Please read accordingly.[7]

This is an autobiographical account written in the twenty-first century. Biographers in antiquity used many of the same literary devices mentioned by Nabeel as well as other devices. Ancient historical literature rarely ever intended to describe events with the precision of a legal transcript. Even modern historical literature often lacks a commitment to such a degree of accuracy.

Truth-telling in ancient historiography permitted the facts to be reported with some elasticity. Sallust commanded one of Caesar's legions and would become one of Rome's finest historians. Tacitus referred to Sallust as "that most admirable Roman historian."[8] The famous Roman rhetorician Quintilian said Sallust was a greater historian than Livy and that "one needs further progress to understand him."[9] Interestingly, Sallust occasionally displaced statements and speeches from their original context and transplanted them in a different one to highlight the true intensity and even the true nature of those events.[10] The finest ancient historians commonly used that technique and others. In my view, this

7. Nabeel Qureshi, *Seeking Allah, Finding Jesus: A Devout Muslim Encounters Christianity* (Grand Rapids: Zondervan, 2014), 19.

8. Tacitus, *Annales* 3.30.

9. *The Institutio oratoria of Quintilian* (*Institutes of Oratory*), 2.5.19, trans. H. E. Butler, 4 vols., LCL 124–27 (London: Heinemann, 1921–22), 124:309.

10. This will be discussed in chapter 6.

does not undermine the overall reliability of the literature in which they appear, as long as we have the understanding that what we are reading was most often intended to convey an accurate gist of the people and events described rather than preserving details with the precision of a legal transcript.

When it came to sticking strictly to the facts, Thucydides (fifth century BC) and Polybius (second century BC) were some of the more scrupulous historians in the Greco-Roman period.[11] Consider the following by Polybius: "The peculiar function of history is to discover, in the first place, the words actually spoken, whatever they were."[12] This does not mean Polybius had in mind that every word must be written precisely as spoken, that paraphrase and approximation were verboten, and that numbers could not be rounded up or down.[13] We get the gist of what Polybius means. That is why it should not worry us when we read Acts 8:32, quoting Isaiah 53:7: "As a sheep, he was led to slaughter, and as a lamb before its shearer is silent, so he did not open his mouth." Luke is thinking in terms of Jesus being generally nonresponsive rather than entirely without words. After all, Luke also reports that Jesus spoke at his arrest, spoke at his trial before the Sanhedrin, spoke at his trial before Pilate, spoke on his way to the cross, and spoke while on the cross.[14]

Around the middle of the second century, Lucian of Samosata wrote a short book describing some of the conventions of his day for reporting history properly. This short book is full of insights pertaining to what was allowable and what was not when writing a history. Here is a small sampling pertaining to accuracy:

---

11. Four-and-a-half to five centuries after Thucydides, two-and-a-half to three centuries after Polybius, and contemporaneous with John's Gospel, Quintilian opined that he had no hesitations matching the histories written by Sallust as being equal in quality with that of Thucydides (Quintilian, *The Orator's Education* 10.1.101).

12. Polybius, *Hist.* (*Histories*) 12.25b. Polybius, *The Histories, Books 9–16*, W. R. Paton, trans., Frank W. Walbank and Christian Habicht, LCL 159 (Cambridge: Harvard University Press, 2011), 413.

13. It is also worth observing that Polybius and Thucydides invented content for their speeches on occasion when the actual content was unknown.

14. See Luke 22:52b–53, 67b–69; 23:3c, 28b–31, 43, 46a. It is uncertain whether Jesus uttered, "Father, forgive them. For they do not know what they are doing" (Luke 23:34). Several significant manuscripts do not include it. However, some scholars believe it is an authentic statement of Jesus that was inserted by a copyist at a later though relatively early time (see Bruce M. Metzger, *A Textual Commentary on the Greek New Testament*, 2nd ed. [New York: United Bible Societies, 1994], 154). The note in the NET Bible for Luke 23:34 explains the difficulty in deciding one way or the other for inclusion. Three of the four Greek New Testaments most widely used by scholars include it with notation (NA[28], Holmes, and the SBL Greek New Testament), while the Cambridge Greek New Testament (Tyndale House) includes it without notation.

> History has one task and one only—what is useful—and that comes from truth alone.[15]

> The historian's one task is to tell the thing as it happened. . . . For history, I say again, has this and this only for its own; if a man will start upon it, he must sacrifice to no god but Truth.[16]

> Above all, let him bring a mind like a mirror, clear, gleaming-bright, accurately centered, displaying the shape of things just as he receives them, free from distortion, false coloring, and misrepresentation. His concern is different from that of the orators—what historians have to relate is fact and will speak for itself, for it has already happened.[17]

But what does Lucian mean when he says the sole task of the historian is "to tell the thing as it happened" in a manner that is "free from distortion, false coloring, and misrepresentation"? Did he have the same standards in mind that we have? We may never know for sure. However, it is noteworthy that Lucian named Herodotus and Thucydides as being among the "best historians" (*hoi aristoi tōn sungrapheōn*).[18] For whereas Thucydides was one to report with accuracy, Herodotus took significant liberties.

Did Jewish historians of that era write with higher standards of accuracy than Greek and Roman historians? Josephus said it was important to report the facts for posterity and for the benefit of the public. He also claims that he will accurately describe what is contained in the Jewish Scriptures without adding to them or subtracting from them.[19] However, Josephus goes on to add and subtract from the Scriptures, though not in a major way. Of Josephus's accuracy, classicist Paul Maier writes,

> Another fault in Josephus is one he shares with most of the ancient historians: a propensity to exaggerate, particularly with numbers. Casualty lists after some of the battles are so implausibly high that even to note such overstatements would clutter too many pages in the text. The reader must also discount such hyperboles as, for example, the claim that so much blood was shed in Jerusalem during its conquest that streams of

15. Lucian, *How to Write History*, 9.
16. Lucian, *How to Write History*, 39.
17. Lucian, *How to Write History*, 50.
18. Lucian, *How to Write History*, 54.
19. Josephus, *Jewish Antiquities* 1:1–4, 17; 4:196.

> gore extinguished fires there. Exaggeration, however, was so common a conceit among most of the ancient sources that if a Herodotus could claim Xerxes invaded Greece with a total force of 5,283,220, Josephus may have felt it unwise to provide accurate figures if such inflation was common fare at the time.[20]

Colin Hemer similarly writes,

> Josephus, while an invaluable witness to matters within his experience, is prone to sensationalize and exaggerate; Luke is restrained. Josephus dwells on the horrors of the famine in doomed Jerusalem (*BJ* 5.10.3.429–38) or the grotesque fates of refugees (*BJ* 5.12.4.548–52), or a mother eating her child, a scene complete with speeches (*BJ* 6.3.3.199–4.213). This problem is especially apparent in the treatment of numbers. In Acts, 4,000 men follow the Egyptian bandit into the desert, and in Josephus, 30,000. Josephus has "not less than three million Jews" in an anti-Roman demonstration; can we accept such a figure?[21]

The only other Jewish historian of that era outside the New Testament literature was Philo. Classicist Brian McGing notes instances where Philo transfers words or deeds to a different character, displaces an event from its true timing and transplants it in a different one, changes the chronological order of events, and expands stories via elaboration.[22] Moreover, Philo changes details found in the scriptural texts in several instances, creating discrepancies between Philo's texts and the Scriptures. Furthermore, Philo and Josephus both recast some of their characters in a slightly different form so that they fit in better with their readers' cultural setting.

Did the authors of the Gospels hold to a higher standard of accuracy than their Greek, Roman, and Jewish contemporaries? Was the truth-telling in their accounts closer to that of modern conventions? Those who answer in the affirmative often appeal to their divine inspiration and view

---

20. Paul L. Maier, trans. and ed., *Josephus: The Essential Works; A Condensation of* Jewish Antiquities *and* The Jewish War (Grand Rapids: Kregel, 1994), 11.

21. Colin J. Hemer, *The Book of Acts in the Setting of Hellenistic History*, ed. C. H. Gempf (Winona Lake, IN: Eisenbrauns, 1990), 97–98.

22. See Brian McGing, "Philo's Adaptation of the Bible in His Life of Moses," in *The Limits of Ancient Biography*, ed. Brian McGing and Judith Mossman (Swansea: Classical Press of Wales, 2006), 117–40. See also Louis H. Feldman, *Philo's Portrayal of Moses in the Context of Ancient Judaism* (Notre Dame, IN: University of Notre Dame Press, 2007). Feldman mentions changes in the order of the plagues, among other changes (361, 363).

such as requiring great precision in accuracy. Sometimes they appeal to John 14:26: "But the Helper, the Holy Spirit, whom the Father will send in my name, that one will teach you all things and will remind you of all the things that I said to you."[23] We should resist the temptation to read more into texts like this than is stated. Jesus is telling his disciples that the Holy Spirit will remind them of what he had taught them so that they may testify about Jesus. However, the texts provide no instructions pertaining to the ways the disciples were permitted to communicate his teachings. And there are no hints that they were forbidden from paraphrasing Jesus's words while maintaining the message behind his words, even expanding them to include their theological implications.[24] Therefore, the only way to answer the question of whether the authors of the Gospels reported facts with a greater precision than other biographers of that era is to observe what the authors of the Gospels do. We will take a close look at this in the chapters that follow. For now, I want to draw attention to two occurrences in the Gospels where the author takes some liberty reporting details in order to make a point. In doing so, he sacrifices accuracy on the ground level of precise reporting while providing his readers with a high-level view of the person and mission of Jesus.

GENEALOGY OF JESUS

Many have attempted to harmonize the differences between the genealogies of Jesus presented by Matthew and Luke (Matt. 1:1–17 // Luke 3:23–38). A popular proposal, though not among scholars, is to say Matthew is tracing Jesus's ancestry through his mother, Mary, whereas Luke is doing so through his earthly father, Joseph. There are numerous challenges to this view.[25] However, I will focus on only one: *Matthew's Math*. Matthew traces Jesus's ancestry back to Abraham, whereas Luke goes all the way back to Adam. If we focus on the generations between

---

23. See Lydia McGrew, *The Mirror or the Mask: Liberating the Gospels from Literary Devices* (Tampa, FL: DeWard, 2019), 129–30.

24. Recall Bruce's assessment that John often gives us "an expanded paraphrase," "a translation of the freest kind," "a transposition into another key," "all this and much more the Holy Spirit accomplished in our Evangelist." See F. F. Bruce, *The Gospel and Epistles of John*, 16. Paul Anderson, an evangelical Johannine specialist asserts that several motifs in John "most likely represents the constructive work of the Evangelist in crafting his own understanding of Jesus' spoken ministry." See Anderson, *Riddles of the Fourth Gospel*, 177.

25. For a good discussion on the two genealogies, see Raymond E. Brown, *The Birth of the Messiah: Commentary on the Infancy Narratives in the Gospels of Matthew and Luke*, updated ed. (New York: Doubleday, 1993), 64–94.

Abraham and Jesus, Luke names fifty-seven whereas Matthew has forty-two. The challenge is that Matthew claims that his genealogy includes *all* of the generations from Abraham to Jesus (Matt. 1:17). Moreover, in his division of the forty-two generations into three sets of fourteen, Matthew uses the name Jechoniah twice. He is the final name in the second set of fourteen generations and the first name in the third set. Given his omission of several names and his lack of care regarding the use of Jechoniah, Matthew appears to be more interested in the number fourteen than in reporting precisely. But why?

Several scholars have proposed that Matthew has employed a rhetorical device known as *gematria* whereby numerical values are assigned to letters: e.g., A = 1; B = 2; C= 3; and so on. Ancient Hebrew had twenty-two letters, all consonants. In addition, letters were often used as numbers. We observe this in Psalm 119, which includes twenty-two sections, each titled by a letter of the Hebrew alphabet. In Hebrew, the name *David* contains three letters: D (*Dalet*), V (*Vav*), D (*Dalet*). *Dalet* is the fourth letter in the Hebrew alphabet and *Vav* is the sixth letter. Assigning numerical values to each letter in the name *David*, we arrive at a total of 14: D (4) + V (6) + D (4). Matthew appears to have arranged his genealogy artistically in order to communicate to his Jewish readers that Jesus is the Son of David, the Messiah. Interestingly, Matthew concludes his genealogy as follows: "and Jacob begat Joseph the husband of Mary, from whom Jesus was begotten who is called Christ [i.e., Messiah]" (Matt. 1:16). Jesus being Messiah is integral to Matthew's portrait of Jesus.

SERMON ON THE MOUNT

There is another item in Matthew that suggests he is more interested in his portrait of Jesus at times than in reporting with precision: Jesus's Sermon on the Mount. The most famous sermon in human history is reported by Matthew and Luke (Matt. 5–7 // Luke 6:20–49). The differences between the accounts have led some to believe Luke is narrating a different event, although most scholars believe Matthew and Luke are reporting the same one. One difference pertains to the content of the sermon. In both Matthew and Luke, the sermon begins with the Beatitudes. However, they are stated and arranged somewhat differently. Matthew gives us eight Beatitudes, whereas Luke gives us four followed by four "woes," each of which parallels a Beatitude. For example, blessed are the poor but woe to the rich (Luke 6:20, 24). Moreover, in Matthew those in view are the "poor in spirit" and those who "hunger and thirst for righteousness," whereas Luke has in mind those living in material poverty and who hunger for food.[26]

Another difference pertains to the length of the sermon. Matthew's version has 1,991 Greek words, while there are only 580 in Luke's version. Let's consider a few possible reasons for this difference. Luke may have substantially abbreviated Jesus's Sermon. Luke's version can be read in under three minutes, whereas Jesus almost certainly spoke much longer on that occasion. Or perhaps Jesus said it as Matthew portrays it in his version of the Sermon on the Mount, then said it as Luke narrates it on a different occasion. It is fine to attempt to harmonize differences. However, more often than not, we must acknowledge that such proposals remain nothing more than unverified speculation and perhaps something worse.

Another possibility, the one held by most New Testament scholars, is that Matthew has gathered a number of Jesus's teachings given on various occasions and artistically combined them with content from Jesus's Sermon on the Mount to produce what we read. This seems likely to me. Several years ago, I memorized Jesus's Sermon on the Mount as presented in Matthew. I spent around forty-five minutes a day for five months to complete the task. It was a wonderful experience. As weeks of repeating the sermon accumulated, I unexpectedly began to see what had previously eluded me: Matthew wove the teachings together in this beautiful sermon with nearly every set of teachings smoothly transitioning to the next.[27]

Perhaps the most interesting difference in the two versions of the sermon is the location where Jesus delivers it.

> Now seeing the crowds, *he went up on the mountain*. And having sat down, his disciples came to him. And he opened his mouth and taught them, saying . . . (Matt. 5:1–2)

Luke appears to narrate the location at a slightly different place. Jesus goes to a mountain and prays all night. When day comes, he chooses the twelve apostles (Luke 6:12–16). Luke then reports the following:

> And *having come down with them, he stood on a level place*. . . . And he looked at his disciples and said . . . (Luke 6:17–20)

26. I understand the Beatitude in Matthew 5:11 to be Jesus expanding the Beatitude in 5:10.

27. Space prohibits touching on this matter further. However, I hope to write a short devotional book on the Sermon on the Mount in the future.

In Matthew, Jesus delivers his sermon on the mountain, whereas Luke has Jesus come down and deliver it from a level place. For this reason, New Testament scholars often refer to Luke's version as the Sermon on the Plain. How should we view this difference between Matthew and Luke?

We may attempt to harmonize the accounts by suggesting Jesus gave two sermons, one from atop the mountain, which Matthew reports, then he proceeded to come down and gave a similar sermon on a plain, which Luke reports. Or we may suggest that while Matthew tells us Jesus was on a mountain, he does not say Jesus was at the top when he delivered his Sermon. He could have been on a level plain on the mountain. While it is possible that one of these suggestions is an accurate description of what occurred, both seem a bit of a stretch to me. Something compels me to think Matthew changed the location.

I have made a few trips to Israel and have been to two locations where some think Jesus may have delivered the sermon, one being the traditional site. I have recited the sermon from memory at both locations and I am fairly confident that neither is where the event took place! When we think of Jesus delivering the Sermon on the Mount, we picture hundreds of people sitting on a slope and Jesus teaching on top or at least from a position higher than those listening. However, the acoustics present at such a location prohibit a large crowd from hearing him.[28] Now if we place Jesus on a plain, as Luke narrates it, and the crowd sitting on the slope of the mountain in a sort of natural amphitheater, Jesus could then be heard by hundreds, probably even by thousands.

Why would Matthew alter such a minor detail as the location where Jesus delivered his sermon? Recall that biographers in antiquity were allowed some freedom in how they reported details in order to make a point more clearly when composing their literary portrait. Many Gospel scholars have proposed that, in addition to presenting Jesus as the Messiah and Son of God, Matthew presents Jesus as the *new Moses*. Consider the following parallels that have been noted between Jesus and Moses: a king seeks to kill them shortly after birth (Pharoah, Herod); both leave Egypt; Moses and Jesus come out from water and into the wilderness (Red Sea, baptism by John); Moses spent forty years in the wilderness, and Jesus spent forty days there; Moses went up on the mountain to receive and communicate God's law; Jesus went up on the mountain to communicate

28. The first occasion when I recited the sermon in Israel was video-recorded and may be viewed at https://youtube.com/watch?v=d1BqDYkV8Jg. With just a little breeze occurring, you will get a very good impression of the poor acoustics at such a location.

God's law. In fact, Matthew uses the same wording in Greek of Jesus going up on the mountain that the LXX most often uses of Moses going up on a mountain.[29]

Although presenting Jesus as a new Moses may be what Matthew had in mind, we should note that some of those details seem forced. Although Moses and Jesus left Egypt, Moses *fled from* it whereas Jesus initially *fled to* Egypt and then left when it was safe to return to Judea. If Matthew intended to draw a parallel between Moses escaping through a parted Red Sea and Jesus's baptism, we might expect him to say the waters were parted when Jesus emerged. Instead, Matthew says that Jesus "came up from the water and *the heavens were opened*" (Matt. 3:16). And there is the important difference: Moses came down from the mountain to give the law to the people, whereas Jesus gave the sermon while on the mountain. We should proceed cautiously to avoid having hermeneutical hallucinations that see more parallels than those to which the author intended to draw our attention. A more cautious approach sees a parallel between God revealing the law to Moses on Sinai and Jesus revealing the correct interpretation of the law to others on the mountain.

The parallels suggest that Matthew may have slightly moved the location of Jesus's sermon from the base of the mountain to its summit in order to assist him in composing a literary portrait of Jesus. Accordingly, I think most scholars are correct in their belief that Matthew and Luke are narrating the same event.

WHY THIS IS IMPORTANT

In the 2004 movie *National Treasure*, the protagonists seek to find treasure hidden by Freemasons during the American Revolutionary War. In the process, they steal the Declaration of Independence because they believe that it contains clues to where the treasure is hidden. The back of the document appears to be blank. However, using special lenses created by Benjamin Franklin, they are able to see numerous symbols and the statement "Heere at the wall" ["Heere" has three *e*'s], which ultimately assist them in finding the treasure.

Some of my fondest memories are of being a young child on Christmas morning. One Christmas I received an odd book. When I opened it,

29. Gk. *anabainō + eis to horos* (Matt. 5:1; cf. Exod. 19:3; 24:12, 13, 15, 18; 34:1, 4; Num. 27:12; Deut. 9:9; 10:1, 3; 32:49).

I observed what appeared to be strange content. Page after page, all I could see were lines jumbled up in a mess. Accompanying the book were two pairs of glasses with cardboard frames. One pair had red lenses; the other had blue lenses. I could view one page through the blue lenses with no discernable difference than when I viewed it without them. However, when I peered at the same page through the red lenses, I could see a clear picture of trees, animals, and people. As in the movie, *National Treasure*, viewing the pages through the correct lenses made a huge difference.

In a similar vein, reading the Gospels through the proper lens will bring into greater focus what their authors intended to communicate, which we may otherwise miss. Rather than a macro lens that focuses very closely only on the written words, it is a wide-angle lens that takes into view the literary conventions of that day, linguistic idioms, and the cultural setting in which the Gospels were written.

If we read the Gospels through lenses prescribed for reading *modern historiography*, we will be able to understand most of what their authors were communicating. However, we are bound to misinterpret a number of items in them. Moreover, many differences in the Gospels will remain difficult to harmonize. But what if some of the differences resulted from intentional altering by the authors? Some harmonizations would be entirely incorrect, though plausible in a technical sense. For example, if what I have suggested above is correct pertaining to Matthew's genealogy of Jesus and the location of the Sermon on the Mount, it would be senseless to attempt to harmonize the details with Luke's accounts since such an exercise would assuredly lead to incorrect solutions. Moreover, we may miss important theological points, such as those Mark makes when reporting Jesus's actions that illuminate a very high Christology. When the Gospels are read through lenses prescribed for reading *ancient biography*, a lot more comes into focus.

My experience of sharing this information over the years informs me that content in this chapter will be unsettling for some modern readers who have viewed the Gospels as reporting every detail as it actually occurred. But such a paradigm is anachronistic, since it was not the objective of ancient historians to report events with that degree of accuracy.[30] Accordingly, reading the Gospels with the expectation of modern precision is to force on them modern conventions that were foreign to the genre

30. In fact, only one historian in the Greco-Roman era attempted to report past events with the degree of accuracy we moderns desire: Quintus Asconius Pedianus, or simply Asconius (AD 3–88). Little of what Asconius wrote has survived.

in which they were written. Robert Stein is an evangelical New Testament scholar who writes,

> It is evident from source criticism that the individual Evangelists "*do not intend to provide us with a record of the precise literal words of Jesus.*" Quite the contrary, they felt free to paraphrase, modify certain terms, and add comments in order to help their readers understand the "significance" of what Jesus taught. The Evangelists had no obsession with the *ipsissima verba* [i.e., the very words], for they believed that they had authority to interpret these words for their audience. Whether we see this approach as an inspired and authoritative interpretation of Jesus' words or as an unauthorized speculation—or even as a corruption—depends, of course, on our theological presuppositions, but the freedom of the Evangelists in handling the words of Jesus and their relative disinterest in simply reproducing them should raise the question of *why* we are pursuing the *ipsissima verba*.[31]

Once, after I had lectured on the matter of Gospel differences, an attorney approached me and said he wanted to believe the Gospels reported the sayings and actions of Jesus with the precision found in the transcript of what a witness says for a modern legal deposition. I answered that although such accuracy would be nice, depositions and biographies belong to different genres and that even modern biographies do not have the objective of reporting with the precision required in a deposition.

Like that attorney, some of you may feel a bit of unease and want to ask, "If the Evangelists exercised some freedom in the manner they reported events, how can I be confident that anything they report is true? And how can I distinguish between what is true and what may not be?" These are reasonable questions. I'll offer a few answers. First, historians have a number of tools that assist in assessing whether a reported item is probably true. Historians will assign more value to a source that was written very close in time to the event alleged to have occurred over a source that was written a century or more later. Historians assign more value to an eyewitness report over one that is not. Historians find value when a report is confirmed by a source that is unsympathetic or even has a hostile attitude toward what it acknowledges. Most of all, historians place

31. Robert H. Stein, *Studying the Synoptic Gospels: Origin and Interpretation*, 2nd ed. (Grand Rapids: Baker Academic, 2001), 168, emphasis in the original.

supreme value when two or more independent sources report an event in a manner that agrees.

Let's look at an example. Jesus's death by Roman execution is reported quite early, within twenty to forty years of the event, by the Gospel of Mark and Paul's letters. It is reported by multiple independent sources, including Mark, Paul, and other New Testament literature written in the first century, as well as a number of non-Christian sources: Josephus (unsympathetic), Tacitus (hostile), Lucian (hostile), and Mara bar Serapion (unknown). Therefore, despite some differences in details among the Gospel narratives of Jesus's crucifixion, historians are quite confident that Jesus was crucified in the first century and died as a result, although they are not as confident that Jesus uttered every word while on the cross that the Gospels attribute to him. Historians are confident regarding the authenticity of many other items related to Jesus's life, although historians cannot come anywhere near to confirming everything in the Gospels. Of course, *the same can be said of virtually all historical literature written in antiquity.*

Second, although some biographers took liberties with their sources that went beyond what was generally acceptable, there were limits beyond which the better ones did not go. Better biographers did not invent events when none had occurred. For the most part, the altering of information occurred only with peripheral details. Craig Keener concludes that, since ancient readers expected biographers to describe actual events while adapting and interpreting them from their particular perspectives, it is reasonable to presume that these expectations follow for ancient readers of the Gospels. It should be no surprise to observe that all four Gospels "fit within the range of variation found in ancient historical sources in general."[32]

Craig Blomberg, another evangelical New Testament scholar, similarly opines that since the Gospels were written a long time ago by people who lived in a culture that was quite different than our own, we should not think of the Gospels in terms of modern, Western biographies. He adds,

> It would be sheer anachronism and a monstrous injustice to evaluate Matthew, Mark, and Luke by twenty-first-century standards of precision, some of which they probably never even could have imagined! . . .

32. Craig S. Keener, *Christobiography: Memory, History, and the Reliability of the Gospels* (Grand Rapids: Eerdmans, 2019), 499–500.

> One of the admirable traits of capable historians or biographers, it was believed, was to so internalize their sources that they could put their own distinctive stamp on their material, writing their works in their own style and with their own language.[33]

Matthew may have arranged his genealogy of Jesus in an artistic manner, but his overall contention remains: Jesus's ancestry goes back to David. Matthew may have moved the location of Jesus's Sermon on the Mount from the summit to the base of the mountain; however, it remains that Jesus delivered his Sermon on or near a mountain. Close readings of the Gospels reveal that Matthew and John take more liberties with the details than do Luke. So while we may not always be reading a precise description of what Jesus said and did in the Gospels, I am convinced that they preserve the main and essential parts of what occurred.[34] In other words, readers get the *gist* of what happened. I am fond of how Christopher Pelling, the world's foremost authority on Plutarch, describes the accuracy with which Plutarch reports. He says his reports are "true enough."[35]

Perhaps a modern analogy between telling stories in either a comprehensive or abbreviated manner will be helpful. Most married couples will be able to relate. The way my wife, Debbie, and I relay a story is different. Debbie likes details, and lots of them. She will tell you what happened, where it happened, when it happened, why it happened, how it happened, who was there, what they were doing, what they were wearing, what they were saying, what they were thinking, and what they were feeling! In contrast, I like bullet points and very often only want the bottom line. When I tell a story to someone, I will sometimes omit details I regard as being unimportant. I will even alter a few minor details to avoid having first to provide five minutes of background information because I suppose, rightly or wrongly, that the other person usually does not care about the exact order of events and precise wording of what was said and done. Those like me are mainly interested in hearing the gist of what happened.

Debbie and I will sometimes go out for dinner with another couple. After ordering, the other couple will usually ask how our kids are doing.

---

33. Craig L. Blomberg, *The Historical Reliability of the New Testament: Countering the Challenges to Evangelical Christian Beliefs*, B&H Studies in Christian Apologetics (Nashville: B&H Academic, 2016), 25.

34. See Michael R. Licona, "Are the Gospels 'Historically Reliable'? A Focused Comparison of Suetonius's *Life of Augustus* and the Gospel of Mark," *Religions*, Special Issue: Current Trends in New Testament Study 10, no. 3, 148 (2019), https://doi.org/10.3390/rel10030148.

35. Pelling, *Plutarch and History: Eighteen Studies* (Swansea: Classical Press of Wales, 2002), 160.

Debbie will light up and have a lot to share about them. But after a few minutes, I'm thinking, "The couple we're with is interested to learn what's up with our kids. But they're not twenty minutes interested." I almost certainly fault in the opposite direction. I may say two sentences about each child then move on to another topic: "How 'bout those Atlanta Braves!"

I have had the experience (many times!) of relaying a story to a friend on the phone when Debbie, who has been listening in the background says, "No! It didn't happen that way. You forgot to mention [blank] and [blank]. And she said [blank] before he did [blank]. And *yada, yada, yada.*" And I'm thinking, "Good grief! I'm not trying to deceive my friend." Generally speaking, I am interested in reporting the relevant facts whereas Debbie wants to report *everything*. And she often insists on doing so with the precision of a legal deposition. That said, this is not a matter of one way being correct or incorrect. It is a matter of having different objectives when telling a story. Ancient biographers would often provide the *abbreviated version* of a story. Accordingly, much of the liberties taken by ancient biographers when composing their literary portraits are similar to the liberties many of us take in everyday, ordinary conversations. So we should recalibrate our expectations for precision when reading the Gospels.

Some readers may still struggle with the Evangelists being somewhat flexible with the details they sometimes report. After all, if the Gospels are divinely inspired, would their authors be allowed to "distort facts" and, thereby, "create error"? One may see or hear the following argument for an error-free Bible:

1. God cannot err.
2. The Bible is the Word of God.
3. Therefore, the Bible cannot err.

This argument has many problems, and we will visit them in chapter 12. For now, I will simply reiterate a principle that I stated near the end of the previous chapter: *our view of Scripture should be consistent with what we observe in Scripture*. People will differ on what should be regarded as an error. Whether you consider the altering of minor details as distorting facts, creating error, or allowable within the context of ordinary reporting today or in antiquity, if we observe the authors of the Gospels being flexible with the details, and if Scripture is divinely inspired, then this is what divinely inspired Scripture looks like. One should feel no guilt in acknowledging this, as though fearing that God will be upset with you.

For if God was behind the composition of the Scriptures as I and most Christians believe, then the Scriptures are as he intended. He was neither surprised nor did he blush as though being caught when the first reader noticed the differences.

SUMMARY

Truth-telling in ancient biography differed somewhat from the literary conventions for reporting in modern biography. Therefore, approaching the Gospels in light of their biographical nature will provide insights related to the degree of accuracy we should expect to encounter in their reporting. We observed two examples where Matthew adapts some minor details to highlight a point he regards as important: his genealogy of Jesus and the location of Jesus's Sermon on the Mount. The authors of the Gospels wrote according to the literary conventions in play in the first century. The matter of divine inspiration allows for the use of those literary conventions. In the next chapter, we will examine some of these conventions, actual techniques that ancient authors were taught for altering texts.

QUESTIONS FOR FURTHER THOUGHT

1. What is the most interesting thing you learned from this chapter?
2. Ancient biography permitted some flexibility in the manner of reporting. Are you troubled by the knowledge that the Evangelists took some minor liberties with the details? Why or why not?
3. How may reading the Gospels in view of the flexibility the genre of ancient biography allowed for reporting events help you gain a better understanding of what their authors are teaching?
4. Name some potential consequences from reading the Gospels anachronistically (i.e., as though they were written with modern conventions of precision in mind).
5. How do you define "divine inspiration"? Do you think it means that God inspired the authors, the literature they composed, or both?

CHAPTER 6

COMPOSITIONAL TEXTBOOKS

Perhaps you have seen the bumper sticker that reads, "If you can read this, thank a teacher!" Most citizens of Western nations are literate. A portion of the taxes paid are used to fund public schools, which are available to everyone. Even illiterate convicts can learn to read and write while in prison. My father-in-law, Eugene Weible, dropped out of school after completing tenth grade. Although he never graduated from high school, he had learned enough that he was known to read the writings of Josephus in his spare time. Those of us who are fortunate enough to live in the West, and even most who live in the East, enjoy the benefits of being literate.

If you had lived in the first century, however, chances are you would have been illiterate. Scholars offer different estimates, but many think that only about 10 percent could read, and only about half of those could also write. There was also basic and advanced literacy. In antiquity, by the time children of well-to-do families reached their midteens, they had already learned how to write and would proceed to the next level where they would be taught to write speeches and various forms of literature. At that stage, they were exposed to compositional textbooks containing writing exercises called *progymnasmata* (pronounced prō-gym-NAS-ma-ta). The earliest of these textbooks that has survived was composed in Greek by a man named Theon, who probably wrote in the first century. The Roman rhetorician Quintilian provided similar exercises in Latin at the end of that same century. And there were others who preceded Theon and Quintilian.[1]

1. Theon said his compositional textbook contained additions to the exercises described by others (Theon, *Prog.* 1 [Kennedy 2003, 3], 59). Unless otherwise stated, the English translations of Theon that follow are that of George A. Kennedy, trans., *Progymnasmata: Greek Textbooks of Prose Composition and Rhetoric*, WGRW 10 (Atlanta: Society of Biblical Literature, 2003).

BASIC PARAPHRASING

In this chapter, I will focus on some of the exercises for varying content provided by Theon. He describes four initial techniques for paraphrasing: "Paraphrase consists of changing the form of expression while keeping the thoughts. . . . There are four main kinds: variation in syntax, by addition, by subtraction, and by substitution, plus combinations of these."[2] Techniques of paraphrasing include changing the syntax (i.e., the grammatical structure), adding to or subtracting from the thoughts expressed, and substituting words with synonyms or synonymous phrases.

Let us consider the technique of *substitution*. My favorite Roman character is Cato Uticensis (pronounced Yu-tee-KEN-sis). He was a Roman senator and is also known in modern literature as Cato Minor or Cato the Younger to distinguish him from his great grandfather Cato the Elder. Although little written about him has survived, our Cato was remembered as having a great deal of integrity. If you were a politician committed to following the law, Cato would stand with you. If you were corrupt, he would oppose you, even if you were a friend. He risked his life to preserve order in the Roman Republic and fight corruption among its leading politicians. Cato had some negative character traits, however. As all of us are aware, being an effective politician often involves compromise. Cato was loath to do so. Sometimes he acted purely out of expedience. Once a man asked Cato for permission to marry the woman to whom Cato was presently married. Now that's an audacious request! After considering the advantages and disadvantages, Cato granted the man's request and divorced his wife.

In 66 BC, Cato was approaching the city of Antioch when he saw a crowd waiting to welcome him enthusiastically at the city's gate. Desiring not to appear haughty, he dismounted from his horse, proceeded on foot, and ordered those accompanying him to do the same. When they arrived at the city's gate, a leader of the welcoming committee asked him where Pompey's freedman Demetrius was. The crowd was disappointed to learn that Demetrius was not among them while failing to recognize that they were speaking to a much greater person. When the men who accompanied Cato observed this, they broke out in laughter, and Cato responded curtly with, "Oh, cursed city!" That is how Plutarch reports what he said in the *Life of Cato Minor*. However, in his *Life of Pompey*, Plutarch

2. Theon, *Prog.* 15 (Kennedy 2003, 70).

substitutes *cursed* with *miserable*: "Oh, miserable city!"[3] Plutarch may have remembered Cato's words differently or chose to translate his source using a synonym. We cannot be certain of his actual reason. However, since substitution is a paraphrasing technique prescribed in the compositional textbooks, the scales tip in that direction for the difference.

ADDITIONAL TECHNIQUES

Changing the syntax, adding, subtracting, and substituting are very basic methods for paraphrasing. Theon goes on to explain that there are even more techniques, many of which we do not use today: "There are other ways of varying the content along the lines discussed in the chapter on narration; for example, recasting an assertion as a question, a question as a potentiality, and similarly other forms of expression that we mentioned."[4]

In the chapter on narrative, Theon writes,

> Since we are accustomed to setting out the facts sometimes as making a straightforward statement and sometimes as doing something more than making a factual statement, and sometimes in the form of questions, and sometimes as things we seek to learn about, and sometimes as things about which we are in doubt, . . . and sometimes as making a command, sometimes expressing a wish, and sometimes swearing to something, sometimes addressing the participants, sometimes advancing suppositions, sometimes using dialogue, *it is possible to produce varied narrations in all these ways.*[5]

The term Theon uses for "vary" is *poikillontas*, which carries the meaning of bringing forth in various colors, to embellish, to adorn, to tell with art and elegance, to change. Theon is saying these techniques are permitted for varying narratives artfully. These paraphrasing and narrative

3. Plut. *Cat. Min.* 13.3 (*kakodaimonos*); *Pomp.* 40.3 (*athlias*). A similar modern and humorous story involves Queen Elizabeth not being recognized by a tourist who is overjoyed to learn that he has met her bodyguard. He then offers his camera to the Queen and asks her to take his photograph with her bodyguard! See https://www.foxnews.com/world/queens-former-bodyguard-recounts-reaction-tourist-didnt-recognize-lovely-sense-humor.

4. Theon, *Prog.* 15 (Kennedy 2003, 70).

5. Theon, *Prog.* 5 (Kennedy 2003, 35), emphasis added. For the Greek text, see James R. Butts, "*The Progymnasmata of Theon: A New Text with Translation and Commentary*" (PhD diss., Claremont Graduate School, 1986), 349, lines 277–78.

techniques in the compositional textbooks are not only for the classroom. They are for historians to use when writing their narratives. And Theon says elsewhere that "historical writing is nothing other than a combination of narrations."[6]

If this is not clear enough, Theon is even clearer in the preface:

> Thought is not moved by any one thing in only one way so as to express the idea [*phantasia*] that has occurred to it in a similar form, but it is stirred in a number of different ways, and sometimes we are making a declaration, sometimes asking a question, sometimes making an inquiry, sometimes beseeching, and sometimes expressing our thought in some other way. There is nothing to prevent what is imagined from being expressed equally well in all these ways. *There is evidence of this* in paraphrase by a poet of his own thoughts elsewhere or *paraphrase by another poet and in the orators and historians*, and, in brief, *all ancient writers seem to have used paraphrase* in the best possible way, *rephrasing not only their own writings but those of each other.*[7]

Evidence of these techniques for paraphrasing may be observed when we compare how a poet states his similar thoughts in more than one place. It may be observed in similar comparisons with orators and historians. The matter concerns how an author states the same thought in a different form. Theon says that *all* ancient writers used these techniques by rephrasing their own writings and the writings of others.

And there is even more! Theon has a chapter on "Elaboration" in which he writes,

> "Elaboration is language that adds what is lacking in thought and expression." What is "lacking" can be supplied by making clear what is obscure; by filling gaps in the language or content; by saying some things more strongly, or more believably, or more vividly, or more truly, or more wordily—each word repeating the same thing—, or more legally, or more beautifully, or more appropriately, or more opportunely, or making the subject pleasanter, or using a better arrangement or a style more ornate.[8]

---

6. Theon, *Prog.* 1 (Kennedy 2003, 4).
7. Theon, *Prog.* 1 (Kennedy 2003, 6), emphasis added.
8. Theon, *Prog.* 16 (Kennedy 2003, 71).

How important was it for a student to learn how to paraphrase? Here is Theon's answer: "Training in exercises is absolutely useful, not only for those who are going to be orators, but also if anyone wants to be a poet *or historian*, or if he wants to acquire facility with some other form of writing. *These things are, in effect, the foundation of every form of writing*."[9]

To summarize, Theon informs us that there were techniques for varying details when writing every form of literature, including historiography. These techniques involved altering the grammatical structure, expanding a thought, abbreviating, using a synonymous term or phrase, recasting a statement as a question, creating a dialogue, elaboration, and several other means. In fact, one is free to combine techniques and come up with others. And Theon says one can observe the use of these techniques when comparing how ancient writers rephrase their own writings and the writings of others.

Given Theon's statements pertaining to the prevalence of paraphrasing by the techniques he mentions, we should be able to identify numerous examples of its use in the ancient literature. Plutarch is regarded by many as the greatest ancient biographer. He wrote in the late first century through the early second century. We will discuss Plutarch much more in the next chapter. For now, here is a brief example of Plutarch paraphrasing by changing a statement to a question: as Julius Caesar continued to increase in power after becoming dictator, some were warning him of Brutus, to which Caesar replied, "Brutus will wait for this shriveled skin." That is what Plutarch reports in the *Life of Caesar* (62.3). However, in the *Life of Brutus* (8.2), Plutarch represents Caesar's reply as a question: "What? Does it not occur to you that Brutus intends to wait for this flesh?"

PARAPHRASING IN THE GOSPELS

Since those who were skilled in literacy were familiar with the above techniques, we may anticipate that the authors of the Gospels—or more likely the secretaries who assisted them—will have used them. Let's consider Jesus's parable of the mustard seed, which is reported by Matthew, Mark, and Luke. Observe how each begins the parable.

9. Theon, *Prog.* 2, emphasis added; cf. *Prog.* 1 (Kennedy 2003, 4).

Matthew 13:31	Mark 4:30–31	Luke 13:18–19
The kingdom of heaven is like a grain of mustard.	How can we compare the kingdom of God, or with what parable may we use for it? It is like a grain of mustard.	What is the kingdom of God like? And to what will I compare it? It is like a grain of mustard.

In chapter 2 we discussed how Matthew and Luke very likely used Mark as their primary source and supplemented it with their own source material. Having this in mind, we can observe Matthew doing two things here with Mark. First, he conflates Jesus's question and statement and presents the two as a single statement: "The kingdom of heaven is like a grain of mustard." Second, instead of saying "kingdom of God," he substitutes "kingdom of heaven." In fact, Matthew has a habit of changing instances where Mark and Luke have "kingdom of God" to "kingdom of heaven."[10] To avoid using the name *God* out of reverence, Jews of that era would often provide a substitution. The academic term for this is *circumlocution*. When speaking to Jews, Jesus may very well have used "kingdom of heaven" instead of "kingdom of God." In that case, Mark and Luke were providing cultural translations by substituting "kingdom of heaven" with "kingdom of God." If this is what occurred, Matthew changed the term back to the one Jesus had actually used. Regardless of his reason, Matthew altered Mark's term "kingdom of God" to "kingdom of heaven."

Jesus's parable of the sower is reported in all three Synoptics (Mark 4:3–9, 13–20 // Matt. 13:3–9, 18–24 // Luke 8:5–8, 11–15). Let's begin by taking a look at Mark's version:

> Listen! Behold, the sower went out to sow. And as he sowed, some [seed] fell along the road, and the birds came and devoured it. Now other [seed]

10. Matthew is the only New Testament author who uses "kingdom of heaven." The phrase appears thirty-two times in his Gospel, whereas he uses "kingdom of God" only four times (12:28; 19:24; 21:31, 43). Two of the four appear in texts with no parallels in the other Gospels (21:31, 43). When parallel passages are taken into consideration, the other two occurrences of "kingdom of God" in Matthew have parallels in the other Gospels (Matt. 12:28 // Luke 11:20; Matt. 19:24 // Mark 10:25 // Luke 18:25). Outside of those two, Matthew always renders "kingdom of heaven" where Mark or Luke or both render "kingdom of God" (Matt. 4:17 // Mark 1:15; Matt. 5:3 // Luke 6:20; Matt. 11:12 // Luke 16:16; Matt. 13:24 // Mark 4:26; Matt. 13:31 // Mark 4:30 // Luke 13:18; Matt. 13:33 // Luke 13:20–21; Matt. 19:14 [cf. 18:3] // Mark 10:14–15 // Luke 18:16–17; Matt. 19:21–23 // Mark 10:23–24 // Luke 18:24–25.)

> fell on the rocky ground where it did not have much soil. And immediately, it sprang up because it did not have deep soil. And it was scorched when the sun rose and withered because it did not have [sufficient] root. And other [seed] fell among the thorns, and the thorns grew up and choked it, and it did not produce fruit. And other [seed] fell on good soil and produced fruit, sprouting and growing and yielding one thirtyfold, one sixtyfold, and one a hundredfold. (Mark 4:3–8)

Matthew's version is very similar. However, observe how his version of the parable ends:

> And other [seed] fell on good soil and produced fruit, one a hundredfold, one sixtyfold, and one thirtyfold. (Matt. 13:8)

Finally, let's observe the ending as told by Luke:

> And other [seed] fell on the good soil and, having grown, produced fruit a hundredfold. (Luke 8:8)

Let's return to Mark, who uses a common rhetorical device called *anabasis*, which is a gradual increase of emphasis. In Mark 13:32, Jesus is speaking of the time when the temple will be destroyed and the Son of Man will return on the clouds. He continues, "Now, concerning that day or hour, no one knows, neither the angels in heaven, nor the Son, but only the Father." We observe a gradual increase of emphasis: no human knows (e.g., prophets); the angels in heaven do not know, even though they are higher than humans (Psalm 8:6 LXX); even the Son of God does not know, even though he is higher than angels. Only the Father knows when these things will occur. In Mark's version of this parable, Jesus uses anabasis: the seed in the good soil grows and produces fruit that is thirty-, sixty-, even a hundredfold. That Jesus told the parable in this manner is very likely since it makes perfect rhetorical sense.

Matthew apparently inverts the order to a hundredfold, sixtyfold, thirtyfold. In doing so, the nice rhetorical flow we see in Mark is now gone. In fact, a decreasing order of emphasis called *catabasis* could be used rhetorically in order to emphasize humiliation or degradation, which is certainly not occurring in this parable. Matthew has very likely inverted the order in Mark merely to paraphrase.

Finally, in Luke's version, Jesus states that the seed that fell on good ground produced fruit a hundredfold. Which technique for paraphrasing did Luke use? I will leave the answer in the footnote below.[11] But try to answer before looking.

Let's now look at an example in the Gospels where several of these techniques are employed: *Jesus's parable of the vineyard and wicked tenants.* This parable is reported in Matthew, Mark, and Luke, with all three locating it after Jesus's triumphal entry on Palm Sunday. Feel free to pause for a moment and read the account in all three Gospels before proceeding (Mark 12:1–12 // Matt. 21:33–46 // Luke 20:9–19).

The parable is most similar in Mark and Luke, where the vineyard owner sends three servants, one at a time. The tenants either wound or kill each servant. Mark adds that the owner also sends many others whom the tenants beat or kill. Mark and Luke then say the owner finally sends his son, whom the tenants kill.

Matthew simplifies the story. Instead of sending three servants, one at a time, Matthew says the vineyard owner sends three servants at the same time whom the tenants wound, kill, or stone. Then he sends more the second time than the first, and the servants are treated in the same manner. Finally, he sends his son whom the tenants kill.

Matthew (21)	**Mark (12)**	**Luke (20)**
3 servants (beaten, killed, stoned)	1 servant (beaten, sent away)	1 servant (beaten, sent away)
–	1 servant (struck head, treated shamefully)	1 servant (beaten, treated shamefully, sent away)
–	1 servant (killed)	1 servant (wounded, cast out)
3+ servants (beaten, killed, stoned)	many others (beaten, killed)	–
son (killed)	son (killed, cast out)	son (cast out, killed)

Matthew, Mark, and Luke then report that Jesus puts a question to those listening to him:

11. If you answered *subtraction*, you are correct!

Matthew 21:40–42	Mark 12:9–11	Luke 20:15b-18
"When, therefore, the owner of the vineyard comes, what will he do to those tenants?" They said to him, "He will put those evil men to a miserable death and lease the vineyard to other tenants who will give him the fruits in their seasons."	"What, therefore, will the owner of the vineyard do? He will come and destroy the tenants and give the vineyard to others.	"What, therefore, will the owner of the vineyard do to them? He will come and destroy those tenants and give the vineyard to others." When they heard this, they said, "Surely not!"
Jesus said to them, "Have you never read in the Scriptures: 'The stone that the builders rejected, this became the cornerstone; this was the Lord's doing, and it is marvelous in our eyes'?"	Have you not read this Scripture: 'The stone that the builders rejected, this became the cornerstone; this was the Lord's doing, and it is marvelous in our eyes'?"	But he looked directly at them and said, "What then is this that is written: 'The stone that the builders rejected, this became the cornerstone'? Everyone who falls on that stone will be broken to pieces, and the one on whom it falls will be crushed."

Let's make note of a few differences between the three texts. Of course, there are some very minor differences in wording. We can see this by comparing the first sentences in all three accounts.

> "What, therefore, will the owner of the vineyard do?" (Mark 12:9)

> "What, therefore, will the owner of the vineyard do to them?" (Luke 20:15)

> "When, therefore, the owner of the vineyard comes, what will he do to those tenants?" (Matt. 21:40)

It is doubtful that any of the Gospels are attempting to provide a perfect transcript of what Jesus said. As basic as that observation may seem, some readers may have previously thought the Gospels were reporting the precise words of Jesus. However, it would have been very difficult for someone to record with inked reed on papyrus in a rapid manner. Moreover, it was not the objective of the ancient biographer and historian to recall the precise words. Furthermore, since Jesus is here speaking to Jewish leaders in the temple complex, the conversation was almost certainly in Aramaic. But the Gospels were written in Greek, eliminating the possibility that the Gospels are relaying to us Jesus's precise words. Even if the exact words of Jesus had been recorded somewhere, the compositional textbooks inform us that good writers were to paraphrase an existing report. Of course, God could have dictated the words to the Gospel writers. But as we observed in chapter 3, the differences make it obvious that God did not choose such a method.

Another difference to which I call your attention is that Matthew creates a bit of a dialogue, as does Luke, though to a much lesser extent. In Mark and Luke, Jesus asks and answers his own question. However, Matthew creates a dialogue by transferring the answer to the Jewish leaders, and he then elaborates their answer with even more vigor than either Mark and Luke narrate Jesus providing (see fig. 4.2). Theon refers to this as creating a dialogue and elaboration.

Lydia McGrew is a Christian philosopher who, like Augustine in antiquity, almost always prefers to harmonize differences. She offers two possibilities for harmonizing the last difference on which we have focused:

> One possibility is that Jesus paused for a moment and that some in the crowd spoke up at approximately the same time that Jesus decided to go ahead and answer his own question. Another possibility is that someone in the crowd spoke up and answered the question approximately as given in Matthew, and that Jesus affirmed, "That's right, he'll come and destroy those tenants," or words to that effect, remembered and recorded by Peter as told to Mark. This sort of natural harmonization hardly stretches the bounds of credibility. In fact, it describes quite a common interactive teaching situation.[12]

Both of McGrew's speculations are *plausible*. However, granting that something is *plausible* is not equivalent to saying it is *probable*. The solution I provided is likewise *plausible*. Unfortunately, we cannot get into a time machine, return to the past, and ask Matthew to render a verdict. So the remaining question is: Which is the more probable solution?

12. Lydia McGrew, *The Mirror or the Mask: Liberating the Gospels from Literary Devices* (Tampa, FL: DeWard, 2019), 267.

Matthew 21:40–44	**Mark 12:9–11**	**Luke 20:15b-18**
"When the owner of the vineyard comes, what will he do to those tenants?"	"What, therefore, will the owner of the vineyard do?	"What, therefore, will the owner of the vineyard do?
They said to him, "He will bring those wretches to a wretched end and give the vineyard to other tenants who will give him his portion at the proper time!"	He will come and destroy the tenants and will give the vineyard to others.	He will come and destroy these tenants and will give the vineyard to others."
		Now when they heard this, they said, "May it never be!"
Jesus said to them, "Have you never read in the Scriptures? '*The stone which the builders rejected, this became the corner stone. This came about by the Lord and is marvelous in our eyes*'? Because of this, I tell you that the kingdom of God will be taken from you and will be given to a people producing its fruit.	Have you not read this Scripture? '*The stone which the builders rejected, this became the cornerstone. This came about by the Lord and is marvelous in our eyes.*'"	And looking straight at them, he said, "What, therefore, is [the meaning of] this that have been written, '*The stone which the builders rejected, this became the cornerstone*'?
And the one who falls on this stone will be broken to pieces and the one on whom it falls will be crushed."		Everyone who falls on that stone will be broken to pieces and the one on whom it falls will be crushed."

Fig. 4.2

In what follows, I will explain why I think McGrew's proposals lead readers down the wrong path.

Let's consider another story from the Gospels and compare how Matthew, Mark, and Luke report Jesus's answer when the high priest commands him to tell the council whether he's Messiah, the Son of God. I have placed in bold and underlined the parallel texts.

Matthew 26:64	Mark 14:62	Luke 22:67–69
"**You have said so.** Only I say to you, from now on you will see the Son of Man sitting at the right hand of Power and coming on the clouds of heaven."	"**I am.** And you will see the Son of Man sitting at the right hand of Power and coming with the clouds of heaven."	"If I told you, you would never believe. And if I asked you, you would never answer. But from now on, the Son of Man will be sitting at the right hand of the power of God." And they all said, "Are you, therefore, the Son of God?" And he answered, **"You say that I am."**

Since Matthew and Luke are very likely using Mark as their source here, we can observe the editorial hands of Matthew and Luke at work. Jesus's simple "I am" answer in Mark becomes "You have said so" in Matthew and placed later in the dialogue in Luke.[13] Intriguingly, Luke's version differs in another way. Matthew and Mark report Jesus saying they will see him "sitting at the right hand of Power." The word *Power* is here used as a circumlocution or synonym for *God* out of reverence. Luke's Gentile patron Theophilus (Luke 1:3; Acts 1:1) may not grasp this so easily. So Luke adds "of God" for clarity (i.e., "the power of God"). Furthermore, when Jesus says they will see him sitting at the right hand of Power, Matthew and Mark report the high priest tearing his clothes, him charging Jesus with blasphemy, and the council condemning Jesus to death. Why such a dramatic reaction? Because in saying he will be sitting at God's right hand and coming on the clouds, Jesus is referring to the divine Son of Man mentioned in Daniel 7:13–14, who will be given a glorious, everlasting kingdom and to whom all people will render service as they would to God. For the high priest, those were clothes-ripping words!

Luke's reader Theophilus was Greek and was likely unfamiliar with the divine Son of Man figure Jesus had claimed to be and why that claim would have elicited the emotion-filled charge of blasphemy. So Luke

13. "You have said so." "You say that I am." These appear to be an idiom of that era simply meaning "yes" (see also Luke 23:3; Mark 15:2; Matt. 26:64, 27:11; John 18:37). It is much like today's American English when someone asks if we will do something and one replies, "You can bet on it," or simply, "You bet!" With this response, we are not encouraging another to place a bet that we will do such and such. Or let us say I have asked a friend to do a favor and he has assured me that he will do it, saying, "You can take it to the bank!" Suppose I understood that literally and went to the bank and said my friend will do it. Can you imagine the look on the banker's face when she answers, "Well, that sounds great for you. But why are you telling me this?"

appears to have provided a *cultural translation*, much like Philo and Josephus do on occasion. There is no tearing of clothes. There is no charge of blasphemy. There is no condemnation of death. Instead, the council follows up by asking Jesus if he is the Son of God—a concept of the divine with which Theophilus would have been familiar. When Jesus answers in the affirmative, the council is satisfied that they now have enough to bring him before Pilate. This looks very much like the technique in the compositional textbooks we observed earlier called *elaboration*.

An example of addition is found in Jesus's teaching on divorce.

Matthew 19:9 (cf. 5:31)	Mark 10:11–12
And I say to you: whoever divorces his wife, except for sexual immorality, and marries another, commits adultery.	Whoever divorces his wife and marries another commits adultery against her, and if she divorces her husband and marries another, she commits adultery.

It is important to note that this is the same occasion in Matthew and Mark, since it occurs in the context where Jesus has just entered the region of Judea beyond the Jordan River (Mark 10:1 // Matt. 19:1). And the stories of the children coming to Jesus and the man who asks Jesus what is necessary for him to have eternal life appear right after our text (Mark 10:13–31 // Matt. 19:13–30). Now, let's read Mark 10:11–12 again, but this time imagine that you are a member of a house church where Mark is being read and Matthew is yet to write his Greek Gospel.

> Whoever divorces his wife and marries another commits adultery against her, and if she divorces her husband and marries another, she commits adultery. (Mark 10:11–12)

Under what conditions are followers of Jesus permitted to divorce *according to Mark*? If you are thinking of the case of sexual immorality, you are thinking of Jesus's statement in Matthew. But Jesus provides no exceptions in Mark's version.

Does Mark's version of Jesus's statement contradict Matthew's version? What is going on here? It is widely accepted by New Testament scholars that Jesus often spoke using hyperbole, since it grabs our attention. Elsewhere Jesus teaches that we must hate our father, our mother, our spouse, and our children if we want to be his disciple (Luke 14:26).

Jesus was certainly not telling us that we should actually hate others, for the same author reports that he had taught precisely the opposite elsewhere (Luke 6:35; 10:27). In teaching on discipleship, Jesus used hyperbolic language to suggest we must love him much more than anyone else if we want to be his disciples. In fact, Matthew has probably redacted Jesus's language by eliminating the hyperbolic element and paraphrasing via substitution. In Matthew 10:37, Jesus says we must *love him more than* our father, our mother, and our children if we want to be his disciple. When Jesus says in Mark that the one who divorces his wife and marries another commits adultery, he almost certainly was using hyperbole. The Jewish leaders of the day were allowing a man to divorce his wife for almost any reason. Jesus was saying precisely the opposite should be the state of marriage. God's plan is that divorce is unallowable in almost all circumstances. Matthew redacts Jesus's words slightly by removing the hyperbolic element and adding an exception clause for clarity. The alert reader also observed that Matthew substituted "sexual immorality" for "adultery."

> Sexual immorality is not the only exception for divorce in the New Testament. In 1 Corinthians 7:12–16, Paul allows for followers of Jesus to divorce if they are married to an unbeliever who desires to leave the marriage. Are there other circumstances whereby a follower of Jesus is permitted in God's eyes to divorce their spouse? While discouraging followers of Jesus from leaving their marriage, Paul says that if a person does, they are not permitted to remarry (1 Cor. 7:10–11). Where does that leave the other spouse who may want to remarry? Paul does not say.
>
> Let's say that a man in California is caught in the act of murdering his boss, who happened to be a woman. He is arrested, convicted, and sentenced to life in prison without chance of parole. Is his wife prohibited from divorcing her husband because he did not rape his female boss prior to murdering her (i.e., "except for the cause of sexual immorality")? In the first century when Jesus lived, the man would have been executed by both Roman and Jewish law. This appears to be an instance where we should apply the *spirit* of Jesus's teachings over the *letter* of them.

We should thank God that the Evangelists made such alterations. Otherwise, we might think that, according to Jesus, we should actually hate our closest family members and have no option of divorcing a spouse who is sexually unfaithful in marriage.

We saw above that Theon asserted that all forms of writing made use of the techniques he describes in his compositional textbook. Ancient historians often made use of these, including elaboration, especially where speeches were involved. In the middle of the second century, Lucian of Samosata wrote a book titled *How to Write History* in which he states that historians have a license to improve a speech: "If a person has to be introduced to make a speech, above all let his language suit his person and his subject, and next let these also be as clear as possible. It is then, however, that you can play the orator and show your eloquence."[14]

We observe some of the finest ancient historians using many forms of the rhetorical devices described in the compositional textbooks. Cornelius Tacitus "was the greatest historian that the Roman world produced."[15] Classicist Ronald Mellor writes of Tacitus,

> His rhetorical training informs every page of his histories, but it is most obvious in his reliance on speeches to shape the historical narrative. Even Rome's enemies are granted an opportunity to speak, and to speak more effectively than they ever actually did on the battlefields of Britain or Germany.[16]

Mellor provides a well-known example where Emperor Claudius delivers a speech in which he contends that nobles of Gaul should be admitted to the Roman senate. He comments,

> It is the only ancient speech that survives both on an official bronze copy (found in Lyons) as well as in an historian's literary version. . . . Though the beginning and other sections of the speech are missing, we can easily compare the first half of Claudius' rambling oration with the first few sentences of Tacitus' version, which describe similar historical precedents. . . . [Tacitus' version] is briefer and the arguments are much more cogently presented. . . . Tacitus is faithful to Claudius' arguments and to the occasion, retaining just a touch of pedantry: where Claudius refers to a speech in Livy, Tacitus consults the speech directly and uses it. Any modern desire for verbal exactitude would have seemed to him

14. Lucian, *How to Write History*, 58.
15. Ronald Mellor, *Roman Historians*, 76.
16. Mellor, *Roman Historians*, 105.

"antiquarian" and unworthy of the literary artistry expected in serious historical writing.[17]

Where did Tacitus learn to improve speeches? We cannot ask him. But we are justified in being confident that it was in his education during his teens where he was required to practice the exercises in the compositional textbooks.

In addition to learning what aspiring historians were taught to do, it is valuable to examine the literature of historians of that time to see what they actually did. Do they invent speeches? Yes. Do they paraphrase and elaborate in order to improve the quality of a speech or even a narrative? Yes. Do they change a statement to a question, and express a thought in any number of different ways? Yes. Do we see them doing this with their own writings? Yes. Do we see them doing this with the writings of others? Yes. Do we observe Matthew and Luke often paraphrasing Mark in these ways? Yes. When we identify the differences in how Matthew and Luke report material for which Mark is their likely source and read the relevant Gospel texts through the lens of the prescribed exercises in the compositional textbooks of that time, what we observe aligns perfectly with what is prescribed in the compositional textbooks.

Referring to the exercises we have discussed in this chapter, Gerald Downing comments,

> The procedures are always so similar that it would be absurd to suppose without massive supporting evidence that the NT evangelists could have learned to write Greek and cope with written source material at all while remaining outside the pervasive influence of these common steps toward literacy.[18]

Accordingly, preferring to harmonize differing accounts in the Gospels over the Evangelists' use of compositional devices is likely to lead one down the wrong road.

---

17. Mellor, *Roman Historians*, 90–92.

18. F. Gerald Downing, "Compositional Conventions and the Synoptic Problem," *JBL* 107, no. 1 (1988): 71. Having conducted an exhaustive treatment pertaining to Luke's preface to his Gospel, Loveday Alexander writes, "Literary and social factors both seem to be converging towards one point: the need to look seriously at the world of the hellenistic schools and their literature as an essential element in the socio-cultural background of the New Testament." See Loveday Alexander, *The Preface to Luke's Gospel: Literary Convention and Social Context in Luke 1.1–4 and Acts 1.1*, Society for New Testament Studies Monograph Series 78 (New York: Cambridge University Press, 1993), 210.

WHY THIS IS IMPORTANT

The techniques taught in the compositional textbooks were used by all ancient writers. Therefore, we should anticipate that the Gospel authors also used them. We can actually observe several instances where it appears they did. If they did, we learn that divine inspiration allowed the Evangelists to make minor changes, even to the words of Jesus, although the underlying message remained similar.

SUMMARY

Students in antiquity who were fortunate enough to receive an advanced education in writing were taught techniques for modifying texts. These techniques were learned by using the compositional textbooks and were to be used in every form of writing. We observe their use by the finest Greco-Roman historians as well as the authors of the Gospels. Reading the Gospels through lenses designed with these techniques in mind can provide greater clarity pertaining to why some of the differences in the Gospels are there.

In the next chapter, we will observe additional techniques employed by the greatest biographer in antiquity and look at a few stories in the Gospels where their authors may very well be employing the same techniques.

QUESTIONS FOR FURTHER THOUGHT

1. What is the most interesting thing you learned from this chapter?
2. Do you think changing details amounts to deceit? If so, why? If not, why not?
3. Are you being deceptive when you do something similar? If not, why not?
4. To what extent would an author need to go before the change becomes deceit?
5. Compare how all four Gospels speak of John the Baptist (Mark 1:2–11 // Matt. 3:1–17 // Luke 3:1–18, 21–22 // John 1:19–34). What differences do you observe, and what compositional devices may account for them?

CHAPTER 7

PLUTARCH AND MORE COMPOSITIONAL DEVICES

For me, the first century BC and the first century AD are the two most fascinating centuries in all of human history. The incarnation, life, death, and resurrection of Jesus, the inception of the Christian church, and the composition of much, if not all, of the New Testament literature occurred in the first century AD. The first century BC contained dramatic events that led the Roman Republic to transition to an empire that are the basis of movies, television drama series, and documentaries.

Less than eighty years after the Jews won their freedom from the Seleucid Empire, a victory celebrated at Hanukkah, their queen Salome Alexandra died, leaving her two sons, Hyrcanus II and Aristobulus II, fighting to possess her throne. In 63 BC, the matter was brought before the Roman general Pompey when he came to Damascus. Pompey ended up siding with Hyrcanus, who in turn surrendered Jerusalem to him. In 54 BC, Crassus, the Roman general who had defeated Spartacus seventeen years earlier, plundered the treasury in the Jerusalem temple. Cassius, one of the conspirators who would later kill Julius Caesar, crushed an insurrection of the Jews in Judea in 52 BC. Three years later (January 49 BC), Caesar crossed the Rubicon and civil war ensued until Caesar defeated Pompey at Pharsalus (August 48 BC). Caesar was assassinated nineteen years later (March 15, 44 BC). Two years after that, Mark Antony and Caesar's nephew Octavian, whom Caesar had adopted and appointed his heir, engaged and defeated the assassins Brutus and Cassius at Philippi (October 42 BC), where, less than a century later, the apostle Paul would establish a church. A letter he wrote to that church is preserved in our New Testament.

The victor Antony went on to have an infamous relationship with Cleopatra. They had children who, as teens, were tutored by Nicolaus of Damascus (or Damascenus). Nicolaus was also a mentor for Herod the

Great, who had been appointed by Antony in 41 BC to be the Jewish tetrarch. With Octavian, Antony arranged for Herod to be recognized by the Roman senate as King of the Jews, a client king of Rome. Relations between Antony and Octavian became increasingly bitter until they met at the Battle of Actium on September 2, 31 BC.

After Octavian defeated Antony, Herod met him and promised to be a friend to him with the same loyalty he had given to Antony. For this gesture, Octavian confirmed Herod's position as King of the Jews. Herod built Masada, rebuilt the temple in Jerusalem, and would later order the killing of infants in Bethlehem. In 27 BC, the Roman senate conferred several honors on Octavian, one of which was giving him the name Augustus, the name by which he is known in Luke 2:1: "Now it came about in those days that a decree went out from Caesar Augustus to register all the world." And in 8 BC, the Roman senate named a month after him that stands to this day. I'll bet you can guess which one!

Herod the Great would go on to engage in actions that placed great strain on his standing with Augustus. When Herod died in 4 BC, Augustus intended to abolish the position King of the Jews and absorb the territory held by Herod to henceforth be under direct Roman rule. But Nicolaus intervened and convinced Augustus to allow Herod's son Archelaus to serve as his successor, according to the terms of Herod's will. However, Augustus abolished the title King of the Jews and divided Herod's kingdom among his three surviving sons. To Archelaus, he bestowed the lesser title *ethnarch* and gave him Judea and Samaria. It was this Herod who was feared by Jesus's father Joseph, who being warned in a dream, avoided Archelaus in Judea and settled in Nazareth (Matt. 2:22). Archelaus ruled so ruthlessly that Augustus removed him in AD 6 in order to avoid a revolt that was brewing. Judea and Samaria were then put directly under the rule of a Roman prefect.

To Herod's other two sons, Philip and Antipas, Augustus bestowed the title of *tetrarch*. Herod Philip received territories located east and northeast of the Sea of Galilee (Mark 6:17 // Matt. 14:3 // Luke 3:1). When Philip died in AD 34, the territory he ruled was added to the Roman province of Syria. Herod Antipas received Galilee and Peraea. This was the Herod who had taken the wife of his brother Philip, had beheaded John the Baptist, and to whom Pilate had sent Jesus. In AD 39, Emperor Caligula deposed and banished Antipas and replaced him with his (i.e., Caligula's) friend Agrippa I, who was Antipas's nephew and brother-in-law. In AD 41, the new emperor Claudius restored to Agrippa I all the territories his grandfather Herod the Great had possessed and bestowed on him the title King of Judea. It was this Herod who persecuted the church, executed James the son of Zebedee, and arrested Peter (Acts 12:1–19). In AD 44, he died of an illness, his last public act being described by Luke in Acts and by Josephus.[1]

Claudius was emperor when Agrippa I died. His son, Agrippa II, was with Claudius at the time. Because of his youth, Agrippa II was not allowed by Claudius to inherit his father's territories, given their importance to Rome. However, in AD 50, Claudius gave Agrippa II a kingdom of lesser importance to Rome, one recently left vacant by the death of another Herod, Herod of Chalcis, who was married to Agrippa II's sister Bernice. Paul as prisoner stood before Agrippa II and his sister Bernice when they visited the Roman governor Festus in Caesarea (ca. AD 56–60; Acts 25:13–26:32).

We can begin to see how interconnected the world of Jesus and the New Testament writers was with the Greco-Roman world. Understanding both worlds can sometimes shed light that assists us when interpreting New Testament texts. Let's look at an example. In the Sermon on the Mount, Jesus speaks of adultery and lust and then says,

> If your right eye causes you to sin, remove it and throw it away. For it is better for you to lose one of your members than for your entire body to be thrown into hell. And if your right hand causes you to sin, cut it off and throw it away. For it is better for you to lose one of your members than for your entire body to go into hell. (Matt. 5:29–30)

Wow! That's serious business! Surely, Jesus does not intend for us to take his words literally. But why not? Nothing in the text itself suggests it should not be understood as a literal command. Now before you gouge out your eye or cut off your hand, let's take a look at what a Roman statesman and Stoic philosopher said in the same century. His name is Seneca, and he wrote the following in a letter to his friend Lucilius: "Vice, Lucilius, is what I wish you to proceed against, without limit and without end. For it has neither limit nor end. If any vice rend your heart, cast it away from you; and if you cannot be rid of it in any other way, pluck out your heart also."[2] Seneca is not actually encouraging Lucilius to kill himself. He is emphasizing the importance of dealing with vice. Jesus is doing the

1. Acts 12:20–23; Josephus, *Ant.* 19:343–51; *Jewish War* 2:219.

2. Seneca the Younger, *Epistulae morales* (*Moral Letters*) 51.13, *Seneca: Epistles 1–65*, trans. Richard M. Gummere, LCL 75 (Cambridge: Harvard University Press, 1917), 343.

same when he instructs those who struggle with lust to rip out their eyes.[3] Your eternal destiny is a very serious matter. So you should take your sanctification seriously! This is an instance where we can say the text "does not mean what it says. It means what it means."[4]

On occasion, interacting with Greco-Roman literature can shed interpretive light on texts whose meaning has remained elusive. In the previous chapter, we observed that those trained to write something as sophisticated as a biography learned various techniques for varying an existing account. To do so was both proper and expected. This is not at all to downplay the importance of recognizing that Jesus was a Jew who preached mainly, though by no means exclusively, to Jews. How did the Jews come to be under Roman rule? What restrictions did Rome place on the Jews? Which customs did they allow the Jews to practice? How warm or cool was Jerusalem's relationship with Rome during the first century? Who were the Pharisees, the Sadducees, and the scribes? What were their roles and beliefs? Understanding the cultural settings of both Jewish and Greco-Roman worlds assists readers in interpreting the Gospels accurately.

Since the Gospels are biographies of Jesus, or at minimum share much in common with the genre of ancient biography, becoming familiar with some additional techniques employed by ancient biographers will assist us in reading the Gospels accurately. So let's spend some time discussing a very important biographer of that era.

PLUTARCH OF CHAERONEA

Plutarch was born sometime before AD 45 in the town of Chaeronea (pronounced keh-rho-KNEE-uh) in central Greece. He came from a wealthy family, studied rhetoric, and became a philosopher of the academy founded by Plato. Plutarch spent most of his life in his hometown and in Delphi, where he served as a priest during the last three decades of his life. Emperor Trajan bestowed on him the honorary title *Advisor of Emperors*.

Plutarch wrote more than sixty biographies, of which forty-eight have survived. Biographies were called "Lives" until only a few centuries ago, so the biographies written by Plutarch are referred to as Plutarch's *Lives*. They were written between ca. AD 90 and ca. AD 120 and "have been the main source of understanding of the ancient world for many readers

---

3. Paul uses still other language to communicate the same thought in Romans 12:1; Colossians 3:5.

4. See Bruce M. Metzger, *Breaking the Code: Understanding the Book of Revelation* (Nashville: Abingdon, 1993), 26–27.

from the Renaissance to the present day."[5] Plutarch has been called "the greatest Greek writer of the post-Classical era."[6] The literature he wrote has been read extensively through the ages.

Of the surviving forty-eight *Lives* Plutarch wrote, nine have main characters who knew one another and even participated in some of the same events. Depending on how one divides the narratives, thirty-six stories appear in two or more of those nine *Lives*. For example, the Catilinarian Conspiracy is mentioned in seven of Plutarch's *Lives*: *Lucullus*, *Crassus*, *Cato Minor*, *Cicero*, *Caesar*, *Brutus*, *Antony*. This affords us with the unique opportunity of comparing how Plutarch reports the same story in all four accounts. This differs from comparing how Caesar's assassination is told by Appian, Cicero, Cassius Dio, Livy, Nicolaus, Plutarch, Suetonius, and Velleius. By focusing on Plutarch's four accounts of Caesar's assassination, we can assess how the same author reported the same story, very often using the same sources and writing around the same time, even simultaneously in some cases.

What I discovered surprised me. Of the thirty-six stories that appear in two or more of the nine *Lives* I examined, thirty contained differences. Plutarch never copies and pastes. In fact, when writing the same story in different *Lives*, he varies the wording to such an extent that close verbal similarities, like those we commonly observe in parallel accounts in the Synoptic Gospels, are absent. Since we can be confident that Plutarch's youthful education included compositional textbooks, we now have the unique opportunity of observing how the exercises in those textbooks play out in the literature he wrote by comparing how Plutarch tells the same story in different *Lives*.

Moreover, classicists have proposed that, in addition to the techniques in the compositional textbooks that were discussed in the previous chapter, several other compositional devices are practically universal in ancient historiography. The following are some of the more prominent ones:

Compression: An author knowingly portrays an event as though it occurred over a shorter period of time than it actually had occurred. New Testament scholars have sometimes referred to this as *telescoping*.[7]

5. D. A. Russell, "Plutarch" in *The Oxford Classical Dictionary*, 4th ed., ed. Simon Hornblower and Antony Spawforth (New York: Oxford University Press, 2005), 1165.

6. Moles, *Plutarch: Life of Cicero*, 5.

7. Looking through a telescope allows one to perceive an object as being closer than it actually is. As a compositional device, *telescoping* narrates an event as being more recent than it actually was. In my opinion, *compression* often more accurately and clearly describes what the author is doing than *telescoping*.

Displacement: An author knowingly removes an event from its original context and places it in a different one. Thus, the time and/or location may be changed.

Transferal: An author knowingly attributes the identity of a person producing or receiving an action to another.

Conflation: An author combines elements from two or more events or people and narrates them as one. Accordingly, some displacement and/or transferal will often occur with conflation.

Simplification: An author omits or alters details that may complicate the overall narrative and may do so merely to abbreviate and communicate only the main ideas.

Literary Spotlighting: An author only mentions the person(s) in focus while being aware that others were present. Think of a theatrical performance. During an act in which several actors are on stage, the lights go out and a spotlight shines on a particular actor. Others are present, though unseen. In literary spotlighting, the author only mentions one of the people present but is aware that others were there.

In this chapter and the two that follow, we will be observing some examples where Plutarch and the Evangelists may very well be employing these devices.

LITERARY SPOTLIGHTING

I begin with literary spotlighting because I observed it being used more than any other compositional device in Plutarch's *Lives*. Let's look at two examples, one from Plutarch and the other from the Gospels.

The Catilinarian Conspiracy[8]

In 64 BC corruption in the city of Rome combined with the absence of Pompey, who was fighting Mithridates in Asia Minor and the Middle East,[9] made Rome fertile ground for a revolution. Revolutionaries

---

8. For a more in-depth treatment, I recommend reading my academic treatment of Gospel differences, Michael R. Licona, *Why Are There Differences in the Gospels? What We Can Learn from Ancient Biography* (New York: Oxford University Press, 2017). The story we are examining here is found on pages 36–41. References in Plutarch's *Lives* are *Cic.* 10.1–22.5; 23.1–3; *Caes.* 7.1–8.4; *Cat. Min*, 22.1–24.3; 26.1–4; *Crass.* 13.2–4; *Brut.* 5.2–3; *Ant.* 2.1–2; *Luc.* 38.3.

9. See the note by John Ramsey in *Sallust: The War with Cataline, The War with Jugurtha*, trans. J. C. Rolfe, ed. John T. Ramsey, LCL 116 (Cambridge: Harvard University Press, 2013), 44n19.

led by the Roman senator Lucius Sergius Catilina (known more simply as Catiline) began plans for taking over the leadership of Rome. That same year, Catiline had stood for consul, the highest elected political office in the Roman Republic, but was defeated by Cicero. The following year, Catiline sought the consulship a second time and lost again. Since the people would not have him lead Rome as a consul, he planned to attack the city and take it by force. As his fellow conspirators began to come together, Marcus Crassus received some letters at his house informing him of the conspiracy. Accompanied by Marcus Marcellus and Metellus Scipio, Crassus went to Cicero's house on the night of October 20 to wake him and bring the letters to his immediate attention. This is the manner that Plutarch reports the event in his *Life of Cicero*. However, in his *Life of Crassus*, Plutarch only mentions Crassus coming to Cicero at night. Plutarch shines a literary spotlight on his biographee Crassus, while choosing to omit mention of the two who had accompanied him.

Fast-forward six weeks. Cicero learns of others who are plotting to overthrow the city. He secures the evidence and calls a meeting of the senate. When the senate meets, Caesar suggests that the property of the conspirators should be confiscated and the conspirators should remain under arrest until Catiline is defeated, after which they would be tried. Caesar's speech persuades most of the senators until Catulus, followed by Cato, passionately opposes Caesar's proposal and convinces Cicero, who was consul at the time, and the senate to execute the conspirators immediately. The conspirators are then condemned and put to death. In Plutarch's *Life of Caesar*, Cato and Catulus oppose Caesar's proposal. In Plutarch's *Life of Cicero*, Catulus is the first to oppose Caesar, followed by Cato. However, in his *Life of Cato Minor*, Plutarch shines his spotlight on his biographee Cato, choosing not to mention Catulus, and leaves the reader with the impression that Cato alone had opposed Caesar.

The Resurrection Narratives in the Gospels

Turning to the Gospels, literary spotlighting is likely responsible for three examples of differences in the resurrection narratives. (1) *The number of women who visited the tomb on Easter morning differs.* The Synoptic Gospels report multiple women discovering the empty tomb. However, only Mary Magdalene is mentioned in John 20:1: "Early on the first day of the week while it was still dark, Mary Magdalene came to the tomb and saw that the stone had been taken away from the tomb." Yet John appears to know of other women who were present since, in the next verse, Mary ran to Peter and the Beloved Disciple and told them, "They have taken the Lord from the tomb and *we* do not know where they have laid him" (emphasis added). To whom does *we* refer? Mary is unlikely to be referring to Peter, the Beloved Disciple, and herself. That would be entirely redundant. Of course Peter and the Beloved Disciple would not know where Jesus's corpse was at that moment, since prior to Mary's early-morning visit, neither was even aware that the tomb was now empty. Furthermore, since all three Synoptic Gospels report the presence of multiple women at the discovery of the empty tomb, it seems likely that John is also aware of the presence of other women and is shining his literary spotlight on Mary Magdalene in his narrative.

(2) *The number of angels encountered at the tomb differs.* Mark 16:5 and Matthew 28:2–4 mention one angel at the tomb, while Luke 24:4 and John 20:12 mention two angels. Mark and Matthew may be shining their literary spotlight on the angel making the announcement.

(3) *The number of male disciples who visited the tomb differs.* John 20:3–20 informs us that *Peter and the Beloved Disciple* ran to the tomb. At first look, this appears inconsistent with Luke 24:12, which only mentions *Peter* running to the tomb.[10] However, only twelve verses later in Luke 24:24, the two Emmaus disciples report that earlier that day, "*some of those with us* went to the tomb and found it just as the women had said" (emphasis added). Luke appears to be shining his literary spotlight on Peter in 24:12.

COMPRESSION

The Assassination of Julius Caesar and the Immediate Aftermath[11]

Julius Caesar was assassinated by a group of conspirators led by Marcus Brutus on the Ides of March (March 15), 44 BC. Nicholas Horsfall wrote, "On the Ides more varied and abundant information survives, I believe, than on any other day in Roman or Greek history. But this evidence is full of obscurities and inconsistencies, largely unexplored."[12] Because there are

10. There is some dispute over whether Luke 24:12 was part of Luke's original text. However, almost all English translations have included it. Metzger, *Textual Commentary on the Greek New Testament*, 157–58, explains why the textual committee included it and assigned it a confidence grade of B. The textual note for Luke 24:12 in the NET Bible opines that "the MS evidence for omission is far too slight for the verse to be rejected as secondary. It is included in P^{75} and the rest of the MS tradition."

11. For a more in-depth treatment, see Licona, *Why Are There Differences in the Gospels?*, 91–98. References in Plutarch's *Lives* are *Caes.* 64.1–68.1; *Cic.* 39.5b–6; 42.3; *Ant.* 13.2–15.1; *Brut.* 11.1–21.1.

12. Nicholas Horsfall, "The Ides of March: Some New Problems," *Greece and Rome* 21, no. 2

so many differences in the way this story is told, all of which are minor, I am going to focus on only one portion of the aftermath.

The most infamous line at the event of Julius Caesar's assassination is uttered by Caesar himself immediately before surrendering to death. Having already been stabbed many times by the group of conspirators, he sees Brutus with dagger in hand approaching to join in the slaughter and utters the Latin words, "Et tu, Brute?" Or so Shakespeare has it in his play *Julius Caesar*. However, Plutarch shows no knowledge of Caesar's utterance. Writing about a decade after Plutarch, Suetonius reports, "And in this wise he was stabbed with three and twenty wounds, uttering not a word, but merely a groan at the first stroke, though some have written that when Marcus Brutus rushed at him, he said *in Greek*, 'You too, my child?'"[13] Unfortunately, none of those sources have survived. A century after Plutarch and Suetonius wrote, Cassius Dio makes mention of the utterance in the same manner as Suetonius, stating that there are some who added that Caesar said to Brutus, "You too, my child?" However, Suetonius and Dio appear to doubt its authenticity.[14]

Upon Caesar's violent death, commotion and confusion raced through the city of Rome. Brutus tried to speak to the senators to explain his actions and those of his coconspirators. But the senators fled in fear. Brutus and the other conspirators then walked confidently to the temple of Jupiter located on a hill called the Capitoline, proclaiming to the people that they were now free from tyranny. Later that day, many senators as well as common folk went up to the Capitoline to hear what the conspirators had to say. Brutus gave a speech, which was well received.

On the following day (March 16), Brutus and the other conspirators walked to the chief public square of the city called the Forum, where he gave a second speech. The Roman people and senators listened to him out

(1974): 191–99. The items considered by Horsfall are limited to only a few. For a treatment that focuses on the hour at which the conspirators met, see John Ramsey, "At What Hour Did the Murderers of Julius Caesar Gather on the Ides of March 44 B.C.?," in *In Pursuit of Wissenschaft: Festschrift für William M. Calder III zum 75, Geburtstag*, ed. Stephan Heilen, Robert Kirstein, R. Scott Smith, Stephen M. Trzaskoma, Rogier L. van der Wal, and Matthias Vorwerk, Spudasmata 119 (New York: Olms, 2008), 351–63.

13. Suetonius, *Divus Julius* 82.2. J. C. Rolfe, trans., *Suetonius*, rev. ed., vol. 1, LCL 31 (Cambridge, MA: Harvard University Press, 1998), 140–41. Although conversant in Greek, Caesar's primary language was Latin. In an environment where Latin was also the primary language of all of the senators in attendance, it is unlikely that Caesar would have switched to Greek to utter, "You too, my child?"

14. Dio, *Hist. rom.* 44.19.5.

of respect, for previously they had held Brutus in high regard. Another of the conspirators, Cinna, spoke after Brutus and denounced Caesar. But the people were greatly angered by Cinna's words and the conspirators fled back to the Capitoline in fear for their lives.

In his *Life of Brutus*, Plutarch narrates the initial progression of events more rapidly than he does in his *Life of Caesar.* In *Brutus* we read that Caesar's assassination, the conspirators' trip to the Capitoline, Brutus's speech to the people from the Capitoline, their invitation for him to come to the Forum, the conspirators' trip to the Forum, Brutus's second speech, Cinna's speech and the people's angry response, and the conspirators' flight back to the Capitoline all occurred on March 15. Plutarch has compressed the account in his *Life of Brutus*. However, these events had actually occurred over a period of two days as narrated in Plutarch's *Life of Caesar.* Let's now look at an example of compression in the Gospels.

Jesus Raises Jairus's Daughter from the Dead

Mark and Luke report that Jairus came to Jesus and said, "My daughter is *about to die*. Please come heal her." Jesus agrees. As they all traveled to Jairus's house, some servants come and tell Jairus that his daughter has just died. Jesus encourages Jairus to have faith. They then go to Jairus's house, and Jesus raises his daughter from the dead (Mark 5:21–43 // Luke 8:40–56).

When Matthew reports the same story (Matt. 9:18–26), Jairus comes to Jesus and says, "My daughter *has just died*. Please come heal her." Jesus agrees, they go to Jairus's home, and Jesus raises the girl from the dead. Matthew does not mention the servants who come to tell Jairus that his daughter had died. After all, there was no need since she was already dead when Jairus approached Jesus in Matthew's version. It appears that Matthew has simplified the story. He has given us the *abbreviated version*.

Lydia McGrew eschews such an approach, instead proposing a way to harmonize the varying accounts:

> If the girl's breathing were slowing and she scarcely seemed to be breathing at all when he left, Jairus may have left his house in a great hurry, hoping to catch Jesus before her death. As Augustine suggests, he may have been mentally despairing. Or he may have been wavering between believing that she was dead and believing that she was not dead yet. This is, after all, a world without stethoscopes or other ways to check vital signs. It is not especially implausible, given the two accounts, that in his mentally agitated state he may have actually said something like this, "My daughter

is dying. She's probably just now died! But if you come and lay your hands on her, she will live." In that case, both Matthew's and Mark's versions of his words would fall well within the range of normal paraphrase, and the differences can easily be attributed to the variations of truthful witness memory. It is interesting that both versions say that the girl will live if Jesus lays his hands on her. A harmonization of this kind takes account of this: If Jesus comes and touches her, she will live, whether she has died already, as Jairus in his fear and grief is inclined to believe, or is alive, as he still partly hopes. This harmonization is one that Licona does not consider.

Whether or not Matthew knew (either from witnessing the scene and/or from Mark's account) that the servants came later and told Jairus that the girl was dead, simply not including that part of the story is not the same thing as deliberately suppressing it to try to make it look like she was dead before Jairus left the house. Omitting that part of the story could be a matter of benign compression—merely telling a story more briefly, without altering facts.[15]

We can acknowledge that McGrew's proposed solution is possibly what Matthew had in mind. However, we should not settle for "possible" when a more plausible way of understanding the Matthean text is available. Classicists and New Testament scholars alike have long recognized that compression is a compositional device employed by ancient writers. In fact, we can observe Matthew's tendency to simplify his accounts using compression elsewhere. We will observe this tendency to compress in the story of Jesus healing the centurion's servant and, in chapter 9, in the stories of Jesus cleansing the temple and cursing a fig tree. Matthew's narrative of Jesus raising the ruler's (i.e., Jairus's) daughter fits perfectly with his tendency to compress. By narrating Jairus as knowing his daughter has already died, Matthew had no need to mention the servants who announce her death to Jairus. In fact, the text would read oddly had he included them:

Jairus: "Jesus! My daughter has just died. Please come heal her."
Jesus: "Take me to her."
Servants arrive and tell Jairus: "Don't trouble Jesus any longer.
Your daughter has just died."

15. Lydia McGrew, *The Mirror or the Mask: Liberating the Gospels from Literary Devices* (Tampa, FL: DeWard, 2019), 383.

Furthermore, in chapter 3, we observed that a relationship exists between the Synoptic Gospels, with Matthew and Luke making robust use of Mark as their primary source. So when Matthew differs from Mark in such minor ways, it's quite probable that Matthew, or more likely the secretary assisting him, was either intentionally providing additional details (something not present in this story), paraphrasing, or correcting Mark. Thus, when Matthew and Luke are likely using Mark, an appeal to "variations of truthful witness memory" should not be the default approach to understanding why such similarities are present in the Synoptic Gospels. It seems far more probable that Matthew has simplified the story of Jesus raising Jairus's daughter by moving the narrative along faster than Mark and Luke narrate it. Most scholars agree.[16]

SIMPLIFICATION

In the above examples, we have observed some occasions where the author simplifies a story by compression or by focusing on a single character to the exclusion of others (i.e., literary spotlighting). However, simplification can also be present when an author alters minor details to make a point more clearly. Simplification may be responsible for the differences in how all three Synoptic Gospels report Jesus's instructions to his disciples when sending them out to preach.

> And he instructed them that they may take nothing on the way *except a staff only*. Not bread, not a bag, not money in the belt. But to *put on sandals* and not wear two tunics. (Mark 6:8–9)

---

16. See Darrell L. Bock, *Luke: Volume 1: 1:1–9:50*, Baker Exegetical Commentary on the New Testament (Grand Rapids: Baker Academic, 1994), 792–93; M. Eugene Boring, "The Gospel of Matthew," in *New Interpreter's Bible*, ed. Leander E. Keck (Nashville: Abingdon, 1994–2004), 245; D. A. Carson, "Matthew," in *The Expositor's Bible Commentary: Matthew–Mark*, ed. Tremper Longman III and David E. Garland, rev. ed. (Grand Rapids: Zondervan, 2010), 269; Craig A. Evans, *Matthew*, New Cambridge Bible Commentary (New York: Cambridge University Press, 2012), 206; R. T. France, *The Gospel of Matthew* (Grand Rapids: Eerdmans, 2007), 359; Donald A. Hagner, *Matthew 1–13*, WBC 33A (Dallas: Word, 1993), 248; Roger L. Hahn, *Matthew: A Commentary for Bible Students* (Indianapolis: Wesleyan, 2007), 128; Craig S. Keener, *The Gospel of Matthew: A Socio-Rhetorical Commentary* (Grand Rapids; Eerdmans, 2009), 302; John Nolland, *The Gospel of Matthew: A Commentary on the Greek Text* (Grand Rapids: Eerdmans, 2005), 394–95; Grant R. Osborne, *Matthew*, Zondervan Exegetical Commentary on the New Testament, Clinton E. Arnold, gen. ed. (Grand Rapids: Zondervan, 2010), 1:346–47; Sharon H. Ringe, *Luke*, Westminster Bible Companion, ed. Patrick D. Miller and David L. Bartlett (Louisville: Westminster John Knox, 1995), 123; Stuart K. Weber, *Matthew* (Nashville: B&H, 2000), 1:127. Leon Morris is open to either abbreviation or imprecise language (*The Gospel according to Matthew* [Grand Rapids: Eerdmans, 1992], 228–29).

"Do not obtain gold or silver or bronze for your belts, not a bag for the way, not two tunics, *not sandals*, *not a staff*. For the worker is worthy of his food." (Matt. 10:9–10)

And he said to them, "Take nothing for the way; *not a staff*, not a bag, not bread, not silver, not to have two tunics." (Luke 9:3)

Did Jesus instruct his disciples to take a staff and wear sandals (per Mark) or not to take a staff (per Matthew and Luke) or sandals (per Matthew)? A variety of explanations for the differences have been suggested. Some scholars think Matthew probably conflated Jesus's instructions given on this occasion where he allows a staff and sandals with Jesus's instruction when he sent out the seventy-two (only reported in Luke 10:1–12), where he does not allow a staff and presumably likewise did not permit the use of sandals.[17] Others have suggested that Matthew and Luke are saying that Jesus was aware that the disciples already had some of these items and was forbidding them from taking extras.[18] Still others have suggested that Matthew preserves Jesus's original instructions and Mark has softened them.[19] Morna Hooker thinks either "Mark's less stringent rules perhaps reflect the conditions of a later missionary journey" or that Matthew's account was later adapted and reflects tradition in the Mishna pertaining to what could be carried when entering the temple mount.[20] All of these suggestions are plausible. For myself, given Markan Priority combined with Matthew's tendency to simplify elsewhere in his Gospel, I am

17. Craig L. Blomberg, *Matthew*, New American Commentary 22 (Nashville: B&H, 1992), 172. See also Craig L. Blomberg, *Historical Reliability of the Gospels*, 2nd ed. (Downers Grove, IL: IVP Academic, 2007), 187–88; Walter L. Liefeld and David W. Pao, "Luke," in *The Expositor's Bible Commentary: Luke–Acts*, ed. Tremper Longman III and David E. Garland, vol. 10, rev. ed. (Grand Rapids: Zondervan, 2007), 168.

18. D. A. Carson, "Matthew," in *The Expositor's Bible Commentary: Matthew–Mark*, ed. Tremper Longman III and David E. Garland, vol. 9, rev. ed. (Grand Rapids: Zondervan, 2010), 285; Daniel J. Harrington, ed., *The Gospel of Matthew*, Sacra Pagina Series 1 (Collegeville, MN: Liturgical, 2007), 140; Ben Witherington III, *Matthew*, Smyth & Helwys Bible Commentary, ed. P. Keith Gammons and R. Alan Culpepper (Macon, GA: Smyth & Helwys, 2006), 220.

19. M. Eugene Boring, "The Gospel of Matthew," in *New Interpreter's Bible*, 256; W. D. Davies and Dale C. Allison Jr., *A Critical and Exegetical Commentary on the Gospel according to Saint Matthew*, vol. 2, *Commentary on Matthew XIX–XVIII*, International Critical Commentary (New York: T&T Clark International, 2004), 171–72; Craig S. Keener, *The Gospel of Matthew: A Socio-Rhetorical Commentary* (Grand Rapids; Cambridge, UK: Eerdmans, 2009); Ulrich Luz, *Matthew 8–20: A Commentary on Matthew 8–20*, trans. James E. Crouch, ed. Helmut Koester, Hermeneia (Minneapolis: Augsburg, 2001), 78.

20. See Morna D. Hooker, *The Gospel according to Saint Mark*, Black's New Testament Commentary (London: Continuum, 1991), 156–57.

inclined to think that Matthew and Luke, or more likely a source from which they both drew, have altered the details to make Jesus's point clearer: Jesus's disciples are to trust God for everything.[21] If this is what occurred, Matthew and Luke—or their source—have simplified their accounts. That said, we can only consider various options here, and although we may have a preference, prudence encourages us not to hold it too tightly.

Thus far, we have observed that the Gospels do not preserve a transcript of Jesus's words. On most occasions, Jesus spoke in Aramaic. But his words are preserved in Greek, with only a few brief exceptions.[22] Moreover, we compared several stories as they appear in more than one Gospel and have observed that Jesus's words often differ slightly between them, most likely because one or more authors or their sources made use of a variety of compositional devices commonly employed by other authors of that era. Some solutions to the differences of whether Jesus instructed his disciples to take a staff and sandals on their journeys suggest one or more of the Evangelists actually edited Jesus's words to communicate the thoughts behind them more clearly.

AUGUSTINE ON WORDS AND MEANING

Some readers will feel uncomfortable with such solutions. Therefore, I would like to acquaint you with the church father Augustine of Hippo (AD 354–430), who can provide a bit of perspective. Augustine had lived a life of sexual immorality and even engaged in theft before becoming a Christian. His subsequent commitment to Christ was both deep and intellectual. Augustine had a high view of Scripture. For him, Scripture is divinely inspired, free from error, authoritative, and trustworthy. He was committed to harmonizing differences that he observed in the Gospels. Sometime between AD 400 and 405 Augustine wrote a lengthy volume titled *Harmony of the Gospels* in which he offered explanations for countless differences. In that volume, Augustine considers the differences in the words of John the Baptist. I will draw our attention to only one item. In Mark, Luke, and John, John the Baptist says he is unworthy even to loose the strap of Jesus's sandal(s), whereas in Matthew John says he is unworthy to carry Jesus's sandals.

21. A major part of the Synoptic problem, though beyond the scope of this book, is whether Luke also used Matthew as a source, or vice versa, or they both made use of a common source to which we no longer have access. We will say more on this in chapter 9.

22. Mark 3:17; 5:41; 7:11, 34; 14:36; 15:34 (cf. Matt. 27:46); Matt. 5:22.

Matthew 3:11	Mark 1:7–8	Luke 3:16	John 1:26–27
I baptize you with water for repentance. But the one coming after me is more powerful than me, of whom I am not worthy *to carry his sandals*. He will baptize you with the Holy Spirit and fire.	One more powerful than me is coming after me, of whom I am not worthy to stoop down and *untie the strap of his sandals*. I baptize you with water. But he will baptize you with the Holy Spirit.	I baptize you with water. But one stronger than me is coming, of whom I am not worthy to *untie the strap of his sandals*. He will baptize you with the Holy Spirit and fire.	I baptize with water. Among you stands one whom you do not know, who is coming after me, of whom I am not worthy to *untie the strap of his sandal*.

Readers can readily observe that the Baptist's words differ in each account, though communicating similar thoughts. Augustine addresses the question of which of the Gospels preserves the actual words of John the Baptist.[23] He says that this is not a problem once we understand that the important element is what the Evangelists report is what John the Baptist meant. Augustine proceeds to contend that since the Gospels are God's Word and possess the highest authority, we should not think that the accounts are unreliable when they use different words to describe the same thing or because one of them omitted something, "nor if the person who has the authority to write the narrative should add not something to the subject but rather some words in order to illuminate and explain his meaning; nor if, although he presents the subject well, he tries but does not succeed in remembering and expressing the exact words he heard with complete accuracy."[24]

Augustine then anticipates those who will reply that there would be no variation in the least among the Evangelists if they had truly been empowered by the Holy Spirit.

> And, if someone says that the evangelists certainly ought to have been given this ability by the power of the Holy Spirit, so that their words would differ in neither kind nor order nor number, then he does not understand that, just as the evangelists' authority is heightened, so too is the credibility strengthened of other people who speak the truth through them.

23. Augustine, *Cons.* 2.12.27.

24. Augustine, *Cons.* 2.12.28 (trans. Paffenroth, "Agreement among the Evangelists," 189).

> For, if several people narrate the same thing, in no way can one of them be rightly accused of falsehood if he differs from another, because the evangelists give a precedent example in his defense. For, just as it is impossible to consider or say that with the evangelists there is anything false, neither does it appear that there is anything false about a writer who has done his work in the same way as we have shown they have done theirs. And, just as it belongs to the highest morality to guard against falsehood, so too ought we to be ruled by so eminent an authority such that we do not suppose that any narratives which we discover contain variations are therefore false, for there are variations among the evangelists.[25]

Augustine has a high view of Scripture. He contends that because we regard the Gospels as God's Word given by the Holy Spirit, we do not accuse them of reporting erroneously when we observe differences among their accounts. In a similar vein, we should not charge one another with error when we vary in recalling the same thing though somewhat differently.

Augustine now returns to the matter of whether John the Baptist spoke of being unworthy to untie Jesus's sandals or to carry them.

> Therefore it may be rightly asked what John said he was unworthy to do—whether to carry the shoes or to unloose the strap of the shoes. For, if he only said one of these things, then the narrative that says what he really said would seem to be the true one; and the other, while not a lie, would nonetheless be a slip of the memory and would be supposed to have said one thing instead of another. But one ought to keep away from the evangelists all charges of falsehood, not only that which comes from lying but also that which comes from forgetfulness. Therefore, if it is relevant to the subject to understand "carrying shoes" to mean one thing, and "unloosing the strap of the shoes" to mean another, then how should one rightly understand it, except that John said both things, either on separate occasions or on the same occasion? For he might have said, "the strap of whose shoes I am not worthy to unloose, and whose shoes I am not worthy to carry," with the result that the one evangelist would have given part of it, and the others the rest, but all would have given truthful accounts. Furthermore, if by mentioning the Lord's shoes John intended to show [the Lord's] greatness and his own lowliness, then, whatever he

25. Augustine, *Cons.* 2.12.28 (trans. Paffenroth, "Agreement among the Evangelists," 189).

> said, whether it was about unloosing the strap of his shoes or carrying his shoes, the sense is preserved by any writer who mentions the shoes in his own words, thereby expressing the same idea of lowliness and not altering his subject's thought. Therefore, this is a useful method, and one especially worthy to be remembered, that, when we speak of the agreement of the evangelists, there is no falsehood, not even if they say that the subject of a narrative said something which that person did not say, as long as they express the same thought as the one of them who does record the actual words. From this we learn the sound lesson that *we ought to seek nothing other than what the person speaking meant.*[26]

At this point, some readers will be wondering why the minor difference of whether the Baptist spoke of being unworthy to carry Jesus's sandals or loose the strap on them was so troubling to Augustine. Other readers will identify with him. Augustine was not open to the possibility that any of the Evangelists were guilty of even a minor error. So in contending that no errors exist in the Gospels, Augustine attempted to harmonize the different ways they often report the same events. In my opinion, he often went too far with this exercise. A good example is observed in how Augustine attempted to reconcile the difference I mentioned at the beginning of this book: Did a rooster crow only after Peter denied Jesus three times (per Matthew, Luke, and John) or once after Peter's first denial and then crowed a second time after Peter's third denial (per Mark)? Augustine suggested that although the rooster did not crow the second time until after Peter's third denial, by the time of his first denial, he was filled with sufficient fear to elicit the second and third denials. Therefore, "it would be neither absurd nor untruthful to say that he denied him three times before the cock crowed." This interpretation of Mark is quite strained. However, Augustine proceeds to offer an alternative interpretation that he seems to have preferred, suggesting that as long as Peter began his series of denying Jesus three times before a rooster crowed the first time, there would be no error present (Augustine, *Cons.* 3.2.7). Augustine then goes on to suggest that Matthew, Luke, and John simply neglect to mention the first crowing of the rooster after Peter's first denial (Augustine, *Cons.* 3.6.22–23).

Despite his occasional strained attempts to harmonize differences in the Gospels' reports, Augustine believed that what matters ultimately is

26. Augustine, *Cons.* 2.12.29 (trans. Paffenroth, "Agreement among the Evangelists," 190, emphasis added).

whether what the evangelist reports is in accord with the *meaning* of what actually occurred and was spoken. Whether the Baptist spoke of untying Jesus's sandals or carrying them is not important. What is important is that both readings communicate the same message: Jesus's superiority to the Baptist and the latter's humility. It is here that Augustine begins to sound more like Origen, who wrote nearly two centuries earlier.[27]

I do not mention Augustine's words to umpire the matter or even to say he was correct. I have brought him into the conversation because his view of Scripture is similar to that held by many of today's theologically conservative Christians. Although Augustine preferred harmonized solutions, even he was not averse to the Evangelists changing and adding to the words so long as the same thought or message was preserved.

WHY THIS IS IMPORTANT

Since compositional devices belong to the fabric of ancient biographical writing, differences resulting from their use should not be regarded as errors. It appears likely that in addition to several of the techniques for paraphrasing that are prescribed in the compositional textbooks, the Evangelists made use of several compositional devices, such as compression, conflation, and literary spotlighting. If they did, attempting to harmonize the differences will take one down the wrong path and yield an incorrect understanding of why the differences are present. Moreover, if the Evangelists employed compositional devices, then God allowed them via divine inspiration.

SUMMARY

Plutarch offers us the rare opportunity of being able to compare how the same author reports the same story on multiple occasions. When we make these comparisons, we understand why, for a long time, classicists and many New Testament scholars have claimed that ancient historians employed a number of compositional devices that resulted in differences between their accounts. In this chapter, we examined some stories in Plutarch's *Lives* and the Gospels where the authors are likely using one or more compositional devices such as literary spotlighting, compression,

27. Origen, *Commentary on the Gospel according to John*, books 1–10, 80:259, book 10, par. 19–20 (Heine).

and simplification. We also saw that even Augustine, who believed the Bible did not contain any errors and was strongly committed to harmonizing Gospel differences, acknowledged that the author was permitted to change and add words to what had been said in order to provide greater clarity. He also stated that the message behind the words is what matters most.

In the next chapter, we will examine some stories in Plutarch and in the Gospels where the use of another compositional device is likely: transferal.

QUESTIONS FOR FURTHER THOUGHT

1. What is the most interesting thing you learned in this chapter?
2. Read Luke 24:1–53. What impression does Luke provide pertaining to the time that elapsed between Jesus's resurrection and ascension?
3. Read Acts 1:11. How long does the author, Luke, say elapsed between Jesus's resurrection and ascension?
4. The Gospel of Luke and Acts were written by the same author. How would you explain the different elapsed times reported between Jesus's resurrection and ascension in Luke and Acts? What compositional device may account for it? Can you think of some reasons why Luke may have used that device?
5. Read the following accounts of Jesus casting out Legion: Mark 5:1–20 // Matt. 8:28–34 // Luke 8:26–39. What do you think may be going on that accounts for the different number of demoniacs?

CHAPTER 8

TRANSFERAL

In the previous chapter, we observed a few instances where Plutarch and the Evangelists appear to use *literary spotlighting*, *compression*, and *simplification*. We also observed that Augustine—who loved to harmonize, was fully committed to the divine inspiration of Scripture, and thought it inconceivable that even the smallest of error could be present in the Bible—concluded that what matters ultimately is whether the evangelist reports in accordance with the *meaning* of what actually occurred and was spoken. In this chapter, we will observe another compositional device: *transferal*.

TRANSFERAL

Transferal is when an author knowingly attributes the identity of a person producing or receiving an action to another.

Pompey Delivers an Illegal Encomium[1]

In 52 BC, Rome was in chaos and Caesar was becoming a threat to the Republic. So the senate took a drastic measure, electing Pompey as sole consul for that year and giving him virtually absolute power. Pompey proceeded to establish a number of new laws to bring about order. One of those laws banned speeches that gave lavish praise to a person, called *encomiums*, from being read at trial on behalf of a defendant. Plutarch reports that shortly after establishing this law, Pompey proceeded to break it when he wrote an encomium and had it read at the trial of his friend Plancus. In Plutarch's *Life of Cato Minor*,[2] Pompey writes the encomium and has an emissary read it at Plancus's trial. But Pompey is not present. This scenario is confirmed by Cassius Dio and Valerius Maximus.[3] However,

1. Plut., *Caes.* 28; *Pomp.* 54–55; *Cat. Min.* 47–48.

2. Plut. *Cat. Min.* 48.4.

3. Dio, *Hist. rom.* 40.55.1–4; Valerius Maximus, *Facta et dicta memorabilia* (*Memorable Deeds and Sayings*) 6.2.5. I am indebted to John Ramsey for alerting me to these references. Valerius reports the

in his *Life of Pompey*, Plutarch reports that *Pompey himself* appeared in court and read his encomium.[4] Plutarch has simplified the narrative by brushing out the emissary from the story and transferring the reading of the encomium to Pompey, who had composed it.

Of course, one could instead suggest the difference resulted from either Plutarch incorrectly recalling the story when writing one of the accounts or his account reflecting new information Plutarch learned after writing his *Life of Pompey*.[5] While such conjectures are *possible*, they fail to consider how the ancients wrote. Christopher Pelling is the foremost authority on Plutarch. He and other classicists have argued that Plutarch's *Lives* featuring those of the late Roman Republic are largely based on a contemporary history of Rome written by Asinius Pollio, whose writings have since been lost. Pelling holds that Plutarch's wide reading of other sources is reflected in not more than 25 percent of his overall narrative. He adds that this practice "is not unique to Plutarch, nor to biography," but is shared by other historians such as Cassius Dio, Livy, Dionysius of Halicarnassus, and even Tacitus.[6] This has implications for the Gospels. Given this practice by ancient historians, should we be surprised when we observe Matthew and Luke making such robust use of Mark and supplementing Mark's Gospel?

Returning to Plutarch, Pelling argues that he composed the *Lives* featuring those of the late Republic as a set, with six of them probably composed simultaneously.[7] If Pelling is correct, it is safest to assume that differences between parallel stories in those six *Lives* resulted from intentional paraphrasing by Plutarch. Accordingly, since *Cato Minor* and *Pompey* are two of those six *Lives*, it is more probable that Plutarch simplified the story of Pompey's encomium in *Pompey* than that he had come across another source since writing *Cato Minor* or had read his source more carefully.[8]

---

story of Pompey's illegal encomium about seventy-five years prior to Plutarch's narratives. Plutarch is aware of Valerius's writings because he mentions them elsewhere. So he probably consulted them during his research phase.

4. Plut. *Pomp.* 55.5.

5. See Lydia McGrew, *The Mirror or the Mask: Liberating the Gospels from Literary Devices* (Tampa, FL: DeWard, 2019), 217.

6. Christopher Pelling, *Plutarch and History: Eighteen Studies* (Swansea: Classical Press of Wales, 2002), 1–44, esp. 19–20; Christopher Pelling, trans., *Plutarch: Caesar* (Oxford: Oxford University Press, 2011), 39–40.

7. Plut. *Pomp.*; *Cat. Min.*; *Crass.*; *Caes.*; *Brut.*; *Ant.* See Pelling, *Plutarch and History*, 2–11; Pelling, *Plutarch: Caesar*, 36. For more on this, see Pelling, *Plutarch and History*, chapters 1 and 3.

8. Pelling (*Plutarch and History*, 12–13) thinks Plutarch may have encountered the Pollio source

Furthermore, the trial at which Pompey's speech would have been read occurred between December 10, 52 BC, and the end of January 51 BC. Pompey likely would have decided to break his own law and have the encomium read only after he had learned that the trial for his friend Plancus was not going as well as he had hoped. This would likely place Pompey's illegal act in January, and, having completed his term as consul in December, Pompey would probably have left the city by that time and taken his proconsulship in a different province.[9] All of this increases the likelihood that Plutarch deliberately simplified his account in his *Life of Pompey* by narrating Pompey appearing in person to read his speech at the trial of his friend Plancus. Let's now turn to some stories in the Gospels where transferal may have resulted in some differences.

Jesus Heals a Centurion's Servant

This story is a very nice parallel to the one with Pompey we just examined. A centurion wanted to ask Jesus to heal his servant who was very sick. Luke 7:1–10 tells us the centurion sent some Jewish elders to make the request on his behalf. They came to Jesus and said, "There is a centurion who has been kind to our people. He has a servant who is sick. Please heal him." Jesus agrees, and they head toward the centurion's house. But when the centurion gets word that Jesus is on his way, he crafts a message and sends some friends who relay it to Jesus: "The centurion says he is not worthy for you to enter his house. But he knows you have authority. So he requests that you only give the command and his servant will be healed." Jesus praises the centurion for his faith and heals his servant without having seen the centurion or his servant. This is Luke's version of the story.

In Matthew's version (Matt. 8:5–13), *the centurion himself* makes the request in person. When Jesus agrees to see the servant, the centurion tells him, "I am unworthy for you to enter my house. But you have authority. So only give the command and my servant will be healed." Jesus praises the centurion for his faith and heals his servant.

Just as Plutarch simplified the story by airbrushing out Pompey's emissary and instead has Pompey deliver his encomium in person, Matthew has simplified the story by airbrushing out the Jewish elders and friends the centurion had sent and instead has the centurion go to Jesus directly to make his request in person. Matthew has transferred the actions of the

---

after writing his *Lives* of *Cicero* and *Lucullus* but prior to the six he likely composed simultaneously.

9. See A. M. Stone, "*Pro Milone*: Cicero's Second Thoughts," *Antichthon* 14 (1980): 88–111. I am grateful to John Ramsey for alerting me to Stone's essay.

emissaries to the centurion. This interpretation is the majority position taken by conservative New Testament scholars.[10]

However, there are three other approaches a minority of scholars have taken for dealing with the differences in this story. A *very* small number have employed *creative harmonization*. These scholars suggest that the centurion sent the Jewish elders, then his friends, then later decided to go see Jesus himself. Chrysostom took this approach in the fourth century.[11] A more recent interpreter who took this approach is Gleason Archer.[12] Such a scenario is not only pure speculation but also wrong. According to Luke, "*the men who had been sent* [by the centurion] returned to the house." Luke does not mention the centurion along with those he had sent because, according to Luke, he apparently did not go to see Jesus.

Another approach also employs harmonizing: *metonymy*. Metonymy is a figure of speech whereby one thing is substituted for another with which it is closely related. For example, the Gospels report that Pilate scourged Jesus (Mark 15:15 // Matt. 27:26 // John 19:1). Most readers understand that Pilate had ordered the scourging rather than being the one holding the whip. Likewise, when the Jewish elders informed Jesus that the centurion had built the synagogue for them (Luke 7:5), readers

---

10. Examples include Darrell L. Bock, "Luke, Acts," in *The Holman Apologetics Commentary on the Bible: The Gospels and Acts*, ed. Jeremy Royal Howard (Nashville: B&H Academic, 2013), 389; F. F. Bruce, *Hard Sayings of the Bible*, ed. Walter C. Kaiser Jr., Peter H. Davids, F. F. Bruce, and Manfred T. Brauch (Downers Grove, IL: InterVarsity Press, 1996), 458–59; D. A. Carson, "Matthew," in *The Expositor's Bible Commentary: Matthew and Mark*, ed. Tremper Longman III and David E. Garland, rev. ed., vol. 9 (Grand Rapids: Zondervan, 2010), 200; R. T. France, *The Gospel of Mark: A Commentary on the Greek Text*, New International Greek Testament Commentary (Grand Rapids: Eerdmans; Carlisle: Paternoster, 2002), 311; David E. Garland, *Reading Matthew: A Literary and Theological Commentary on the First Gospel* (Macon, GA: Smyth & Helwys, 2001), 94–95; Robert H. Gundry, *Matthew: A Commentary on His Handbook for a Mixed Church under Persecution*, 2nd ed. (Grand Rapids: Eerdmans, 1994), 141–43; Donald A. Hagner, *Matthew 1–13*, World Biblical Commentary 33A (Nashville: Nelson, 1993), 202; Walter L. Liefeld and David W. Pao, "Luke," in *The Expositor's Bible Commentary: Luke–Acts*, ed. Tremper Longman III and David E. Garland, rev. ed., vol. 10 (Grand Rapids: Zondervan, 2007), 143; I. Howard Marshall, *The Gospel of Luke: A Commentary on the Greek Text*, New International Greek Testament Commentary (Carlisle: Paternoster Press; Grand Rapids: Eerdmans, 1978), 278; Leon Morris, *The Gospel according to Matthew*, in Pillar New Testament Commentary (Grand Rapids: Eerdmans; Leicester, England: Inter-Varsity Press, 1991), 228–29; Robert H. Stein, *Luke*, New American Commentary 24 (Nashville: B&H, 1992), 218–19; Mark L. Strauss, *Mark*, Zondervan Exegetical Commentary on the New Testament 2, ed. Clinton E. Arnold (Grand Rapids: Zondervan, 2014), 489n7; Michael Wilkins, "Matthew," in *The Holman Apologetics Commentary on the Bible: The Gospels and Acts*, 65.

11. Chrysostom, *Hom. Matt.* 26.3.

12. Gleason L. Archer, *Encyclopedia of Bible Difficulties* (Grand Rapids: Zondervan, 1982), 321–22. See also Norval Geldenhuys, *Commentary on the Gospel of Luke: The English Text with Introduction, Exposition and Notes*, New International Commentary on the Old and New Testament (Grand Rapids: Eerdmans, 1952), 220.

naturally understand that the centurion had funded or had overseen the project rather than having completed all of the work single-handedly. With metonymy, Matthew is doing something similar when he says that the centurion went to Jesus. The centurion sent others to Jesus to deliver a message on his behalf. But Matthew is not saying the centurion appeared before Jesus in person. This approach was proposed by Augustine and Calvin and is held today by Vern Poythress.[13]

The suggestion that metonymy is being used here by Matthew is problematic. While one can easily see how saying the centurion had built a synagogue would have been understood by others to mean the centurion had funded or delegated the task, it is a bit of a stretch to claim this is what Matthew was doing pertaining to the centurion's communications with Jesus. Consider the following statement: "The president attempted to negotiate North Korea's nuclear disarmament with Kim Jong Un." This statement could easily be understood to mean that he sent his secretary of state to do the work on his behalf. However, it would be a quite different matter if the statement were: "The president *went* to Singapore to negotiate North Korea's nuclear disarmament with Kim Jong Un." In this case, we would think the president himself had gone.

Additional clues suggest that Matthew has specified how the centurion's request reached Jesus and is, therefore, not using metonymy: Matthew first tells us the centurion went to Jesus and made the request (Matt. 8:5). He then writes, "And Jesus said *to the centurion*, 'Go! It is done for you as you believed'" (Matt. 8:13). Notice what the text says. Jesus spoke directly *to the centurion*. This is immediately followed by the instruction to "Go," which is a singular rather than plural verb in the Greek. Matthew would have used the plural verb if he had been referring to a group of emissaries. Jesus immediately follows his instruction to go with the encouragement, "It is done *for you* [singular pronoun in Greek] as *you believed* [singular verb in Greek]."[14] He did not say, "It is done *for him as he believed*." Matthew narrates Jesus speaking directly to the centurion who has appeared before him. Moreover, Matthew does not mention emissaries. So everything in Matthew's report suggests that Matthew intended to communicate that the centurion came to Jesus in person and Jesus spoke with him directly.

Another option is that Matthew may simply be mistaken. This is the

13. Vern S. Poythress, *Inerrancy and the Gospels: A God-Centered Approach to the Challenges of Harmonization* (Wheaton, IL: Crossway, 2012), 20–22.

14. Gk. "go" (*hypage*), "for you" (*soi*), "you believed" (*episteusas*).

opinion of Christian philosopher Lydia McGrew.[15] I am not aware of any New Testament scholar who shares her view—conservative, atheist, or anywhere in-between. She also holds that Matthew would have engaged in "fictionalization" and a "misleading activity" had he employed transferal as previously suggested.[16] Vern Poythress disagrees, however.

> Some may boldly claim that Matthew has "committed an error" and say that he has not truthfully represented the facts. But Matthew is completely true. The difficulty actually lies in fallible human expectations about Matthew and the other Gospels. People have expectations as to what, in their minds, constitutes a trustworthy account. These expectations may sometimes go astray and create an unnecessary difficulty.[17]

Moreover, I see no good reason to think Matthew erred here when a simple explanation is readily available and is in accord with what other biographers of the same era were doing: Matthew simplified the story by eliminating the Jewish emissaries and friends and has the centurion make the request in person to Jesus (transferal).

In my opinion, the option that most likely provides an accurate description of the cause for the difference is that Matthew has simplified the account, having streamlined it by eliminating the emissaries and transferring the messages from the emissaries to the centurion, who expresses them in person to Jesus. However, we are not ready to move on because there is another option that may change the scenario considerably: John's Gospel narrates a healing miracle that may actually be a different version of the same story.

> Therefore, [Jesus] came again into Cana of Galilee where he turned water into wine. Now there was a certain royal official whose son was sick in Capernaum. When this one heard that Jesus had come from Judea into Galilee, he went to him and asked him to come and heal his son. For he was about to die. So Jesus said to him, "Unless you see signs and wonders, you will never believe." The royal official said to him, "Lord, come before my child dies." Jesus said to him, "Go. Your son will live." The man believed the word that Jesus said to him and went. And while

15. McGrew, *The Mirror or the Mask*, 375–81, 391.
16. McGrew, *The Mirror or the Mask*, 378.
17. Poythress, *Inerrancy and the Gospels*, 48.

> he was on his way, his servants met him and said that his child is alive. Therefore, he inquired from them the hour in which he began to recover. And they said to him, "The fever left him yesterday at the seventh hour." Then the father recognized that it was at that hour in which Jesus said to him, "Your son will live." And he believed and his entire household. And this was the second sign Jesus performed, having come from Judea into Galilee. (John 4:46–54)

There are numerous differences between this story in John and the one narrated by Matthew and Luke. In John, the one coming to Jesus is a "certain royal official," whereas he is a centurion in Matthew and in Luke. In John, his son is sick, whereas in Matthew and Luke, his servant is. The royal official begs Jesus to come to his house, whereas the centurion specifically asks Jesus not to come to his house. The royal official leaves Capernaum, goes to Jesus in Cana, and asks him to come to Capernaum; whereas in Matthew, the centurion came to Jesus after Jesus had entered Capernaum. In Luke, the language is ambiguous and would be consistent with the centurion sending the elders either when Jesus was in Capernaum or when he was giving the Sermon on the Mount. That said, Capernaum was not a large town. Therefore, to send elders to invite Jesus and then, upon hearing he was on his way to his house, send friends to dissuade him from coming fits very well with John's version, perhaps even more than it does Luke's.

Many scholars think John is presenting another version of the same story.[18] The similarities are intriguing: one who is near death with sickness is in Capernaum, and a person of rank in Capernaum asks Jesus to heal one for whom he cares deeply. Jesus heals the sick person without seeing him. The healing occurs toward the beginning of Jesus's ministry. John 4:54 says this was the second sign Jesus did while in Galilee, the first being when he turned water into wine (John 2:1–11; 4:46), while Matthew and Luke both report that Jesus entered Capernaum and healed the centurion's servant shortly after delivering his Sermon on the Mount, which was close to the beginning of his ministry (Matt. 8:1–5 // Luke 7.1). It is the timing of the event in Matthew, Luke, and John—toward the beginning of Jesus's ministry—that almost makes it too much to ask

---

18. François Bovon, *Luke 1: A Commentary on the Gospel of Luke 1:1–9:50*, ed. Helmut Koester, Hermeneia (Minneapolis: Fortress, 2002), 259. Ringe, *Luke*, Westminster Bible Companion, 98. Bock says this is the view of most scholars; however, Bock thinks John preserves a different event (see Bock, *Luke: 1:1–9:50*, vol. 1, 631–32).

to interpret the story in John as being a different event, given the other similar details.

If John is narrating the same event, then it is far less likely that Matthew is simplifying the story and transferring the action and words of the centurion's emissaries to the centurion, unless both Matthew and John have simplified the story in the same manner. It would also be unlikely that metonymy is present for the same reasons it would be absent in Matthew: singular pronouns and a singular verb are used. Moreover, the conversation suggests direct correspondence: "Lord, come before *my child* dies," and "Go. *Your son* will live," rather than "Lord, come before *his child* dies," and "Go. *His son* will live." Furthermore, there is no indication whatsoever that the royal official sent others. One could charge Matthew, Luke, or John with error, innocent or otherwise. However, most scholars who have spent a significant amount of time studying John's Gospel are of the opinion that John often adapts his stories about Jesus. Recall F. F. Bruce's description of John's version as "an expanded paraphrase," "a translation of the freest kind," "a transposition into another key," "all this and much more."[19]

If John is narrating the same event reported by Matthew and Luke, we may not have an example of Matthew simplifying and transferring since John would have engaged in similar editing. However, we would then observe either how the story had changed in the time between when Matthew and Luke wrote or, more likely, the additional extent of freedom John would take when reporting a story. Craig Blomberg writes,

> If they are variant accounts of the same event, as I have tentatively favoured, then . . . we have a good example of the freedom that John felt to bring out different details and emphases in stories already commonly known from early Christian oral tradition, if not from the final form of the Synoptics themselves. This measure of freedom will recur in subsequent passages in John that are demonstrably describing the same events as their synoptic counterparts.[20]

If John is reporting the same story as Matthew and Luke, we must also consider the possibility that *Luke added the emissaries* to the story. Why would he do that? One may only speculate, of course. It has been

19. Bruce, *The Gospel and Epistles of John*, 16. See page 46.

20. Craig L. Blomberg, *Historical Reliability of John's Gospel* (Downers Grove, IL: IVP Academic, 2001), 107.

suggested that Luke invented the emissaries to minimize contact between Jesus and gentiles.[21] We are unlikely to arrive at a conclusion we are justified to hold with confidence. There is no consensus among scholars on the matter.[22] However, by now it is clear that ancient biography had literary conventions that permitted biographers to alter peripheral details and that they did so to varying degrees. Ancient biographers did not have the objective of reporting with the same precision we desire of modern biographers.

Jesus's Baptism: To Whom Did God Speak?

Although *transferal* usually involves attributing the words spoken or actions performed by one person to another, it can also involve changing the recipient of words or actions. The Synoptic Gospels recall differently what God's voice said at Jesus's baptism. Mark and Luke report God saying, "*You* are my beloved Son. With *you* I am well-pleased" (Mark 1:11 // Luke 3:22). God is speaking directly to Jesus. However, Matthew reports God saying, "*This* is my beloved Son. With *him* I am well-pleased" (Matt. 3:17). God is speaking directly to the crowd. Given Markan Priority, it appears that Matthew has transferred the recipient of the message. Instead of to Jesus, God speaks to the crowd. Why would Matthew do this? One can only guess. Perhaps, as Augustine suggested, Matthew desired to make God's message more personal to his readers.[23] To me, this seems more plausible than what appears to be an attempt to harmonize the difference, an attempt we observe in the apocryphal *Gospel of the Ebionites*.

> When the people had been baptized, Jesus also came and was baptized by John. And as he came up from the water, the heavens opened, and he saw the Holy Spirit in the form of a dove descending and entering him.

---

21. Bovon, *Luke 1*, 259; Christopher M. Tuckett, *Luke*, T&T Clark Study Guides (1996; repr., New York: T&T Clark, 2000), 53.

22. John Chrysostom and Origen hold that John is narrating a different event, whereas Irenaeus appears to think John is narrating the same event, since he refers to the royal official in John as the "centurion" (*Adv. Haer.* 2.22.3). Therefore, Irenaeus either confuses the Johannine story with the story of the centurion in Matthew and Luke, or he thinks John reports the same event. See John Chrysostom, *Homilies on the Gospel of John* 35.2 (John Chrysostom, "Homilies of St. John Chrysostom, Archbishop of Constantinople, on the Gospel of St. John," in *Saint Chrysostom: Homilies on the Gospel of St. John and Epistle to the Hebrews*, ed. Philip Schaff, trans. G. T. Stupart, vol. 14 of *A Select Library of the Nicene and Post-Nicene Fathers of the Christian Church*, First Series [New York: Christian Literature Company, 1889], 123–24); Origen, *Commentary on John*, 13.446, 80:162 (Heine).

23. Augustine, *Cons.* 2.14.31.

> A voice from heaven said: "You are my beloved son, in you I am well pleased." And again: "Today I have begotten you." And immediately, a great light shone around the place. Seeing this, John says to him, "Who are you, Lord?" And again a voice from heaven said to him: "This is my beloved son, in whom I am well pleased."[24]

In this *Gospel of the Ebionites*, God's voice speaks directly to Jesus ("You are my beloved son") and then directly to John ("This is my beloved son").[25]

WHY THIS IS IMPORTANT

In this chapter and the previous two, we have observed that compositional devices are the outworking of the liberties allowed ancient biographers when writing their accounts. Modern readers should, accordingly, read ancient biographies in view of the conventions in play when they were written rather than imparting our modern ideas of precision upon them.

Thus far in our journey, we have observed numerous techniques for paraphrasing prescribed in the compositional textbook by Theon. The techniques were for use in all forms of writing, explicitly mentioning historical writings, and other compositional devices employed by Plutarch and the Evangelists. Given that such editorial work was prescribed and appears to have been common practice in that era, it seems naïve to insist that the resulting surface differences are errors.

SUMMARY

In this chapter we observed a story from Plutarch's *Lives* in which Plutarch appears to have simplified one of his accounts by employing *transferal.*

---

24. The *Gospel of the Ebionites* is usually dated to the first half of the second century and has been lost. Only seven fragments have survived in Epiphanius' *Panarion* (ca. 376–78 AD). See Petri Luomanen, "Jewish-Christian Gospels," in *Early New Testament Apocrypha*, ed. J. Christopher Edwards, Ancient Literature for New Testament Studies 9 (Grand Rapids: Zondervan Academic, 2022), 98; Bart D. Ehrman, *Lost Scriptures: Books That Did Not Make It into the New Testament* (New York: Oxford University Press, 2003), 13; J. K. Elliott, *The Apocryphal New Testament: A Collection of Apocryphal Christian Literature in an English Translation Based on M. R. James* (New York: Oxford University Press, 1993), 6. Andrew Gregory opines, "It could hardly have been written much before the end of the first century, and probably sometime later than that," in "Jewish-Christian Gospels" in *The Non-Canonical Gospels*, ed. Paul Foster (New York: T&T Clark, 2008), 62. The above English translation is that of Luomanen (99).

25. Note also the addition of "Today I have begotten you" from Psalm 2:7 and also used by the New Testament authors in Acts 13:33, Hebrews 1:5 and 5:5.

We also observed two examples in the Gospels, one in which an evangelist may have transferred the words or actions of some persons to another and another in which the evangelist changed the recipient of those words or actions. In the next chapter, we will examine some more stories in Plutarch's *Lives* and in the Gospels where the use of another compositional device is likely: *displacement*.

QUESTIONS FOR FURTHER THOUGHT

1. Read Matthew 20:20–28 and Mark 10:35–45. What is the main difference in these accounts? What compositional device may account for it?
2. Read Mark 12:28–34, Matt 22:35–40, and Luke 10:25–37. Do you think transferal is occurring in Luke's rendition? What detail is similar in Matthew and Luke but different in Mark?
3. In this chapter, we discussed the story of Jesus healing the centurion's servant in Matthew and Luke where I contended that the best explanation for the difference is that Matthew simplified the story, streamlining it by transferring the words and actions performed by the emissaries to the centurion who sent them. However, we also considered the very good possibility that John is reporting the same story, which is closer to Matthew's account and would mean that Luke may have instead added the emissaries. Go back and consider the striking similarities between Matthew and John. Do you think Matthew and John simplified their accounts or that Luke amplified his? Why?

CHAPTER 9

DISPLACEMENT

When my wife, Debbie, and I married in 1987, I was not earning much money. I had only recently earned a black belt in the Korean martial art of Taekwondo and had opened a school. But I had a problem: I had no training in how to run a business. Fortunately, I didn't have much overhead. Calvary Road Baptist Church in Alexandria, Virginia, permitted us to use their gymnasium for a small fee. Still, I didn't have a sufficient number of students for the school for it to be my sole source of income. So I also worked forty hours a week as a security guard.

During that time, Debbie and I went on a weekend business trip and stayed at a very nice hotel. Debbie and I both came from blue-collar, middle-class families. Other than the first night of our honeymoon (we stayed for free because the hotel manager was a family member), neither of us had ever stayed at a very nice hotel. When we checked in on our business trip, a bellhop took our bags to our room. Arriving at the room, I reached into my wallet and took out two dollars and gave it to him. That wasn't much even then. But at that time, we were on a very tight budget and giving someone two dollars meant having to cut back on something else. I'm sure that some of you can sympathize.

After we unpacked and dressed for the evening seminars, we left the room, had dinner, and then attended several lectures. Late that evening when we returned to our room, I immediately noticed that someone had been there while we were gone.

Mike: "Debbie. Someone has been in our room!"
Debbie: (Alarmed) "Why do you say that?"
Mike: "The radio is playing and the light is on. Neither were on when we left."

I looked under our bed and behind the shower curtain to ensure the trespasser was no longer there, then called the front desk. The call went something like this:

> **Front Desk:** "Good evening, Mr. Licona. Can I help you?"
> **Mike:** "Yes! Someone has been in our room!"
> **Front Desk:** "What makes you think that, Mr. Licona?"
> **Mike:** "When we left the room before dinner, none of the lights were on and the radio was not playing. We just returned to our room and immediately noticed that a light was on and the radio was playing. Hey, and someone pulled down the sheets on our bed, and just to ensure we knew they were here, they placed a mint on each of our pillows!"
> **Front Desk:** "Mr. Licona, that's our turn-down service. We do that for all of our guests."
> **Mike:** "Oh, . . . okay. . . . Well, . . . thanks."
> **Front Desk:** "You're welcome, Mr. Licona. Have a good night."

It's embarrassing to admit it, but, yes, that actually occurred. And I'm sure the folks at the front desk that evening had a wonderful laugh at my expense!

My wife and I both remember that story well. We both agree on all of the details . . . except one: she recalls that the event occurred in Richmond, Virginia, whereas I recall that it happened in Dallas, Texas! Because we attended business meetings in both cities, Debbie confused the occasion on which the turn-down service occurred (well, maybe I'm the one who's confused), displacing it from its true context and transplanting it in another. It's an easy mistake, one that does not really matter in this particular instance. Displacement can occur with the geographical or chronological location of an event.

INTENTIONAL DISPLACEMENT

Displacement can occur by accident, as it did in my story. It can also be intentional. There are reasons to think ancient biographers occasionally displaced the timing or location of a story and did so for one of any number of reasons. John Ramsey is a classicist, now retired, who taught Greek and classics at the University of Illinois Chicago. He possesses special expertise related to literature written by Cicero and the Roman historian

Sallust. The latter was recognized by his peers as being a great historian, even superior to Livy.[1] Ramsey observes that Sallust sometimes moves speeches to a different occasion. In one case, he moves a campaign speech given by the Roman senator Catiline one whole year earlier, and in another instance, he moves a threatening remark made by Catiline in the Roman senate to several months later. Ramsey suggests that Sallust did so to make his account of events more effective, to turn it into a better story.[2]

We observe another example of displacement in Plutarch's *Lives*. In late 45 BC, the Roman senate voted to confer extravagant honors upon Julius Caesar. They approached him in an impressive processional to confer the honors on him. Caesar refused to stand in respect, treated them as if they were common folks making a request of him, and rejected their act. Other Romans who were present felt insulted by Caesar's arrogance. Many left. When Caesar became aware of his *faux pas*, he pulled back the toga from his neck and invited anyone who desired to strike and kill him.[3] A few months later on February 15, one month prior to being assassinated, Caesar was seated in regal attire for all to see at the Lupercalia Festival. At the event's culmination, Antony took a diadem that was intertwined in a wreath and placed it on Caesar's head—a gesture suggesting that Caesar should be made king. It was a daring move and was likely preplanned by Caesar and Antony. Creating a kingship meant replacing the republican form of government with a monarchy. When Antony's gesture did not receive the positive response from the people for which he and Caesar had hoped, Caesar removed the diadem. The move elicited hearty applause from most of those present. Antony again attempted to place the diadem on Caesar's head to which some in the crowd responded with approval. But when Caesar again declined the diadem, the majority expressed their strong approval. Caesar then rose from his seat and left, greatly disappointed.[4] This is how Plutarch narrates both events in his *Life of Caesar*: the procession of the senators and Antony's gesture with the diadem.

In his *Life of Antony*, Plutarch does not report the senate's attempt to confer extravagant honors on Caesar, since that event has little to do with his main character in that biography. However, when he reports Antony's multiple attempts to place a diadem on Caesar's head at the Lupercalia

1. Quintilian, *Inst.* 2.5.19 (Butler, LCL).

2. John Ramsey, email message to the author, November 14, 2015, quoted in Licona, *Why Are There Differences in the Gospels?*, 188.

3. *Caes.* 60.3–5.

4. *Caes.* 61.4–5.

and the positive responses of the crowd when Caesar refused it, Plutarch reports that Caesar rose from his seat vexed, pulling back the toga from his neck, and inviting any who desired to strike and kill him. Caesar then left.[5] Plutarch appears to like the story of Caesar offering his neck. Although Caesar exposing his neck may have occurred on both occasions, Plutarch has likely displaced it from the original context of the senate conferring extravagant honors on Caesar and transplanted it at the Lupercalia.[6]

We will soon turn to the Gospels for examples. Before we do, I want to touch on the subject of chronology. Determining the chronology of reported events is a matter with which historians must sometimes wrestle. On occasion, the time and order of events are not clear to historians. Authors can report events in a chronological manner, lump events together according to a theme, or describe them with no particular order in mind.

There are three types of chronological reporting. The first is "floating chronology," where the timing of an event is not stated. The second is "explicit chronology," where the timing of an event is clearly stated (e.g., "it was two days before Passover" or "later that evening"). The third is "implicit chronology," where the timing of an event may be implied but is unclear. There are different degrees by which timing can be implied. In some instances, the implication that *Event B* had occurred immediately following *Event A* may be present but not strong. The story of Jesus healing a man with a withered hand is a good example of an implied chronology. In all three Synoptic Gospels the story appears immediately after a dispute between Jesus and some Jewish leaders over why his disciples were picking grain on the Sabbath. Immediately following his narration of the dispute, Luke reports that Jesus went into a synagogue *on a different Sabbath* and healed a man's withered hand (Luke 6:6). Mark presents the same progression of events; however, he says nothing of the chronology ("and he entered the synagogue again"). Jesus has just spoken to the Pharisees on the Sabbath, and Mark follows it with Jesus going into the synagogue and healing a man with a withered hand, which also would have occurred on a Sabbath. Although Mark does not explicitly say the synagogue healing occurred on the same day as Jesus's disciples picking grain on the Sabbath, readers get the impression that it did.

---

5. *Ant.* 12.1–4.

6. Another example in Plutarch's *Lives* that includes several instances of displacement but involves too many details for this volume may be seen in my 2017 book on this subject, *Why Are There Differences in the Gospels?*, 61–67. See also "Chapter 5: Synthetic Chronological Placement in the Gospels" in the same book for more examples in the Greco-Roman literature and in the Gospels.

Matthew also reports the same progression of events. However, his wording implies more strongly than Mark's that the healing occurred on the same Sabbath on which the dispute with the Jewish leaders had occurred: "*And going down from there*, he went into their synagogue" (Matt. 12:9; emphasis added).[7] Matthew and Mark may have implied that the healing occurred on the same Sabbath, however, they fall short of explicitly stating that it did.

In other instances, the implication that *Event B* occurred immediately following *Event A* may be so strong as to be virtually explicit. In this chapter I want to focus on a few occasions in the Gospels where a strongly implied chronology in one Gospel stands in conflict with the strongly implied or explicit chronology in another. Let's take a look at four examples.

A WOMAN ANOINTS JESUS

> Now it was two days before the Passover and the Feast of Unleavened Bread. And the chief priests and the scribes were seeking how they might arrest him secretly and kill him. For they were saying, "Not during the feast lest the people riot." And while Jesus was in Bethany, in the house of Simon the Leper, and while reclining, a woman came having an alabaster jar of very expensive ointment of pure nard. (Mark 14:1–3a; cf. Matt. 26:6–7a)

Mark then relates that the woman poured the ointment on Jesus's head and that some present became angry and objected saying her deed was a waste because the ointment could have been sold and the proceeds given to the poor. Jesus rebuked them saying the poor will always be with them, but he will not, and that the woman had anointed his body for burial beforehand (Mark 14:3b–9 // Matt. 26:7b–13). Mark follows this with a short story of Judas going to the chief priests and arranging to betray Jesus (Mark 14:10–11; cf. Matt. 26:14–16). Now notice the verse that follows:

7. Other than Matt.12:9, the phrase "and going down from there" (*kai metabas ekeithen*) appears in the New Testament only in Matt. 15:29 and Acts 18:7. Matt. 15:29 has a parallel in Mark 7:31 and appears in the same context, although the phrase is absent. The chronology in Mark is linked with the event that follows in an implied sense though not strongly so. However, in Acts 18:7 the chronology seems to be immediately linked to the event that follows, since Paul has been teaching in the synagogue and then visits Titius Justus, whose house was next to the synagogue.

> Now on the first day of the [Feast of] Unleavened Bread when the Passover [lamb] is sacrificed, his disciples were saying to him, "Where do you want us to go and prepare so that you may eat the Passover?" (Mark 14:12)

Given the progression of the narrative in Mark 14:1–12 (two days before Passover, anointing, Judas discusses betraying Jesus, Passover), I understand Mark to be stating explicitly that the event of the woman anointing Jesus and the discussions among the Jewish leaders pertaining to how they might arrest Jesus had both occurred during the two days preceding Passover, perhaps even on the second day prior to Passover. I encourage you to read Mark 14:1–12. While doing so, keep in mind that the chapter and paragraph divisions in our present Bibles did not appear until more than a thousand years later.[8] In fact, the ancient Greek language did not have punctuation marks. There were not even spaces between words! Ask yourself whether you think Mark intends for his readers to understand that the anointing had occurred within two days of Passover.[9]

Now let's look at the parallel text in John 12:1–3 (and 12:4–7):

> Therefore, six days before the Passover Jesus came to Bethany, where Lazarus lived, whom Jesus had raised from the dead. So they prepared for him a dinner there. Martha served, and Lazarus was one of those reclining with him [at the table]. So Mary took a pound of expensive ointment of pure nard. . . .

John appears to be locating the anointing six days prior to the Passover meal. Also noteworthy is that the anointing in John occurs *prior* to Jesus's triumphal entry to Jerusalem on Palm Sunday whereas it occurs *after* it in Mark and Matthew. Did the anointing occur two or six days before the Passover? Or were there two anointings?

Three noteworthy differences between the stories in Mark/Matthew and John may suggest John is reporting a different event. First, as already

---

8. See also Matt. 16:1–19. Chapter divisions and numbers were added to some New Testament manuscripts by Stephen Langton near the beginning of the thirteenth century. This mainly affected Latin Bibles but very few Greek Bibles. Verse numbers were added in 1551 by Robertus Stephanus. The Geneva New Testament of 1557 is the first to include them. I am indebted to Daniel Wallace for this information.

9. Mark 14:1 / Matt. 26:2. "after two days" (*meta duo hēmeras*). Compare with John's use of the term "after two days" (*meta de tas duo hēmeras*) in 4:43 (cf. 4:40; 11:6).

noted, the timing of the event differs: two days and six days before Passover. Second, whereas Jesus appears to know the woman in John, nothing in Mark/Matthew suggests Jesus knew her. Third, the woman anoints Jesus's head in Mark/Matthew, whereas she anoints his feet in John. Notwithstanding, the number of similarities John's account shares with Mark/Matthew makes it very likely that they are all referring to the same anointing. (1) Immediately preceding the story of the anointing, the Jewish leaders plot to kill Jesus. (2) The anointing occurs during Passover week. (3) The anointing takes place in Bethany. (4) A woman pours costly ointment on Jesus. (5) The ointment is of the same approximate value. (6) The anointing raises the displeasure of some in the room who object to the woman's act as waste and suggest the ointment could have been sold and the proceeds given to the poor. (7) Jesus responds by telling those objecting to leave the woman alone for there will always be the poor among them but he will not always be among them. The anointing was for his burial. (8) The anointing is immediately followed by another mention of the plans of the Jewish leaders to kill Jesus. These similarities seem to be far more than coincidental. Therefore, it is my view that either John or Mark has displaced the event.[10] But who and why?

Mark may have displaced the anointing and transplanted it between plans to have Jesus killed, since it fits thematically. However, I lean toward thinking it was John who displaced the anointing. Most scholars think John displaced another event, relocating Jesus's temple cleansing from the final week of his life, where the Synoptic Gospels locate it, to the beginning of his ministry. If he did, displacement is something for which John was not averse.

Moreover, it would have been proper practice for John to displace the anointing from its original context and transplant it where he does. In his book *How to Write History*, written in the middle of the second century, Lucian of Samosata recommended that stories be joined together in a narrative like links in a chain and with overlapping material when possible.[11] The great Roman rhetorician Quintilian encouraged something quite similar, using the metaphor of men linking their arms together to lend one another mutual support.[12] It is worth observing that just prior to the

---

10. Luke's Gospel includes a story of a woman who anoints Jesus. However, a number of reasons have persuaded me that it is probably a different event. See Licona, *Why Are There Differences in the Gospels?*, 149–50.

11. Lucian, *How to Write History*, 55.

12. Quintilian, *Inst.* 9.5.129.

anointing in John, Jesus raised Lazarus from the dead in the presence of Lazarus's sisters, Mary and Martha (John 11:1–44). At the beginning of the story of Jesus raising Lazarus, John mentions ever so briefly that Mary is the one who anointed Jesus (11:1–2), a story he will later narrate. Perhaps having just told the story of Jesus raising Lazarus, John knows that he has the story of Mary's anointing, which he has already mentioned. So he tells it here, linking the two stories closely together with Mary serving as the overlapping content.

JESUS CLEANSES THE TEMPLE AND CURSES A FIG TREE

Mark 11:1–23 narrates that after making his triumphal entry on Palm Sunday, Jesus goes into the temple, looks around, and then leaves. He and his disciples then go to Bethany, where they spend the night. On Monday morning Jesus and his disciples return to Jerusalem, and on the way Jesus curses a fig tree because it has not born fruit. When they arrive in Jerusalem, he makes a second trip into the temple. This time he becomes angered over the corrupt Jewish leadership of that day, which held control over the temple system.[13] Jesus overturns the tables of the money changers and drives them away along with the merchants who are selling animals to be sacrificed. Later that day, Jesus and his disciples return to Bethany, where they spend another night. On Tuesday morning, they are returning once again to Jerusalem when they notice that the fig tree Jesus had cursed on the previous day has withered and died.

Matthew 21:1–21 narrates the events differently. He also has Jesus going into the temple on Palm Sunday after his triumphal entry. However, Matthew displaces the temple cleansing from Monday, relocates it on Sunday, and conflates it with the first temple visit reported by Mark. The two events now become one. On Monday morning Jesus and his disciples are returning to Jerusalem when he curses the fig tree, and it withers immediately. Once again Matthew combines two events into one. In doing so, he also compresses these events to have occurred over a period of two days (Sunday and Monday) rather than the three days mentioned in Mark (Sunday through Tuesday). Matthew does not explicitly state that Jesus cleansed the temple immediately following Jesus's triumphal entry on Palm Sunday or that the fig tree withered before their very eyes. Yet both are so strongly implied that those who would contend otherwise

13. Keener, *The Gospel of John*, 524.

bear a very heavy burden of proof.[14] Accordingly, in this story we observe Matthew using displacement, conflation, and compression.

JESUS HEALS A LEPER

This story appears in all three Synoptic Gospels (Mark 1:40–45 // Matt. 8:1–4 // Luke 5:12–16). In Mark 1:21–28, Jesus arrived in Capernaum, entered a synagogue, and cast a demon out of a man in attendance. Mark then writes, "And immediately he left the synagogue and entered the house of Simon and Andrew," where he healed Simon's mother-in-law (1:29–31).[15] This is followed by: "When evening came and the sun had set," people came to Jesus, bringing the sick and demon-possessed (Mark 1:32–34). This is followed by: "in the early morning while it was still dark," Jesus got up and went to a secluded place to pray (Mark 1:35–38). He then left Capernaum and went throughout Galilee, preaching in their synagogues (Mark 1:39). Over the course of this journey, Jesus healed a leper (Mark 1:40–45). In the verse that follows, Mark says that Jesus returned to Capernaum "after some days" and healed a paralytic (Mark 2:1–12). Therefore, Mark's chronology is fairly explicit that (1) Jesus entered Simon's house and healed his mother-in-law immediately *after* leaving the

---

14. The chronology in Matthew is implied so strongly that even the staunch conservatives Norman Geisler and Thomas Howe are willing to acknowledge that Matthew moved the day on which Jesus cleansed the temple from Monday to Sunday. See Norman L. Geisler and Thomas Howe, *The Big Book of Bible Difficulties: Clear and Concise Answers from Genesis to Revelation* (Grand Rapids: Baker, 1992; previously published under the title *When Critics Ask*), 354. Gleason Archer likewise held this view in his *Encyclopedia of Bible Difficulties* (Grand Rapids: Zondervan, 1982), 335. It is, therefore, odd that Geisler criticized me so strongly for suggesting (with many scholars) that John probably moved the temple cleansing to the beginning of Jesus's ministry and that he slightly moved the day and time of Jesus's crucifixion. (For a detailed statement of that view, see Brown, *The Gospels as Stories*, 128–35, esp. 131–2 and Keener, *The Gospel of John*, 1129–1131.) Augustine attempts to harmonize the accounts by proposing a solution that is quite complex (Augustine, *Cons.* 68). Paul Anderson (*Riddles of the Fourth Gospel*) states that "most scholars side with the Synoptics, which locate the event during Jesus' last days (following Mark 11:15–18), arguing that such a Temple disturbance would not have gone unpunished for two or three years; discipline would have been swift and decisive" (51).

15. Scholars have often observed that Mark has a practice of transitioning to another story with "and immediately" in order to move his narrative along rapidly. Of course, this does not eliminate its chronological sense. And chronology sense is the focus of this chapter. "Immediately" (*euthys*) appears forty-one times in Mark (1:10, 12, 18, 20, 21, 23, 28, 29, 30, 42, 43; 2:8, 12; 3:6; 4:5, 15, 16, 17, 29; 5:2, 29, 30, 42 [twice]; 6:25, 27, 45, 50, 54; 7:25; 8:10; 9:15, 20, 24; 10:52; 11:2, 3; 14:43, 45, 72; 15:1). *Euthys* appears far less often in the other Gospels: Matthew 3:16; 13:20; 14:27; 21:3; Luke 6:49; John 13:30, 32; 19:34. Matthew prefers *eutheōs*, using it thirteen times (4:20, 22; 8:3; 13:5; 14:22, 31; 20:34; 21:2; 24:29; 25:15; 26:49, 74; 27:48. Mark uses it once (7:35); Luke uses it six times (5:13; 12:36, 54; 14:5; 17:7; 21:9); and John uses it three times (5:9; 6:21; 18:27).

synagogue and that (2) Jesus healed the leper *after* he had healed Simon's mother-in-law (3) *prior* to healing a paralytic (i.e., synagogue → mother-in-law → leper → paralytic). Furthermore, when one reads Mark's text in a straightforward manner, it is implied that Jesus healed those who came to him on the evening of the same day he healed Simon's mother-in-law and that Jesus got up early on the following morning and prayed.

In Luke, Jesus entered Capernaum and cast a demon out of a man in their synagogue (4:31–37). This is followed by: "And having left the synagogue, he entered the house of Simon" and healed his mother-in-law (4:38–39). This is followed by: "as the sun was setting," people came to Jesus and he healed them (4:40–41). "And when day came," Jesus went to a desolate place to pray, then left with his disciples to preach "to the other towns" (4:42–44). "While in one of those towns," Jesus healed a leper (5:12–14). He then healed a paralytic (5:17–26).

Luke follows Mark's order for the events. Luke uses similar yet somewhat-weaker language to imply that Jesus healed those who came to him on the evening of the same day he healed Simon's mother-in-law, that Jesus rose early on the following morning and prayed, and that he healed the leper afterward. Luke also locates Jesus healing a paralytic after him healing a leper. However, unlike Mark and Matthew (9:1), Luke does not indicate that Jesus had returned to Capernaum before he healed the paralytic. However, Luke's chronological progression is clear and identical to Mark's: synagogue → mother-in-law → others healed that evening → leper → paralytic.

In Matthew, the healing of the leper appears to have occurred during an earlier period than we find in Mark and Luke. After Jesus's Sermon on the Mount, Matthew reports, "Having come down from the mountain, large crowds followed him" (8:1). This information is followed by the story of a leper who approached Jesus and was healed (8:2–4). Jesus then returned to Capernaum, where he healed a centurion's servant (8:5–13) and then healed Peter's mother-in-law, who was also in Capernaum (8:14–15). "When evening came," people came to Jesus and he healed them (8:16–17). The phrase Matthew uses here, "when evening came" (*opsias de genomenēs*), clearly refers to the evening of the day Jesus healed Peter's mother-in-law. In the New Testament, this phrase appears seven times: six in Matthew and once in Mark (Matt. 8:16; 14:15, 23; 20:8; 26:20; 27:57; Mark 1:32). Bracketing Matthew 8:16 and Mark 1:32, which are parallel texts, every instance clearly refers to the evening of the same day. There is no reason to think these two texts are any different. Although

Matthew's language surrounding Jesus healing the leper is neither explicit nor strongly implied, he at least weakly implies the timing, locating it prior to Jesus healing Simon's mother-in-law (i.e., leper → centurion's servant → mother-in-law → others healed that evening).

There is another reason that suggests Matthew probably placed the healing of the leper chronologically prior to Jesus healing Simon's mother-in-law. In Matthew 8:1, Jesus came down from the mountain after preaching the Sermon on the Mount. A large crowd was following him, perhaps consisting of those who had attended the sermon. Verse 2 begins with "and behold" (*kai idou*), which is followed by Jesus healing a leper. The phrase "and behold" occurs twenty-eight times in Matthew,[16] of which twenty-three clearly refer to an event occurring where its timing is clear. Of the five exceptions, two have parallels in Mark and Luke where explicit chronology is present.[17] So although Matthew's chronology is not explicit in these two instances, the parallels in Mark and in Luke are. Since Matthew is likely using Mark as his source, he probably intends to communicate that these two events occurred in the same chronological sequence stated by Mark. Of the three that remain, one is our reference in question, Matthew 8:2: Jesus healing a leper. Another is located in Matthew 9:2, which introduces the story of Jesus healing a paralytic after Jesus had just crossed the Sea of Galilee to come to his own city (Capernaum). Although the passage contains no explicitly chronological terms, it is clear that Matthew is narrating Jesus's healing of the paralytic to have occurred in Capernaum, shortly after Jesus had arrived there: "And embarking on a boat, he crossed over and came to his own city [i.e., Capernaum]. *And behold*, they brought to him a paralytic lying on a bed. And seeing their faith, Jesus said to the paralytic, 'Take heart, child. Your sins are forgiven'" (Matt. 9:1–2).

Only the third, Matthew 19:16, is not chronologically linked to the preceding event in a clear manner. What does this tell us? Of the twenty-eight occurrences of "and behold" (*kai idou*) in Matthew, twenty-three are clearly to be understood in a tight chronological sense. Matthew probably intends for two of the remaining five to be understood in an explicit chronological sense. This means that twenty-five

16. Matt. 2:9; 3:16, 17; 4:11; 7:4; 8:2, 24, 29, 32, 34; 9:2, 3, 10, 20; 12:10, 41, 42; 15:22; 17:3, 5; 19:16; 20:30; 26:51; 27:51; 28:2, 7, 9, 20.

17. Hemorrhaging woman in Matthew 9:20: Mark 5:27 // Luke 8:49 explicitly connect it chronologically to the story of Jairus. Blind men/man in Matthew 20:30: Mark 10:46 // Luke 18:35 explicitly connect it chronologically to Jesus's trip to Jericho.

of the twenty-eight occurrences of "and behold" (*kai idou*) in Matthew probably appear in a context in which the chronology is meant to be understood. Of the remaining three, one appears in a context where the chronology is clear (Matt. 9:1–2), one is quite ambiguous pertaining to its chronological setting (Matt.19:15–16), and the other is the one we are assessing (Matt. 8:1–2). In other words, bracketing the occurrence in question (Matt. 8:2), the time at which the event had occurred within its context is clear in twenty-six of twenty-seven occurrences of the phrase "and behold." When one then comes to Matthew's account of Jesus healing a leper in 8:1–4, in my opinion, the chronological placement of the story is no less clear than we observe in 9:1–2. Although certainty is not possible, we can at least acknowledge that a straightforward reading of Matthew's account suggests he reported Jesus healing the leper to have occurred prior to healing Peter's mother-in-law. Despite the fact that the language does not explicitly state that such-and-such occurred "on the same day" or "on the following day," the language used by Matthew and Mark strongly implies that they have located the healing of the leper at different times.

One might instead suggest that Jesus healed more lepers than this one and Matthew is probably narrating a different healing. However, such a suggestion can be quickly abandoned when one observes the same conversation between Jesus and the leper occurring in all three Synoptics.

FOXES, BIRDS, AND BURYING THE DEAD

Closely related to the previous story in which Jesus heals a leper is this one about foxes, birds, and burying the dead (Matt. 8:14–23 // Luke 9:51–62; cf. Mark 1:29–33).

My translations of both texts above are somewhat wooden so that you will be able to observe their verbal similarities. Where the Greek words in both are exactly the same, my translation is italicized. In both Matthew and Luke, two or three people (all have a masculine pronoun in Greek and are, therefore, men) express to Jesus an interest in following him, and Jesus responds to each. However, this event seems to occur in a different context in Luke than it does in Matthew. So there are two questions we need to address: (1) Are the people in Matthew who are expressing an interest in following Jesus different from those described in Luke? (2) If they are the same people in both, have Matthew and Luke explicitly located this event at different times and locations?

Matthew 8:14-23

And when Jesus came into the house of Peter, he saw his mother-in-law laying down with a fever. He grasped her hand, and the fever left her. And she rose and served him. When evening came, they had brought to him many who were demon-possessed. [Mark 1:32 says here, "And the whole town was gathered together at the door."] He cast out the spirits with a word, and he healed everyone having sicknesses, so that the word of Isaiah the prophet may be fulfilled, saying, "He took our sicknesses and bore our diseases." Now seeing a crowd around him, Jesus commanded [his disciples] to go to the other side. And a scribe came and said to him, "Teacher, *I will follow you wherever you may go." And Jesus* said *to him, "Foxes have holes and the birds of heaven have nests. But the Son of Man has nowhere to lay his head."* And another of his disciples said to him, "*Lord, let me first* go and *bury my father*." But Jesus said to him, "Follow me and *let the dead bury their dead*." And when he embarked on the boat, his disciples followed him.

Luke 9:51-62

And when the days had come for him to be taken up [into heaven], he was determined to go to Jerusalem. And he sent messengers ahead of him. And they went and entered a village of Samaria to prepare for him. And they did not receive him because he was determined to go to Jerusalem. And when the disciples James and John saw it, they said, "Lord, do you desire that we may tell fire to come down from heaven and destroy them?" But he turned and rebuked them. And they went to another village. And as they were going along the road, someone said to him, "*I will follow you wherever you may go." And Jesus* said *to him, "Foxes have holes and the birds of heaven have nests. But the Son of Man has nowhere to lay his head."* And he said to another, "Follow me." But that one said, "*Lord, let me* go *first to bury my father*." But he said to him, "*Let the dead bury their dead*. But you, go and proclaim the kingdom of God." And even another said, "I will follow you, Lord. But first let me say 'Goodbye' to those in my house." But Jesus said to him, "No one putting his hand upon a plow and looks at the things behind him is fit for the kingdom of God."

Let's begin by focusing on the first question. The first two men in Matthew and in Luke speak to Jesus using the same reasons and with virtually the same words. In both texts, Jesus responds with the same answers and with virtually the same words. Now which of the following do you think is more likely?

1. Matthew and Luke are recalling two different events whereby the two men in each communicate the same messages to Jesus, who responds with the same answers. The words of each have been

recalled independently by Matthew and Luke, decades later, and the words we are reading, though strikingly similar, may not have been the same in the original Aramaic before being translated into Greek.
2. Matthew and Luke are recalling the same event.

In my opinion, the same messages of the men, Jesus's responses to them, and virtually the same wording all strongly suggest that Matthew and Luke are recalling the same event. This creates a tension with the different time and location of the event and brings us to our second question: Have Matthew and Luke intentionally located this event at different times and locations?

Matthew locates this event in Capernaum very early in Jesus's ministry. Jesus had recently delivered the Sermon on the Mount and came into Capernaum, where he healed Peter's mother-in-law as well as many others. Because of the crowd that evening, Jesus told his disciples to go to the other side of the Sea of Galilee. It is then that Matthew has two men expressing to Jesus their interest in following him. Jesus answers them, then he gets into a boat with his disciples, and they cross the sea.

Luke locates the event near the end of Jesus's ministry ("when the days had come for him to be taken up") and somewhere south of Capernaum. Luke tells us that Jesus and his disciples were rejected by a village of Samaria. (Samaria is located approximately halfway between Capernaum and Jerusalem.) So they started walking to another village, and while they were on the road, Luke portrays the men being interested in following Jesus. So Matthew locates the event in Capernaum just prior to crossing the Sea of Galilee near the beginning of Jesus's ministry, while Luke locates it south of Capernaum while they are walking between villages and near the end of Jesus's ministry.

So what exactly is going on? There are several possibilities. (1) Matthew and Luke are describing different events in which very similar discussions occurred. (2) Matthew and Luke are describing different events and have conflated what was said at both (e.g., one man approached Jesus at Capernaum while the other [plus a third] approached Jesus while they were walking between villages). (3) The discussions actually occurred at Capernaum early in Jesus's ministry as reported by Matthew, but Luke has displaced it to a different time and location. (4) The discussions actually occurred in or near Samaria near the end of Jesus's ministry as reported by Luke, but Matthew has intentionally displaced it to a different time and location. (5) The displacement by Matthew or Luke could have been unintentional, perhaps due to a memory lapse on the part of one of them.

(6) The event was an anecdote known by Matthew and Luke for which the time and location were not included, and each wove the story into their biographical narrative at places and times of their choosing. (7) Matthew and Luke formed a committee that discussed what they could do to mislead future historians. I am sure we could come up with some other options.

In my opinion, the seventh is absurd, and the remaining are all possible. However, I regard the sixth option to be the most plausible. My reason for preferring it goes beyond what we have discussed thus far in this book. Without going into a lot of detail that would pull us too far away from the main question of this book, when scholars and theology students discuss the Synoptic problem, they also recognize a collection of Jesus's sayings that make up over 230 verses shared by Matthew and Luke that are absent from Mark. In many cases, the verbal similarities once again suggest that a relationship of some sort is present. Because the verses are absent from Mark, Mark cannot be the source. This leaves us with three options: (1) Luke used Matthew as a source for these verses; (2) Matthew used Luke as a source for these verses; (3) Matthew and Luke used another source, which we no longer have. What would we call such a source? Well, the German word for "source" is *Quelle* (pronounced QUELL-eh). Scholars abbreviate that word as simply *Q* to represent a hypothetical source used by Matthew and Luke. The *Q* material is almost entirely comprised of sayings of Jesus unconnected to a narrative, similar to someone putting together a document containing individual quotes of Winston Churchill and not mentioning the contexts in which Churchill had uttered them. Given Jesus's popularity and remarkable deeds, it is likely that some of what he said was written down even before he died, perhaps even by one of his twelve disciples or one or more in the larger group of seventy (Luke 10:1, 17). If so, could this belong to the *Q* material?

It is possible that Papias (*Frag.* 3.16) and some of the early church fathers are referring to what scholars now call "*Q*" when they mention a Gospel of Matthew written in Hebrew. However, the matter is debated. Several scholars who specialize in *Q* studies have rejected this idea,[18] while other scholars do not find their case compelling and hold that the *Q* = *Hebrew Matthew* hypothesis remains a plausible possibility.

---

18. For arguments against *Hebrew Matthew* = *Q*, see Edwards, *The Hebrew Gospel and the Development of the Synoptic Tradition*, 242. John S. Kloppenborg Verbin, *Excavating Q: The History and Setting of the Sayings Gospel* (Minneapolis: Fortress, 2000), 72–80.

The *Q* material in Matthew and Luke differs in interesting ways from the content in Mark that appears again in Matthew and Luke, which scholars refer to as the "triple tradition." The latter is usually found in the same order as we observe in Mark. However, the *Q* material is peppered throughout Matthew and Luke, usually in different places and in a different order.

The matter of how best to explain the relationship of this content is by no means settled. Outstanding New Testament scholars can be found in different camps. That said, most of today's New Testament scholars think that there was a *Q* source (the third option above), while a significant minority believe Luke used Matthew (the first option). A very small minority prefer the second option, that Matthew used Luke.

Since I am persuaded that Matthew and Luke drew upon a *Q* source, I think the sixth possibility above is the most plausible explanation: Jesus's interactions with those expressing an interest in following him but who wished to be excused temporarily belongs to the *Q* material. It is an anecdote known by Matthew and Luke for which the time and location were not included, and Matthew and Luke each wove the story into their biographical narrative at places and times of their choosing.

"AN ORDERLY ACCOUNT"

What of Luke's claim "to write an orderly account"? There is no widespread agreement among scholars pertaining to what Luke means by *orderly*. However, many do not think he has precise chronology in mind.[19] F. F. Bruce understood Luke to be saying he will be arranging many of Jesus's teachings in "topical groupings" to facilitate a clearer understanding of them. He then writes,

> [We do not] necessarily get the exact setting in which Jesus said all of the material. To do that would likely have made the material harder to understand, for it would have been split over large portions of the Gospel. Exact chronology is a relatively modern fixation; ancient writers were very

19. In her monograph pertaining to the preface to Luke's Gospel, Alexander thinks Luke may be contrasting his written work with oral storytelling about Jesus, the former being arranged "'one after another' in a narrative sequence" (Alexander, *The preface to Luke's Gospel*, 136). Bock suggests, "One can answer this question [of what is meant by "orderly"] only by examining what Luke has done." He then concludes, "the order of Luke's account works on many levels. It is broadly chronological and geographic, and deals with sacred history." (Bock, *Luke: 1:1–9:50*, vol. 1, 62–3).

> happy to compromise chronology if by so doing readers got a better grasp on the inner meaning and real significance of the facts.[20]

From what we have observed in this chapter, chronological displacement appears to have been a compositional device that was used by a number of ancient biographers, including the Evangelists.

WHY THIS IS IMPORTANT

I was brought up in a theologically conservative Christian home. I was taught that the Bible is divinely inspired and without any error. I believed that all of the events in the Bible happened precisely as the Bible describes them. I believed that Jesus spoke the precise words as reported in the Bible. However, as I have studied Scripture over the years, I have come to understand that some of these beliefs cannot be true. Matthew, Mark, and Luke report Jesus saying something on the same occasion but often recall him using slightly different words. In those instances, they cannot all be recalling Jesus's precise words. This becomes even clearer when we understand that Jesus most often spoke in Aramaic, that his words have been translated into Greek, and that many are now reading them after being translated again into English. Now I am by no means suggesting that Jesus's message has been corrupted. I am saying that I was mistaken to think that when I read the Gospels, in Greek or in English, I am reading the precise words that Jesus spoke on that occasion. But this does not mean that I am not reading the essence of what Jesus said on that occasion or on another one.

Something similar may be stated about some of the narratives in the Gospels. I used to think that the narratives in the Gospels describe exactly how the events occurred. However, as we have seen in this chapter, that cannot always be the case. The Evangelists were not poor historians. They were not deceivers. They did not form a committee with the objective of planning how they could mislead their readers. They were following the literary conventions that were in play when they wrote. They wove stories of Jesus into their biographies of him, sometimes placing stories in their actual historical context, sometimes placing them in a different one. We do not find ancient biographers adding footnotes or comments such as,

---

20. F. F. Bruce, "Luke" in Walter C. Kaiser Jr., Peter H. Davids, F. F. Bruce, and Manfred T. Brauch, *Hard Sayings of the Bible* (Downers Grove, IL: InterVarsity Press, 1996), 454–55.

"I do not know when this event actually occurred, so I have placed it here for convenience." The objective of ancient biography was to provide a literary portrait of the main character. So ancient readers did not demand or expect the same level of precision that we moderns desire.

I have spent countless hours over the years pouring over the matter of differences in the Gospels and in other ancient literature. Moreover, I have spent considerable time reading what scholars have said on the matter. I have had lots of time to allow the data to marinate in my mind and wrestle with the subject. Many of you who are reading this book are learning a lot of new things all at once. I realize it can be a daunting experience. Depending on your background and how you have viewed the Bible, some of you may be struggling with some of the solutions to the differences I have provided. After all, other solutions have been proposed and even taken for granted over the years. It would be a wonderful experience to get into a time machine, return to the first century, and ask the Evangelists to explain to us what led to particular differences! Since we cannot do that, the question we should ask is which solution is the most plausible one. We should resist the temptation to accept an explanation merely because it is *possibly true* and is compatible with what we have thought about the Bible.

Years ago, I became friends with a Mormon couple. They are good people who cared about me as much as I cared about them. Because they cared for me, they wanted to share Mormonism with me with the hope that I would join the Mormon Church. When they asked if I would be willing to speak with some Mormon missionaries, I agreed to do so. A couple of weeks prior to the first meeting with the missionaries, I began to do my own study on Mormonism. As one who is passionately interested in the historical data pertaining to the origins of Christianity, specifically, what we can verify about Jesus, I began investigating the historical data pertaining to the origins of Mormonism to learn what can be verified about its foundation claims. I ended up writing a short book that reveals what I found, which is available for free download at my website.[21]

The *Book of Mormon* claims there was a major battle that took place on the Hill Cumorah near the beginning of the fifth century and asserts that the enemy had swords, bows and arrows, axes, and "all manner of weapons of war." It also claims that more than 200,000 Nephites were killed in

21. Michael R. Licona, *Behold, I Stand at the Door and Knock: What to Say to Mormons and Jehovah's Witnesses When They Knock on Your Door* (1998), https://www.risenjesus.com/wp-content/uploads/behold-i-stand-at-the-door-and-knock.pdf.

that battle and their corpses left unburied (Mormon 6:9, 15). The Hill Cumorah referred to is almost certainly to be identified with the Hill Cumorah in Palmyra, New York, near Rochester.[22] Now if such a battle had actually occurred on that hill, we should be able to find some artifacts. However, no weapons of war, even as much as an arrowhead, have ever been unearthed there. Despite the claim that more than 200,000 Nephites died there and were left unburied (not to mention the Lamanites who were also alleged to have been killed in that battle), no human bones have ever been found on that hill.

I pointed out to my Mormon friends that this creates a terrible problem for them. What happened to all of those bones? The response I received was, "Maybe God took them." That's *possible*, of course, and such a claim cannot be disproved. However, the answer has the strong appearance of trying to rescue a view that is in serious trouble. We should consider all available options. However, when we are addressing some of the most important questions we can ask, we should not be willing to settle for an answer that is merely *possible* (even though it allows us to maintain our present belief) when an answer that is *more probable* is available.

The same can be said of some solutions used to address differences in the Gospels. One can come up with a seemingly infinite number of ways to harmonize differing accounts, many of which have the strong appearance of trying to rescue a Bible in trouble. However, *it is not the Bible that is in trouble. Instead, it is one's present concept of the Bible that is being challenged.*

SUMMARY

In this chapter, we discussed the compositional device known as *displacement*, whereby an author changes the geographical or chronological location of an event. We observed that the finest Greco-Roman historians and biographers sometimes displaced events and did so intentionally. There are three types of chronological reporting:

1. *Floating chronology:* The timing of an event is not stated.
2. *Explicit chronology:* The timing of an event is clearly stated.
3. *Implicit chronology:* The timing of an event may be implied but is unclear.

22. See this article: "Hill Cumorah," Mormon Stories, https://www.mormonstories.org/truth-claims/the-books/the-book-of-mormon/hill-cumorah.

We examined four stories in the Gospels where at least one of the Evangelists has probably displaced an event: a woman anoints Jesus, Jesus cleanses the temple and curses a fig tree, Jesus heals a leper, and Jesus's statement pertaining to foxes, birds, and burying the dead. Recognizing that ancient historians and biographers, including the Evangelists, occasionally displaced events is important because it assists us in recalibrating our expectations when reading the Gospels and in formulating a more accurate doctrine of Scripture.

QUESTIONS FOR FURTHER THOUGHT

1. What is the most interesting thing you learned in this chapter?
2. Do you feel troubled when learning that ancient authors, including the authors of the Gospels, sometimes displaced an event from its actual geographical or temporal location? Why or why not?
3. While reading this chapter, are there one or more things you have observed in the Gospels that have challenged what you think about the Bible? If so, name one and describe why you feel challenged by it. Also reveal whether you feel encouraged or troubled by the challenge and describe why you feel this way.
4. Some readers will be surprised by the kind of liberties the authors of the Gospels sometimes took when reporting the words and actions of Jesus. Do you think any of those liberties surprised God? Why or why not?
5. The story of Jesus telling Peter he will deny him three times appears in all four Gospels (Mark 14:22–31 // Matt. 26:26–35 // Luke 22:14–34 // John 13:1–38, 18:1). Read these accounts and note when Jesus uttered the prediction in each. Do you think displacement is occurring? Why or why not?

CHAPTER 10

THE OUTER LIMITS OF COMPOSITIONAL DEVICES

I have lectured all over the world on the topic of Gospel differences. Whether in North America, Scandinavia, Africa, or southeast Asia, the responses have been quite similar. If readers of this book respond in a kindred manner, they will typically fall into one of three groups. Those of you in the first group have had your eyes opened to a new way of reading the Gospels. You are thrilled because so much in the Gospels now makes sense to you that was cloudy before reading this book.

Those of you in the second group feel troubled by some of the concepts in this book. Those concepts have challenged the paradigm you have held for a long time related to what divinely inspired Scripture looks like. You previously may not have given much thought to the process of divine inspiration and now may be wondering whether these concepts are even compatible with the divine inspiration of Scripture. You also had no idea that the human element played a part in Scripture to the extent you have observed.

Finally, some of you are members of a third group who have found portions of what we have discussed to be eye-opening and other portions not as convincing, and you need time to allow these matters to marinate in your mind as you read through the Gospels again. Reading the Gospels will never be the same for many of you, regardless of whether you find yourself in the first, second, or third group. Going forward, you will be more perceptive when noticing differences. It will be an exciting adventure, like reading the Gospels for the first time . . . again!

To be transparent with you, I have felt uncomfortable at times—and still do—about the degree of flexibility many ancient historians and biographers took when writing. I want to know exactly how events transpired. I want to know precisely what was said, especially what Jesus said, so I can study his words in a microscopic manner and discover additional meanings to be found between the lines. But the Gospel authors, like every other ancient author of historical literature of that era, paraphrased and altered the words of their characters to make points more clearly. This was consistent with the literary conventions they were taught and were expected to follow.

So I sometimes feel frustration. That said, I should not impose my own desires on texts written nearly 2,000 years ago by those who wrote with purposes that differ slightly from my own. I should not become frustrated with the Bible at times because it does not report events in the manner I may prefer or how I think it should report them. The Bible is not the problem. My expectations are.

Moreover, if Jesus were to address the frustration I sometimes feel because I can't always satisfy my desire to study his words to the nth degree, I think he would say, "Son, you're not even doing all of the things I've taught in a single sermon, my Sermon on the Mount. Why don't you work on those things for a while? After you've got a good handle on them, we can look at some of my other teachings you can work toward mastering."

I am committed to discovering and following what I believe to be true. If I downplay or brush away observations that appear to be in tension with what I presently believe, I may very well be preventing myself from resolving the tension or discovering that a belief I have held needs to be revised or abandoned. Therefore, I am guided by a principle, which I have mentioned earlier. Since I will present another principle later in the final two chapters, I will refer to this as principle 1:

> My view of Scripture should be consistent with what I observe in Scripture.

If Scripture teaches something about itself that appears to be inconsistent with what I observe in Scripture, I will have to consider either (A) I have an incorrect view of what Scripture teaches about itself, (B) my interpretation of what I observe in Scripture is incorrect, or (C) Scripture is, in fact, inconsistent with itself and, therefore, incorrect on a particular matter.

During our journey in this book, we have learned some important points that should inform our view of Scripture:

1. God was able to give us the Gospels without their authors using sources. However, he did not choose to go that route.

2. Most, if not all, of the Evangelists probably used secretaries to compose their Gospels.
3. The authors of the Gospels often quote from the ancient Greek translation of the Old Testament (LXX), which many times differs in its wording from the corresponding Hebrew text.
4. Whatever we may say about the nature of the divine inspiration of the Bible, it should acknowledge that the end product possesses distinct human elements that are sometimes imperfect, such as awkward grammar and editorial fatigue. (The latter I will cover below.)
5. Compositional textbooks prescribed that authors *should* alter what their sources report for the purposes of making points clearer and composing a good narrative. We observe Matthew and Luke altering Mark, although they often do so to a lesser extent than we observe other ancient biographers doing with their sources.
6. It appears likely that the Evangelists made use of several compositional devices, such as literary spotlighting, compression, conflation, transferal, and displacement. If Scripture is divinely inspired, then divine inspiration allowed for these techniques.

There are other phenomena that need consideration when reflecting on our view of Scripture. A very important one is how the New Testament uses the Old Testament. I want to focus on two phenomena we often observe when this occurs: *repurposing Scripture* and *composite citations*. We will then consider a third phenomenon known as *editorial fatigue*.

REPURPOSING SCRIPTURE

Occasionally, a New Testament author will repurpose a text in the Old Testament, assigning a meaning to it that is foreign to its original one. Let's suppose that I were to say the following:

> Matthew reports that after the magi had departed, an angel appeared to Joseph in a dream and said, "Wake up. Take the child and his mother and flee to Egypt. Stay there until I tell you. For Herod is about to search for the child to kill it." Thus, the Scripture was fulfilled which says, "At that time the one born according to the flesh persecuted the one born according to the Spirit."

Here I have quoted Matthew 2:13. I then added Galatians 4:29 while assigning it a meaning foreign to its original one. In the latter, Paul is referring to Ishmael persecuting his half-brother Isaac. But I have employed it to refer instead to Herod the Great persecuting Jesus and repurposed it to suggest Herod's action fulfilled prophecy. Today, such a move is called *proof texting* and is a shunned practice.

Those who seek a responsible explanation of the meaning of a text must consider what the text means within its original context. Otherwise, we can make the text say whatever we want it to say. Although such may help us arrive at an interpretation that allows us to do something we may want to do, it may very well lead us away from what God wants for us. For example, a person who is unsatisfied in their present marriage might appeal to a portion of Jesus's words out of context to justify divorcing their spouse: "Now it was said, 'Whoever divorces his wife, let him give her a certificate of divorce'" (Matt. 5:31). I actually know a man who sent an email to his wife that expressed his decision to divorce her and claimed the email served as a certificate of divorce. He used Matthew 5:31 to assert that he now had biblical justification to divorce her and was therefore free to date a girl in his church with whom he had fallen in love. However, he used Matthew 5:31 out of its context, which actually prohibits divorce unless one's spouse has been sexually unfaithful. Had he taken the text seriously and read the verse that follows, he would have seen that Jesus was not sanctioning his action. New Testament scholar Ben Witherington writes, "I tell my students all the time that a text without a context is just a pretext for what we want it to mean, and thus the New Testament text must be read in its historical, rhetorical, literary, social, and religious contexts."[1]

We would not approve of someone proof texting today in a sermon or Bible study. However, surprisingly, such a practice is not uncommon for the New Testament authors. Let's look at a few examples. Matthew reports that an angel warned Joseph in a dream to take his family and flee to Egypt in order to escape Herod's attempt to kill the Messiah. They would later return to Judea after Herod's death. Matthew reports that this fulfilled prophecy: "And he rose up, took the child and his mother while it was night and departed to Egypt. And he was there until the death of Herod, in order that the word spoken by the Lord through the prophet may be fulfilled, saying, 'Out of Egypt, I called my son'" (Matt. 2:14–15).

---

1. Ben Witherington, III, *The Individual Witnesses*, vol. 1, *The Indelible Image: The Theological and Ethical World of the New Testament* (Downers Grove, IL: IVP Academic, 2009), 41.

Matthew cites Hosea 11:1, "When Israel was a child, I loved him, and out of Egypt I called my son." To his original readers, Hosea is unambiguously referring to God bringing the Jewish people out of their bondage in Egypt. No distinctly Jewish uses before or after the first century link Hosea 11:1 with the Messiah.

There are a number of ways to understand what Matthew is doing here. Many scholars suggest that the relationship Matthew is drawing between Jesus and Israel in Hosea is one of analogy that some scholars refer to as "typology," which serves as a type of prophetic symbolism.[2] They are probably correct. Jeannine Brown comments, "By drawing on Israel's foundational story of redemption from Egypt, Matthew intentionally draws a parallel between their story and God's providential rescue of Jesus from Herod's clutches by taking Jesus' family to Egypt and back."[3] In essence, Matthew sees a "theological analogy" between what God did with Israel and what he is doing now in Jesus.[4] Regardless of what Matthew is doing with Hosea 11:1, one thing is clear: Matthew is engaged in a creative hermeneutic, whereby he takes an Old Testament text, assigns it a meaning that is entirely foreign to its original one, and then repurposes it to his context.

Hebrews 1:5 provides another example of repurposing: "For to which of the angels did he ever say, 'You are my Son; today I have begotten you'? And again, 'I will be his Father, and he will be my Son.'" The author of Hebrews is quoting two texts from the Old Testament. This first is Psalm 2:7: "You are my son. Today, I have begotten you." Psalm 2 was written to celebrate the coronation of a new king in Israel. The new king was appointed by God and, in that sense, became God's son on the day he was inaugurated. Hebrews 1:5 applies this statement to Jesus. Jesus is God's Son in the sense that God exalted him after he made the purification of sins. "You are my son" carries the meaning of being divinely appointed in Psalm 2:7 and in Hebrews 1:5. However, the author of Hebrews has taken a text that originally references Israel's new king and applies it to Jesus in a far more exalted sense.

---

2. Blomberg, *Matthew*, 67; Carson, "Matthew," in *The Expositor's Bible Commentary*, 118–19; R. T. France, *The Gospel of Matthew*, New International Commentary on the New Testament (Grand Rapids: Eerdmans, 2007), 80–81; Hagner, *Matthew 1–13*, 36; Keener, *The Gospel of Matthew*, 108; Morris, *The Gospel according to Matthew*, 43–44; Grant R. Osborne, *Matthew*, Zondervan Exegetical Commentary on the New Testament 1 (Grand Rapids: Zondervan, 2010), 99.

3. Jeannine K. Brown, *The Gospels as Stories: A Narrative Approach to Matthew, Mark, Luke, and John* (Grand Rapids: Baker Academic, 2020), 109.

4. J. Brown, *The Gospels as Stories*, 121.

The second Old Testament text quoted in Hebrews 1:5 is from 2 Samuel and its parallel text in 1 Chronicles: "I will be his Father, and he will be my Son." In its original context, the prophet Nathan tells David that the Lord says one of David's descendants "will build a house for my Name, and I will establish the throne of his kingdom forever. I will be his father, and he will be my son. When he does wrong, I will punish him with a rod wielded by men, with floggings inflicted by human hands" (2 Sam. 7:13–14; cf. 1 Chron. 17:12–13a NIV). Solomon is the descendant to which Nathan is referring (1 Kings 11:14, 23–26). He cannot be referring to Jesus, since, through Nathan, God immediately goes on to say that he will punish this descendant when he does wrong, while the author of Hebrews who repurposes this text informs us elsewhere that Jesus was sinless.[5] Notwithstanding, Hebrews 1:5 applies this text to Jesus.

Let's look at one more example. Acts 2:22–32 takes places on the day of Pentecost, which was a festival celebrated on the fiftieth day after Passover. After the Holy Spirit came upon Jesus's apostles, they were miraculously speaking in tongues publicly so that others whose primary language was not Aramaic could understand them in their own language. Some accused the apostles of being drunk. So Peter preached to them. In the midst of his sermon, he says the following:

> Men of Israel! Hear these words! Jesus the Nazarene, a man attested to you by God with miracles and wonders and signs, which God performed through him in your midst, just as you yourselves know. This man, delivered over by the predetermined plan and foreknowledge of God, having been nailed to a cross by the hands of lawless men, you killed him. But God raised him, releasing him from the agony of death, because it was not possible for him to be held by it. For David says about him,
>
> "I saw the Lord always before me.
> For he is at my right hand, so that I will not be shaken.
> Because of this, my heart was glad and my tongue rejoiced.
> My flesh also will dwell in hope.
> For you will not abandon my soul to Hades.
> Nor will you allow your holy one to experience decay.
> You have made known to me the paths of life.
> You will make me full of joy with your presence." (Acts 2:22–28)

5. See Heb. 4:15; 7:26; 9:14. See also 2 Cor. 5:21; 1 Pet. 1:19; 2:22; 1 John 3:5.

In verses 25–28, Luke has Peter quoting Psalm 15:8–11 verbatim from the LXX (Ps. 16:8–11 in Hebrew[6]). The psalmist speaks of trusting God to deliver him from death and from being in Hades where he would be separated from God's presence. Peter repurposes the text to be referring to Jesus and his resurrection instead of to David. Let's now look at another way the New Testament authors occasionally use the Old Testament in a free manner.

> In Greek mythology, *Hades* is the god of the underworld. The realm he ruled also came to be called by his name. All of the dead go to Hades where they live a shadowy existence. Greeks and Romans later viewed it as a place where the dead are either rewarded or punished. The translators of the LXX rendered the Hebrew term *Sheol* as *Hades*. *Sheol* referred both to the underworld (Gen. 37:35) and to the grave (Ps. 89:48). In the New Testament, Hades could refer simply to *death* (Rev. 1:18), the *realm where all the dead exist* (Acts 2:27, 31), and the *place where the wicked are punished after death* (Luke 16:23).

COMPOSITE CITATIONS

Sometimes an ancient author takes portions from two or more texts, combines them, and presents them as a single text. This produces a *composite citation*. Suppose I were to say the following:

> When I was a student in Baltimore City public schools in the 1960s, I was required every morning to stand and recite the Pledge of Allegiance:
>
> > I pledge allegiance to the flag of the United States of America
> > What so proudly we hailed at the twilight's last gleaming.

Those of you who are patriots noticed something strange. What I have cited is only partially from the Pledge of Allegiance. I have actually conflated the first sentence of the pledge with the second sentence of "The

6. The numbering of the Psalms in the LXX often differs from that found in our English Bibles, which is based on the Hebrew text. This is because the LXX sometimes combines what the Hebrew text has as two psalms. For example, Psalm 9 in the LXX has what the Hebrew text has as Psalms 9 and 10. The converse is also true: the Hebrew text sometimes combines what the LXX has as two psalms. For example, Psalm 116 in the Hebrew text has what the LXX has as Psalms 114 and 115. Only Psalms 1–8 and 148–150 are identical in both the Hebrew text and the LXX.

Star-Spangled Banner" and attributed both to the pledge. Now let's go to the Bible and suppose I were to write the following,

> Scripture must be fulfilled. Thus, it is written in the Gospel of Mark, "Salt is good; but if salt becomes unsalty, with what will you make it salty again? Have salt in yourselves. Consider Lot's wife. She looked back and became a pillar of salt."

Here I created a composite citation of Mark 9:50 and Genesis 19:26. It is a strange combination because I have taken the latter reference concerning Lot's wife out of context, given it a positive meaning not present in its original context, and credited the entire quotation to Mark.

We occasionally observe a similar practice by the New Testament authors. The most radical example is found in Matthew. After narrating Judas throwing the thirty pieces of silver in the temple sanctuary, Matthew writes, "Then was fulfilled what was spoken by Jeremiah the prophet, saying, 'And they took the thirty pieces of silver, the price of him on whom a price had been set by the sons of Israel. And they gave them for the potter's field, just as the Lord instructed me'" (Matt. 27:9–10). The careful reader will search in vain to find this text in Jeremiah. That is because Matthew is quoting Zechariah 11:13. Let's examine what's going on in its context in Zechariah.

God tells Zechariah that he is removing his favor from Israel and Judah. The unity between them will be ruined. Zechariah feels pity on the oppressed and serves as a political leader for the group. But the people reject his leadership. So he resigns his position and asks them to pay him an amount that they think his services were worth:

> I told them, "If you think it best, give me my pay; but if not, keep it." So they paid me thirty pieces of silver. And the Lord said to me, "Throw it to the potter"—the handsome price at which they valued me! So I took the thirty pieces of silver and threw [*emballō* LXX] them to the potter at the house of the Lord. (Zech. 11:12–13 NIV)

The book of Zechariah is beset with numerous interpretive challenges, some appearing in the context in which these verses occur. However, the essence communicated by this text is that when Zechariah asks the people to pay him what they think the services he rendered were worth, they paid him thirty pieces of silver, which Zechariah sarcastically calls a "handsome price," because at that time it was the typical price for purchasing a slave. God then commands Zechariah to throw the money to the potter. In the context of Zechariah, "to throw" carries the meaning of simply giving. The "potter" likely refers to the person at that time who, though a potter by trade, was serving as temple treasurer. So Zechariah's assertion that he "took the thirty pieces of silver and threw them to the potter at the house of the LORD" likely means that he gave the thirty pieces of silver to the temple via the treasurer, who was a potter.

How does Jeremiah play into this? Matthew probably has Jeremiah 32:9 in mind. Before we look at that text, let's consider its background. It's a little more than a century before Zechariah will resign his position and give the thirty pieces of silver he was paid to the temple. Zedekiah, king of Judah, is a client king of Nebuchadnezzar, king of Babylon. When the people urge King Zedekiah to align Judah with Egypt against Babylon, the prophet Jeremiah opposes the plan, warns Zedekiah that such would be a mistake, and is put in prison for his opposition.[7] Now that's a clear instance of "ancient cancel culture"! During Jeremiah's imprisonment, the Lord informs him that the son of his uncle is coming to him and will ask him to purchase his field. With the fall of Jerusalem to the Babylonians being imminent, this would typically be the very worst of times for a person to purchase land that is about to go to the enemy. It would be similar to purchasing stock once a company has declared it is going out of business. Nevertheless, Jeremiah obeys the Lord and purchases the field for seventeen shekels of silver. That's seventeen pieces of silver, not thirty. It is a sign from the Lord that the Judeans will return to the land. And they do about fifty years later when Babylon is defeated by Assyria in 539 BC and King Cyrus allows the Jews to return to Jerusalem about a year after that. With this background in mind, here is the text in Jeremiah:

> Jeremiah said, "The word of the LORD came to me: Hanamel son of Shallum your uncle is going to come to you and say, 'Buy my field at Anathoth, because as nearest relative it is your right and duty to buy it.'
>
> "Then, just as the LORD had said, my cousin Hanamel came to me in the courtyard of the guard and said, 'Buy my field at Anathoth in the territory of Benjamin. Since it is your right to redeem it and possess it, buy it for yourself.'
>
> "I knew that this was the word of the LORD; so I bought the field

7. In 588 or 587 BC, the Babylonians place Jerusalem under siege and eventually take it.

> at Anathoth from my cousin Hanamel and weighed out for him seventeen shekels of silver. I signed and sealed the deed, had it witnessed, and weighed out the silver on the scales. I took the deed of purchase—the sealed copy containing the terms and conditions, as well as the unsealed copy—and I gave this deed to Baruch son of Neriah, the son of Mahseiah, in the presence of my cousin Hanamel and of the witnesses who had signed the deed and of all the Jews sitting in the courtyard of the guard.
>
> "In their presence I gave Baruch these instructions: 'This is what the LORD Almighty, the God of Israel, says: Take these documents, both the sealed and unsealed copies of the deed of purchase, and put them in a clay jar so they will last a long time. For this is what the LORD Almighty, the God of Israel, says: Houses, fields and vineyards will again be bought in this land.'" (Jer. 32:6–15 NIV)

Now let's look again at what Matthew writes related to the action of Judas:

> Then when Judas, who had betrayed him, saw that Jesus was condemned, he regretted what he had done and returned the thirty pieces of silver to the chief priests and the elders, saying, "I have sinned, having betrayed innocent blood." And they said, "What is that to us? See to it yourself." And he threw [*hriptō*] the silver pieces into the temple and left. And going away, he hanged himself. Now the chief priests took the silver pieces and said, "It is not lawful to put [the Greek word for throw—*ballō*—is here translated "put"] this into the treasury, since it is blood money." After consulting together, they bought the potter's field from the silver pieces as a burial place for foreigners. Therefore, that field has been called the Field of Blood until this day. *Then was fulfilled what was spoken by Jeremiah the prophet, saying, "And they took the thirty pieces of silver, the price of him on whom a price had been set by the sons of Israel. And they gave* [*didōmi*] *them for the potter's field, just as the Lord instructed me.*" (Matt. 27:3–10; emphasis added)

Notice what Matthew did. He borrowed the word *field* from Jeremiah (32:9), inserted it in the text from Zechariah, loosely paraphrased the text, attributed it to Jeremiah, interpreted it to say something quite different from the original meaning of either text, and then claimed Scripture had been fulfilled.

What are we to think of such practices as repurposing Scripture and composite citations? I have to admit that this use of the Old Testament makes me somewhat uncomfortable. Is this what is meant by Jesus fulfilling prophecy in the Old Testament? In some instances, yes. Admittedly, such fulfillment does not impress. So I will offer a few comments related to these phenomena. First, the free artistic use of texts, as you have just observed, was not unique to the New Testament authors. In a volume titled *Composite Citations in Antiquity: Jewish, Greco-Roman, and Early Christian Uses* edited by Sean Adams and Seth Ehorn,[8] we learn that composite citation was a common literary practice and was sometimes used in the free sense that we observe Matthew doing. While we might scold a pastor today for doing something similar in his sermons, it was an acceptable practice in antiquity for Christians, Jews, Greeks, and Romans.[9]

Second, there might have been different types of messianic prophecies in that period: some clearly related to the Messiah, such as those found in Isaiah;[10] others symbolically prophetic (i.e., typology), such as we observed with Matthew's use of Hosea 11:1; and a third type, of a creative and free sort, such as we observed pertaining to Judas and the thirty pieces of silver. The manner in which some of the New Testament authors interpret Old Testament texts sometimes seems odd to us modern readers. However, the New Testament authors were not taking liberties that were unique to them. During the Second Temple period, several Jewish writers used interpretive methods similar to what we observe the New Testament authors using.[11]

Third, although this sort of prophecy may have little value in our minds related to Jesus actually fulfilling it, it has value for historical research. Why would the Evangelists go to such lengths to find texts in the Old Testament that they must take out of context and freely reinterpret? In my opinion, the most plausible explanation is that they were attempting to make sense of actual historical events. The story of Judas's betrayal of Jesus may serve as an example. Portions of the story, such as Judas receiving

8. Sean A. Adams and Seth M. Ehorn, eds., *Composite Citations in Antiquity*, vol 1, *Jewish, Graeco-Roman, and Early Christian Uses*, Library of New Testament Studies 525 (London: Bloomsbury T&T Clark, 2016).

9. Adams and Ehorn assert that of the 288 occasions that the New Testament authors cite the Old Testament, 54 (18.75 percent) are composite citations. See Sean A. Adams and Seth M. Ehorn, *Composite Citations in Antiquity*, vol. 2, *New Testament Uses* (New York: T&T Clark, 2018), 210. They add that "composite citations appear much more frequently in the New Testament than for works outside the New Testament" (215; cf. 248).

10. Isaiah 52:13–53:12 is considered to be the strongest single prophecy, gaining further strength from the related passages in chapters 42, 49, and 50. I am indebted to Michael L. Brown for this insight. For more information, see his debate with Rabbi Daniel Freitag: "Is Jesus the Jewish Messiah?" at Kennesaw State University, March 23, 2017, https://youtu.be/t_oCkfe4ivQ, accessed August 10, 2021.

11. See Peter Enns, *Inspiration and Incarnation: Evangelicals and the Problem of the Old Testament*, 2nd ed. (Grand Rapids: Baker Academic, 2015), 103–52.

thirty pieces of silver for betraying Jesus, which he later returned before hanging himself, are only found in Matthew. If Matthew had been willing to fabricate such elements of the story to assert that Jesus had fulfilled prophecy, why not think of some better ones for which he could find an Old Testament text that would fit much more cleanly? Why not say that Jesus had walked with a limp, his head was physically deformed, and that he had a cleft palate? He could then write, "Thus, was fulfilled the words of Isaiah the prophet, 'he had no beauty or majesty to attract us to him, nothing in his appearance that we should desire him'" (Isaiah 53:2b NIV). Such fabricated details would be a much easier fit with Isaiah 53:2b than what Matthew had to do in order to match the story of Judas's betrayal with Scripture. To me, it seems more plausible to hold that the story of Judas's betrayal of Jesus for thirty pieces of silver that he returned is true, and Matthew sought to find a text in the Old Testament that would make sense of it. Granted, guessing the thoughts and motives of an ancient author can be a chancy exercise. Nevertheless, the point still stands that Matthew's creation of a composite citation from two repurposed texts that have been liberally paraphrased and assigned a distorted interpretation suggests Matthew was searching for Scriptures that may have had Judas's treachery in view and, thereby, supports the historicity of the betrayal.

Finally, our observations in this chapter thus far should lay to rest any lingering reservations toward affirming that the Evangelists would use compositional devices to alter minor details pertaining to the words and actions of Jesus. For, *since we observe the Evangelists redacting Old Testament Scriptures on occasion, which they regarded as God's Word, why should we think they regarded redacting Jesus's words and descriptions of his actions as being off-limits?*

We have just examined several instances where the New Testament writers use the Old Testament and have seen that they sometimes repurpose a text by assigning it a meaning that is foreign to its original one. The presence of repurposing Scripture should caution us against appealing to some prophecies as evidence that Christianity is true. If you are going to appeal to prophecy, go with the strongest: Isaiah 52–53. We have also observed that the New Testament authors did what other historians and biographers in that era did. They combined elements from two texts to form a composite citation.

I want to touch on another phenomenon. It has nothing to do with a compositional device. However, it does provide insight into why there are some differences in the Gospels. It will also contribute toward a better understanding of what it means to say Scripture is divinely inspired.

EDITORIAL FATIGUE

Since we are examining some of the more radical edits by the Gospel authors in this chapter, I think this is an appropriate place to discuss another factor that results in a difference between two texts: *editorial fatigue*. New Testament scholar Mark Goodacre writes,

> When one writer is copying the work of another, changes are sometimes made at the beginning of an account that are not sustained throughout. The writer lapses into docile reproduction of the source. Like continuity errors in film and television, editorial fatigue results in unconscious mistakes, small errors of detail that naturally arise in the course of constructing a narrative. This phenomenon of "fatigue" is thus a telltale sign of a writer's dependence on a source.[12]

Goodacre provides several examples, some of which are far more compelling than others.[13] I think the clearest and most interesting example of editorial fatigue is found in Luke's version of Jesus's parable of the minas. A nearly identical parable appears in Matthew. Let's take a look at both.

Matthew 25:14–30	Luke 19:12–26
For it [i.e., Jesus's return] is like a man going on a journey, who summoned his slaves and entrusted his property to them. To one he gave five talents, to another two, and to another one, each according to his ability. Then he went on his journey. The one who had received five talents went off right away and put his money to work and gained five more. In the same way, the one who had two gained two more. But the one who had received one talent went out and dug a hole in the ground and hid his master's money in it.	Therefore he said, "A nobleman went to a distant country to receive for himself a kingdom and then return. And he summoned ten of his slaves, gave them ten minas, and said to them, 'Do business with these until I come back.' But his citizens hated him and sent a delegation after him, saying, 'We do not want this man to be king over us!'

12. Goodacre, *The Synoptic Problem*, 71–72.

13. Goodacre, *The Synoptic Problem*, 72–76. Also see Mark Goodacre, "Fatigue in the Synoptics" in *New Testament Studies* 44 (1998): 45–58, http://www.markgoodacre.org/Q/fatigue.htm.

Matthew 25:14–30 ***(continued)***

After a long time, the master of those slaves came and settled his accounts with them. The one who had received the five talents came and brought five more, saying, "Sir, you entrusted me with five talents. See, I have gained five more." His master answered, "Well done, good and faithful slave! You have been faithful in a few things. I will put you in charge of many things. Enter into the joy of your master." The one with the two talents also came and said, "Sir, you entrusted two talents to me. See, I have gained two more." His master answered, "Well done, good and faithful slave! You have been faithful with a few things. I will put you in charge of many things. Enter into the joy of your master." Then the one who had received the one talent came and said, "Sir, I knew that you were a hard man, harvesting where you did not sow, and gathering where you did not scatter seed, so I was afraid, and I went and hid your talent in the ground. See, you have what is yours." But his master answered, "Evil and lazy slave! So you knew that I harvest where I didn't sow and gather where I didn't scatter? Then you should have deposited my money with the bankers, and on my return I would have received my money back with interest! Therefore take the talent from him and give it to the one who has ten. For the one who has will be given more, and he will have more than enough. But the one who does not have, even what he has will be taken from him. And throw that worthless slave into the outer darkness, where there will be weeping and gnashing of teeth."

Luke 19:12–26 ***(continued)***

When he returned after receiving the kingdom, he summoned these slaves to whom he had given the money. He wanted to know how much they had earned by trading. So the first one came before him and said, 'Sir, your mina has made ten minas more.' And the king said to him, 'Well done, good slave! Because you have been faithful in a very small matter, you will have authority over ten cities.' Then the second one came and said, 'Sir, your mina has made five minas.' So the king said to him, 'And you are to be over five cities.' Then another slave came and said, 'Sir, here is your mina that I put away for safekeeping in a piece of cloth. For I was afraid of you, because you are a severe man. You withdraw what you did not deposit and reap what you did not sow.' The king said to him, 'I will judge you by your own words, you wicked slave! So you knew, did you, that I was a severe man, withdrawing what I didn't deposit and reaping what I didn't sow? Why then didn't you put my money in the bank, so that when I returned I could have collected it with interest?' And he said to his attendants, 'Take the mina from him, and give it to the one who has ten.' But they said to him, 'Sir, he has ten minas already!' 'I tell you that everyone who has will be given more, but from the one who does not have, even what he has will be taken away.'"

There are several differences in Luke's version of the parable. I will draw your attention to five. First, there are ten slaves in Luke, whereas there are three in Matthew. Second, the slaves are given *minas* in Luke, whereas they are given *talents* in Matthew. Third, in Luke, each of the slaves are given the same amount, one mina, whereas each slave receives a different amount in Matthew: five, two, and one talent. Fourth, the three slaves on whom Luke focuses yield ten minas, five minas, and preserves the one, whereas the three slaves in Matthew yield five talents, two talents, and preserves the one.

And fifth, the locations where Matthew and Luke place the parable, although close, are not the same. In Matthew, Palm Sunday has already occurred. Later that week, Jesus and his disciples are leaving the temple complex when his disciples comment on the beauty of the buildings. Jesus responds by telling them of the temple's forthcoming destruction. On Wednesday, his disciples come to him and ask when the temple will be destroyed. Jesus provides a lengthy answer that takes up two complete chapters and is referred to as his Olivet Discourse (Matt. 24–25). Jesus's parable of the talents appears within this discourse. After the completion of the discourse, the following verse says, "And it came about that when Jesus finished saying all of these things, he said to his disciples, 'You know that the Passover comes in two days, and the Son of Man will be handed over to be crucified'" (Matt. 26:1–2). Therefore, Matthew *explicitly* places Jesus teaching the parable of the talents within Jesus's Olivet Discourse uttered on Wednesday after Palm Sunday.

Luke also includes the Olivet Discourse after Palm Sunday (Luke 21:5–36). However, he *explicitly* locates the parable of the minas shortly before Palm Sunday (19:11–27). For the very next verse reads, "And having said these things, he went on ahead, going up to Jerusalem" (19:28), at which time Jesus's triumphal entry on Palm Sunday occurs.

Of course, it is entirely possible that Matthew and Luke are narrating two different occasions. After all, Jesus no doubt gave the same sermons countless times during his ministry, and it would have been entirely normal to vary how one tells a story, especially a parable. That said, two details in these parables suggest that something else is behind the difference. The first concerns the number of slaves. In Matthew, there are three. In Luke, there are ten. Luke's wording at one point appears to suggest he was familiar with Matthew's version of the parable.

The first (*ho prōtos*) came before him . . . (Luke 19:16)

And the second (*ho deuteros*) came, saying, . . . (Luke 19:18)

And the other (*ho heteros*) came, saying, . . . (Luke 19:20)

It is interesting to observe how major English translations have rendered the third servant (Luke 19:20):

"Then another servant came and said, . . ." (New International Version, 2011)
"Then another came, saying, . . ." (English Standard Version)
"And then another came, saying, . . ." (New American Standard Bible 2020)
"And another came, saying, . . ." (King James Version)
"Then another slave came and said, . . ." (NET Bible, 2nd ed.)
"But the third servant . . ." (New Living Translation)
"Then the other came, saying, . . ." (New Revised Standard Version, Updated ed.)
"Then the other servant came and said, . . ." (New American Bible, Revised ed.)
"Next came the other, . . ." (New Jerusalem Bible)
"And another came and said, . . ." (Christian Standard Bible)
"Another servant came and said, . . ." (Common English Bible)
"Another came, saying, . . ." (World English Bible)
"The third came and said, . . ." (Revised English Bible)

Here is the relevant text in Greek with a literal translation:

kai ho heteros ēlthen legōn, . . .
"And the other came saying, . . ."

Contrary to how the large majority of English translations have rendered the term, the definite article in Greek preceding the noun *other* is best translated "*the* other." I understand how *another* may sound better. There are ten servants with three being mentioned. However, those translators rendering the translation as *another* have overlooked Luke's editorial fatigue in this text. In the New Testament, *ho heteros* is almost always translated with a definite article ("the other").[14] The translation is important because had Luke meant to say *another*, he could easily have not included the definite article, as was his practice many times throughout his Gospel.[15] His inclusion of the definite article here may suggest he has only three slaves in mind, whereas *another* can easily refer to another of the ten.[16]

The other item in Luke's version of this parable that suggests the presence of editorial fatigue is the verb for *making* or *earning*. When the first servant gives an account to his master, he says that his mina has *earned* ten more. The Greek term here is *prosergazomai*. It means "to make, to earn in addition, to work besides."[17] The corresponding noun *prosergon* refers to "earnings, interest upon money."[18] The one mina has earned an additional ten. The servant now has eleven minas. The second servant says his mina has earned five more. He now has six minas. When "the other" servant returns the one mina his master had given him without it having earned any return, his master rebukes him strongly and then orders, "'Take the mina from him and give it to the one having ten minas.' But they said to him, 'Lord, he [already] has ten minas'" (Luke 19:24–25). The item of interest here is that the first servant has eleven minas, not ten. The one having ten is the first servant in *Matthew's version* of the parable: "Therefore, take the talent from him and give it to the one who has ten talents" (Matt. 25:28). Both items—"the other" and "the one having ten minas"—suggest editorial fatigue.

So how do we account for the fatigue? There are a few possibilities.

---

14. The following includes every occurrence in the New Testament of *heteros* with the definite article: Matt. 6:24; 10:23; 11:16; 21:30; Luke 4:43; 5:7; 16:13; 17:34; 18:10; 19:20; 23:40; Rom. 2:1; 13:8; 1 Cor. 4:6; 6:1; 10:24, 29; 14:17; 2 Cor. 8:8; Gal. 6:4; Phil. 2:4.

15. For a quick sampling, see Luke 14:19, 20; 20:11; 22:58.

16. See how Luke uses the singular *ho heteros* (with article) and *heteros* (without article). With article: Luke 5:7; 7:41; 16:13 (twice); 17:34 (twice); 18:10; 19:20; 23:40. All of these involve two parties (i.e., the first and then "the other"). Without a definite article: Luke 6:6; 8:6 (thrice); 9:29, 56, 59, 61; 14:19, 20, 31; 16:7, 18; 20:11; 22:58. In the plural: Luke 3:18; 4:43; 8:3; 10:1; 11:16, 26; 22:65; 23:32; all of which lack a definite article except 4:43. Given how Luke uses *ho heteros* and *heteros* in the singular throughout his Gospel, *heteros* is probably what we would be reading in 19:20 if editorial fatigue was not present. Matthew 10:23 and Romans 2:1 and 13:8 can be understood as "another" of several. Still, Luke does not use it in this sense, and there is an additional item that suggests editorial fatigue in this text which we will examine next. The combination of both makes the case much more likely that editorial fatigue resulted in both items in Luke's text.

17. Liddell et al., *Greek-English Lexicon*, 1510; William Arndt et al., *A Greek-English Lexicon of the New Testament and Other Early Christian Literature* (Chicago: University of Chicago Press, 2000), 878.

18. Liddell et al., *Greek-English Lexicon*, 1510.

Jesus's parable may have been remembered differently by Matthew and Luke because he had told it differently at times. In this case, Luke is familiar with both versions. He chose one version to include in his Gospel but accidentally included some of the details from the other. Another possibility is that Luke was familiar with the parable in Matthew's Gospel or in another source we no longer have (remember *Q* in the previous chapter?) and altered it intentionally while accidentally retaining some of the details from the original version.[19] In both scenarios, Luke appears to have been familiar with the version of the parable found in Matthew's Gospel and has either confused details with another version of the parable or neglected to clean up a few details that no longer fit after his edits. In summary, there are two possibilities:

1. Jesus told the parable differently at times. Luke included one of the versions and confused some details with those in another version.
2. Luke, his secretary, or his source altered the parable and neglected to clean up a few minor details that no longer fit.

What is today's equivalent value of a talent and a mina? It is difficult to estimate the talent's value Jesus has in mind. A talent was the weight of a precious metal, such as silver or gold. And the metal Jesus has in mind is not stated. Regardless, a talent was a significant amount of money that could take a day laborer several decades to earn! In contrast, a mina was worth approximately 100 denarii. A day laborer earned one denarii a day. So 100 denarii (or one mina) was approximately what a laborer would earn over the course of four months, assuming he rested one day a week.

The presence of editorial fatigue, though fairly rare in the Gospels, demonstrates that a human element is present in the composition of the Gospels that resulted in imperfect editing. However one thinks of divine inspiration, we can see that it allowed for imperfect editing on the part of the human writer.

19. Goodacre also observes that the 10:1 ratio is characteristic of Luke (see Luke 15:8; 17:11–19). See Mark Goodacre, "The Farrer Hypothesis," in *The Synoptic Problem: Four Views*, ed. Stanley E. Porter and Bryan R. Dyer (Grand Rapids: Baker Academic, 2016), 57.

WHY THIS IS IMPORTANT

I realize that this chapter has been a difficult one to read for many of you. Observing how the New Testament authors sometimes used the Old Testament (e.g., repurposing Scripture, composite citations) and editorial fatigue can be troubling. I sympathize because some of the more radical examples make me uncomfortable too. As unsettling as some of this may be, and as much as we may wish it were otherwise, it is clear that some of the New Testament authors engaged in these things. Although Scripture informs us it is divinely inspired, it does not tell us how it is inspired or how inspiration occurred. The presence of editorial fatigue reveals that the human element in Scripture produced imperfections. Therefore, by whatever means God inspired Scripture, it was rarely if ever accomplished by God somehow dictating the words for the biblical authors to write.

If these observations are correct, they contribute to forming a view of the Bible or to fine-tuning our present view. For this is what divinely inspired Scripture looks like at times. But what are we to make of this? How do the phenomena we have discussed in this chapter and the other compositional devices we have discussed throughout this book fit with the divine inspiration of Scripture? My objective in the next chapter is to cast some light on the matter.

SUMMARY

Repurposing and composite citations form the outer limits of the flexibility of ancient compositional devices. These were acceptable practices for the ancients. Editorial fatigue is occasionally present in the Gospels. It reveals that the human element of Scripture sometimes results in imperfections that extend beyond the mere awkward grammar discussed in chapter 3. The divine inspiration of Scripture allows for these phenomena.

QUESTIONS FOR FURTHER THOUGHT

1. What are your thoughts about repurposing Scripture and composite citations?
2. God allowed awkward grammar in Mark and editorial fatigue in Luke. Do you regard these human imperfections as errors? Why or why not?

3. Since we observe the presence of human imperfections in Scripture, do you think their presence disqualifies Scripture as being divinely inspired? Why or why not?
4. Propose a scenario in which the divine inspiration of Scripture can accommodate poor grammar and editorial fatigue.
5. Do you think divinely inspired Scripture can accommodate errors in minor details? Why or why not?
6. Can you think of a way God could be involved in the creation of divinely inspired Scripture that allows for errors in minor details?

CHAPTER 11

FINE-TUNING OUR DOCTRINE OF SCRIPTURE: INSPIRATION

Several years ago, upon learning that I would be in a particular country, the dean of a large Muslim university in that country invited me to deliver a lecture to its theology students. Walking through the university to the theology department, I noticed students gazing at me, surprised that a White Westerner was on their campus. I was informed later that several new ISIS fighters were initiated on the campus that same day and that I was the first Christian ever to lecture there. Despite the university being Islamic, I was treated with kindness and hospitality, never feeling in danger. Following my lecture in which I laid out a historical case for the death and resurrection of Jesus of Nazareth, a professor at the university gave a response. This was followed by a period for audience questions during which a few students engaged me and were visibly upset by the historical case I had laid out. At the conclusion of the event, the dean who had invited me told the students that he admired my approach to my Scriptures: I was willing to look at the Scriptures through a critical eye, seeing what could be established using the tools of historians while considering the possibility of certain skeptical views being true. He said that if he were to take a similar approach to the Qur'an . . . then he slowly dragged a finger across his neck, signifying that he would be beheaded.

The question of why there are differences in how the Gospels report the same events is one over which many early church fathers and modern scholars have wrestled. Just as I used a critical eye when approaching the question of whether Jesus rose from the dead, I have approached the matter of Gospel differences with a critical eye and posited what I think are the most probable causes for many of the differences. We have observed compositional devices in the Gospels that are bound to make a number of readers uncomfortable. How is it that at least some of the Evangelists felt free to alter the words of Scripture? Since they were willing to do so, should we be surprised when we see them altering Jesus's words and other details in their stories about him? Why should we trust anything they wrote? Since they often report items in ways that are different than how they had actually occurred, can we still view the Bible as God's divine Word? These are fair questions. And it is my intent to answer them in this chapter and the next.

In this book, we have been discussing the human element in the composition of the Gospels. This was not at all to diminish the divine element to which pride of place is usually given. My focus on the human element is to give attention to a quality of the Gospels that is often overlooked by evangelicals. This human element provides insight for understanding why many of the differences in the Gospels are present. The Gospels were not dictated by God or by an angel to their authors. God could have employed any number of means to communicate Scripture to us, such as parting the clouds and having a bright beam of light shine on a location where a book made of imperishable materials and containing everything he desired to communicate to us would be found. But the one he chose included human beings. This book has focused on just a few items of that human element.[1]

That said, we must not forget the divine element. In writing on this subject, Christian philosopher and theologian William Lane Craig affirms that "Scripture is the product of dual authorship, human and divine."[2] This is referred to as the *confluence* of Scripture. Why think there is a divine element? And how do the divine and human elements fit together in a plausible concept of the divine inspiration of Scripture—in other words, the *why* and the *how* of divine inspiration? Let's begin with the *why*.

---

1. Oral tradition and memory are some others. See Kenneth E. Bailey, *Poet and Peasant* (Grand Rapids: Eerdmans, 1976); Richard Bauckham, *Jesus and the Eyewitnesses: The Gospels as Eyewitness Testimony*, 2nd ed. (Grand Rapids: Eerdmans, 2017); Samuel Byrskog, *Story as History, History as Story: The Gospel Tradition in the Context of Ancient Oral History* (Boston: Brill Academic, 2002); James D. G. Dunn, *Jesus Remembered: Christianity in the Making*, vol. 1 (Grand Rapids: Eerdmans, 2003), 192–253; Craig S. Keener, *Christobiography: Memory, History, and the Reliability of the Gospels* (Grand Rapids: Eerdmans, 2019), 365–496; Werner H. Kelber and Samuel Byrskog, eds., *Jesus in Memory: Traditions in Oral and Scribal Perspectives* (Waco, TX: Baylor University Press, 2009); Robert K. McIver, *Memory, Jesus, and the Synoptic Gospels* (Atlanta: Society of Biblical Literature, 2011).

2. William Lane Craig, "'Men Moved by the Holy Spirit Spoke from God' (2 Peter 1.21): A Middle Knowledge Perspective on Biblical Inspiration," *Philosophia Christi* 1, no. 1 (1999): 45–82. This article may now be viewed at https://bit.ly/32u8Rya.

WHY THINK SCRIPTURES ARE DIVINELY INSPIRED?

Historians do not possess tools capable of verifying theological claims. Take, for example, the statement "Jesus died for our sins." Historians can verify that Jesus died. They can verify that the early Christians *believed* Jesus's death atones for our sins. However, they do not possess tools capable of verifying that Jesus's death truly has atoning qualities. This does not mean that, as Christians, we cannot or should not believe Jesus's death atones for sins. It is merely to say *historians* are incapable of verifying that it does. Similarly, historians do not possess tools capable of verifying the theological claim that Scripture is divinely inspired. However, I think it is rational for a Christian to believe that it is. And I am going to provide reasons that ground belief in the divine inspiration of Scripture.

In what follows, I provide *four building blocks* that, when taken together, provide a rational foundation for belief in the authority and divine inspiration of Scripture.

Building Block 1: Jesus Rose from the Dead

If Jesus rose from the dead, we have a good reason for devoting our serious consideration to his teachings. Is there respectable historical evidence that suggests the resurrection of Jesus actually occurred? I believe there is. Consensus is all too frequently absent among historians. Mark Gilderhus served as chair of the History Department at Colorado State University before holding the Lyndon Baines Johnson Chair in History at Texas Christian University. In his history primer, *History and Historians: A Historiographical Introduction*, he writes, "We no longer possess a past commonly agreed upon. Indeed, to the contrary, we have a multiplicity of versions competing for attention and emphasizing alternatively elites and nonelites, men and women, whites and persons of color, and no good way of reconciling all the differences."[3] Chris Lorenz, professor of philosophy of history and historiography at Vrije University in Amsterdam, makes a similar comment:

> [A proper philosophy of history] must elucidate the fact that historians present reconstructions of a past reality on the basis of factual research and discuss the adequacy of these reconstructions; at the same time it must

3. Mark T. Gilderhus, *History and Historians: A Historiographical Introduction*, 7th ed. (Upper Saddle River, NJ: Prentice Hall, 2010), 107.

> elucidate the fact that these discussions seldom lead to a consensus and that therefore pluralism is a basic characteristic of history as a discipline.[4]

Given the frequent lack of consensus among historians even on nonreligious matters, we should not be surprised to find so many different opinions about Jesus shared by historians. That said, virtually all historians of Jesus, including those who are rather skeptical, agree upon a number of items about Jesus. They agree that Jesus lived in Palestine in the early first century AD, that he believed he had a special relationship with God who had chosen him to usher in his kingdom, that he taught in parables, that he performed deeds that astonished crowds, that he, his followers, and many others regarded as divine miracles and exorcisms, that the Jewish leadership in Jerusalem handed him over to the Roman prefect Pontius Pilate, who, in turn, had him crucified. Moreover, it is nearly universally agreed by historians of Jesus that, shortly after his death, many if not all of his disciples had experiences they interpreted and sincerely believed were of Jesus who had risen from the dead and appeared to them. They also agree that a man named Saul of Tarsus, who was persecuting Christians, had an experience that he likewise interpreted and sincerely believed was of the risen Jesus who had appeared to him. Though not nearly all historians agree that some of these experiences involved groups of people seeing Jesus, a large majority do.

The task of the historian is to formulate hypotheses that attempt to account for the known facts. The hypothesis doing this better than competing hypotheses is regarded as what probably occurred. I will not assess numerous hypotheses here, though interested readers may read where I do so elsewhere.[5] What I will do here is compare the Resurrection Hypothesis with the most common alternative offered by skeptical scholars: the Hallucination Hypothesis.

At first look, the Hallucination Hypothesis may appear quite probable. After all, grief hallucinations are quite common, with some reports estimating as high as 50 percent of those who are grieving over the loss of a

4. Chris Lorenz, "Historical Knowledge and Historical Reality: A Plea for 'Internal Realism,'" *History and Theory* 33, no. 3 (1994): 326.

5. See Michael R. Licona, *The Resurrection of Jesus: A New Historiographical Approach* (Downers Grove, IL: IVP Academic, 2010). See also Gary R. Habermas and Michael R. Licona, *The Case for the Resurrection of Jesus* (Grand Rapids: Kregel, 2004); William Lane Craig, *The Son Rises: Historical Evidence for the Resurrection of Jesus* (1981; repr., Eugene, OR: Wipf and Stock, 2000); Andrew Loke, *Investigating the Resurrection of Jesus Christ: A New Transdisciplinary Approach* (Abingdon, UK: Routledge: 2020); N. T. Wright, *The Resurrection of the Son of God* (Minneapolis: Fortress, 2003).

loved one subsequently experiencing a hallucination of that person. Surely, Jesus's disciples would have been in such a state of mind, having just seen their beloved leader suddenly and brutally executed.

But there are many reasons to give one pause before concluding the disciples and Saul experienced hallucinations of a risen Jesus. For one, the number of those required to have experienced a hallucination of Jesus is far too high. Hallucinations come in many forms: visual, auditory, gustatory (taste), olfactory (smell), tactile (touch), kinesthetic (sense of motion), and a sense that the person is in the room though not perceivable by the percipient's natural senses. That said, only a small portion, seven percent, of those experiencing a hallucination of their deceased loved one do so in a *visual* sense. This is a challenge to the Hallucination Hypothesis because many of the reports of Jesus's postmortem appearances have him appearing to 100 percent of his disciples, which does not fit well with hallucinations but fits very well with actual appearances.

Second, hallucinations are not experienced by groups. Hallucinations are false sensory perceptions of something that is not actually present. They occur in the mind of an individual and have no external reality. In this sense, they are like dreams. I can no more share a hallucination with someone than I can share a dream with someone. For example, let's suppose that I am dreaming I am on a beach in Hawaii, enjoying a breathtaking sunset. Let's also suppose that upon awakening from my dream at 3:00 a.m., I immediately wake up my wife Debbie and say, "Honey, I've been dreaming I'm in Hawaii! Go back to sleep, join me in my dream, and we'll have a free vacation!" Even if we both fell back asleep immediately and both dreamed we were in Hawaii, it would not be the same dream. Now imagine that a group of people in a room all took a sleeping pill and were intentional in thinking of Hawaii as they were falling asleep. Not all would then dream of being in Hawaii. Those who did dream of Hawaii would not experience the same dream. Thus it is with hallucinations. Although all of Jesus's disciples would have been grieving over Jesus's death, only perhaps seven percent—or one of the eleven—would experience a hallucination of Jesus. And it is doubtful that the content of their hallucinations would be so similar that they would be convinced that they saw the same thing. That some groups—especially the one consisting of Jesus's main disciples, although the early oral tradition preserved in 1 Corinthians 15:3–7 mentions others—appear to have had experiences that they interpreted as the risen Jesus appearing to them fits far more comfortably with the Resurrection Hypothesis than with the Hallucination Hypothesis.

Third, the conversion of Saul of Tarsus poses a significant challenge to the Hallucination Hypothesis. Saul believed Jesus was a failed Messiah and a false prophet who had rightfully experienced God's judgement by being crucified. Saul wanted to destroy the religious sect Jesus started. Therefore, there is no good reason to think Saul would have been grieving over Jesus's death, which resulted in a grief hallucination. Other proposed reasons for why Saul may have experienced a hallucination of the risen Jesus are highly speculative and result from a skeptical scholar engaging in psychohistory, which is frowned upon by historians. Why? Mental health professionals very often find it difficult to accurately diagnose a willing patient sitting across from them. In contrast, historians engaged in psychohistory almost never have training in diagnosing mental health issues yet are attempting to do just that for a person they have never met who lived 2,000 years ago in a foreign culture. To do so accurately would be far more impressive than a magician telling you which card you are thinking of!

The Hallucination Hypothesis does a terrible job of accounting for the facts that are widely and nearly unanimously agreed upon by a heterogeneous consensus of historical-Jesus scholars. In contrast, the Resurrection Hypothesis quite comfortably accounts for all of those facts. One may reject the Resurrection Hypothesis on philosophical grounds (e.g., one is an atheist or deist) or on theological grounds (e.g., one is a Muslim or Buddhist). But the Resurrection Hypothesis is, in my opinion, the best explanation of the known facts on historical grounds.[6]

Now if Jesus rose from the dead as the historical evidence suggests, he must have been more than a remarkable person and we should be interested to learn what he had to say!

Building Block 2: The New Testament Preserves Significant Information Pertaining to Jesus's Claims

Historians of Jesus do not have the luxury of assuming the divine inspiration, infallibility, or inerrancy of Scripture. Those acting in their capacity as historians in a responsible manner will consider the data apart from such assumptions and seek to conclude what the data suggest. Using common-sense criteria, such as multiple independent sources, unsympathetic sources, eyewitness sources, and other criteria, we can render a

6. Discussing arguments contending for the existence of God would take us far off topic. Those interested should consult any number of good books on Christian apologetics where such arguments can be found.

number of conclusions about the life of Jesus that possess various degrees of confidence.[7] I noted a number of these conclusions above. Moreover, a growing number of historians think the historical evidence is sufficient to establish that Jesus claimed to be divine in some sense and that he predicted his imminent death and subsequent resurrection.[8] Accordingly, if Jesus rose from the dead, as the evidence suggests, it becomes quite probable that he truly had a special relationship with God, that his astonishing deeds were truly divine in nature, and that his claims of being divine are correct.

Building Block 3: Jesus Believed That the Old Testament Scriptures Are Divinely Inspired

Historical inquiry also reveals that *Jesus believed that the Old Testament Scriptures are divinely inspired*. Jesus saw his life as fulfilling prophecy (Mark 14:49; Matt. 26:54, 56; Luke 4:18–21; 22:37; John 13:18; 17:12; 19:28). He appealed to Scripture when tempted (Matt. 4:1–11 // Luke 4:1–13). Craig observes that "Jesus' successive citations of Deut 8.3; 6.13; 6.16,

---

7. Some scholars think the criteria either have very limited value or should be abandoned altogether. See Chris Keith and Anthony Le Donne, eds., *Jesus, Criteria, and the Demise of Authenticity* (London: T&T Clark, 2012). However, many scholars, this author included, argue that, while the criteria are not foolproof, they provide a commonsense means for assessing whether a saying or act of Jesus is a genuine historical recollection. For a defense of the criteria, see Darrell L. Bock and J. Ed Komoszewski, eds., *Jesus, Skepticism, and the Problem of History: Criteria and Context in the Study of Christian Origins* (Grand Rapids: Zondervan Academic, 2019).

8. For more on the idea that Jesus claimed to be divine in some sense, see Richard Bauckham, *Jesus and the God of Israel: God Crucified and Other Studies on the New Testament's Christology of Divine Identity* (Grand Rapids: Eerdmans, 2008); Michael F. Bird, ed., *How God Became Jesus: The Real Origins of Belief in Jesus' Divine Nature* (Grand Rapids: Zondervan, 2014); Robert M. Bowman Jr. and J. Ed Komoszewski, *Putting Jesus in His Place: The Case for the Deity of Christ* (Grand Rapids: Kregel, 2007). Bowman and Komoszewski have just completed a revised and greatly expanded edition as I write this, and their new edition may now be available under the title *The Incarnate Christ and His Critics: A Biblical Defense* (Grand Rapids: Kregel, 2024). In addition, see Raymond E. Brown, *An Introduction to New Testament Christology* (New York: Paulist, 1994); David B. Capes, *The Divine Christ: Paul, the Lord Jesus, and the Scriptures of Israel* (Grand Rapids: Baker Academic, 2018); Gordon D. Fee, *Pauline Christology: An Exegetical-Theological Study* (Peabody, MA: Hendrickson, 2007); Simon J. Gathercole, *The Preexistent Son: Recovering the Christologies of Matthew, Mark, and Luke* (Grand Rapids: Eerdmans, 2006); Murray J. Harris, *Jesus As God: The New Testament Use of* Theos *in Reference to Jesus* (Grand Rapids: Baker, 1992); Larry W. Hurtado, *Lord Jesus Christ: Devotion to Jesus in Earliest Christianity* (Grand Rapids: Eerdmans, 2003); Michael R. Licona, "Did Jesus Think He Was God?," in *T&T Clark Companion to Christology*, ed. Chris Tilling and Darren Sumner (London: Bloomsbury T&T Clark, 2023); Ben Witherington III, *The Christology of Jesus* (Minneapolis: Fortress, 1990). On Jesus predicting his imminent death and resurrection, see Hans F. Bayer, *Jesus' Predictions of Vindication and Resurrection: The Provenance, Meaning and Correlation of the Synoptic Predictions* (Tübingen: Mohr Siebeck, 1986); Licona, *The Resurrection of Jesus*, 284–302. See also Mike Licona: "Did God Become Jesus? (Did Jesus Claim to be God?)," Mike Licona (YouTube channel), posted July 8, 2017, YouTube, https://youtu.be/gT2TN6kA5kY.

as well as Satan's quotation of Ps 91.11–12 are noteworthy because they do not represent direct divine discourse but rather Moses' admonitions to the people and the Psalmist's reflections."[9] This strongly suggests that Jesus believed that Scripture possesses divine authority. Craig notes several other examples where Jesus appeals to the authority of Old Testament texts, even though God is not said to be the one speaking (Matt. 12:3; cf. 1 Sam. 21:1–6; Matt. 12:5; cf. Num. 28:9–10; Matt. 19:4; cf. Gen. 1:27; 2:24; Matt. 21:16; cf. Ps. 8:2).

Even more impressive are instances where Jesus quotes the Old Testament and says that God had said it. For example, in Matthew 19:4–6, Jesus quotes Genesis 2:24 when answering the Pharisees pertaining to their understanding of when divorce is permissible. What makes this relevant is the text Jesus quotes does not portray God speaking directly but is rather the author's conclusion pertaining to what God had said and did when creating Eve. To be fair, the verb appears in the third person and does not indicate gender. In this context, the verb could mean either *he (i.e., God) said* or *it (i.e., Scripture) said.* Moreover, in Mark's parallel text (10:3–9), Moses says it rather than God. Bracketing theological preferences, we should acknowledge that Matthew has possibly imported *his view* of Scripture into Jesus's teachings. But there are also some clear texts in which the interchangeability between God and Scripture goes in the other direction, so that what the Old Testament reports God saying, the New Testament reports Scripture saying (e.g., Exod. 9:16 / Rom. 9:17; Gen. 12:3 / Gal. 3:8).

Then there are statements where Jesus says, "Scripture cannot be broken" (John 10:35), and "it is easier for heaven and earth to pass away than for one stroke of a letter of the law to fail" (Luke 16:17). Jesus is unambiguously depicted as believing that the Scriptures are authoritative. Of course, it can be none other than God who gives them authority. Scripture is in that sense divinely inspired.

Jesus's statements pertaining to his view of the Scriptures are important if he truly said them. But did he? Because the historian's tools are often too blunt or the data is too thin, the historian is often unable to verify the authenticity of many of these individual sayings of Jesus. However, the data is sufficient and the tools are effective enough to establish a broader conclusion. Jesus's belief that the Scriptures are divinely inspired is so strongly evidenced by such a clear motif permeating all four Gospels

9. Craig, *Systematic Philosophical Theology.*

that it is rightly concluded as being an authentic element of the historical Jesus. Notice that we arrive at this conclusion by using the tools of historians—without circular arguments that the Scriptures are divinely inspired because they claim to be.

The New Testament authors believed that the Scriptures are divinely inspired. God or the Holy Spirit is said to speak through the Old Testament prophets (Acts 28:25–27 / Isa. 6:9–10; Heb. 9:8) and through the Psalms, sometimes specifying David (Acts 1:16 [Psa. 69:25]; 4:25–26 [Psa. 2:1–2]; 13:32–35 [Psa. 2:7; 16:10; Isa. 55:3; 16:10]; Heb. 4:7 [Psa. 95:7b–8a]), while other Scriptures attribute them to the actual words of the Holy Spirit or God (see Heb. 1:6–13 / Deut. 32:43b [LXX]; Psa. 104:4; 45:6–7; 102:25–27; 110:1; Heb. 3:7–11 / Psa. 95:7b-11).

> When the phrase "it is written" appears in the Bible, it always refers to Scripture included in the Bible (Protestant, Catholic, and Orthodox Bibles) with one exception. In 2 Samuel 1:18, the phrase points to the book of Jashar, which is also mentioned in Joshua 10:13 and has since been lost. The phrase "it is written" appears fairly often throughout the Apostolic Fathers, where it almost always refers to the Old Testament Scriptures.[10] However, there are a few exceptions. Barnabas 4:14 (probably late first century after AD 70 but possibly as late as AD 140) cites Jesus's saying reported by Matthew 22:14, "As it is written, 'Many are called, but few are chosen.'" In Barnabas 16:6, the source is unknown but may be a free paraphrase of Daniel 9:24. In Barnabas 11:1 and 14:6, "it is written" refers to the broader teachings of Scripture. And 1 Clement 46:2 reads, "For it is written, 'Follow the saints, for those who follow them will be sanctified.'" However, the source from which it quotes is unknown. In the Shepherd of Hermas 7:4, the phrase is referring to the book of Eldad and Medad.

From where did the early Christians get this view? Judaism in the first century held a similar view of Scripture.[11] Pious Jews held that the Scriptures are authoritative because they come from God. Thus, to disobey Scripture is to disobey God. This was the understanding of the Jewish leaders who confronted Jesus when he healed on the Sabbath, which they claimed was to break God's law (Mark 3:1–6; Luke 13:10–17; 14:1–6; John 5:2–17; 9:1–38). Jesus did not correct their view of Scripture.

---

10. 1 Clem. 4:1; 14:4; 17:3; 29:2; 36:3; 39:3; 48:2; 50:4, 6; Ign. *Eph.* 5:3; Ign. *Magn.* 12:1; *Barn.* 4:14; 15:1.

11. Jos. *Ant.* 12:37; *Apion* 1.37–43.

But he corrected their interpretation of it. Although the high view of Scripture held by first-century Judaism would have influenced the earliest Christians, who were pious Jews, it is not quite enough to settle the matter, since Jesus and the early church had major disagreements with several views of the Jewish leadership at the time. However, had Jesus not held a view of Scripture similar to that of Judaism, the early church likely would not have done so. This indirectly attests to Jesus's view of Scripture as being divinely inspired.[12]

Building Block 4: Divine Teachings Are Preserved in the New Testament

What we have just discussed concerns the divine inspiration of the Old Testament Scriptures. What about the New Testament? Is it divinely inspired? If Jesus was God's uniquely divine Son, his teachings are divinely authoritative. Although it is unlikely that the Gospels preserve precise transcripts of Jesus's teachings—in fact, as we have observed in this book, they clearly do not in most instances—I am persuaded for a number of reasons that the Gospels, at the very minimum, preserve an essentially faithful representation of what Jesus taught.[13] And some occasions the words they contain may even be close to Jesus's actual words.

If Jesus is divine, his teachings are authoritative, and we would expect for him to have commissioned his disciples to pass them along. And he does (Mark 13:9–11; Matt. 28:18–20; Luke 24:44–49 // Acts 1:8; John 14:26; 15:25–16:3; 20:21). This commissioning bestowed authority on his apostles. Accordingly, to the extent that the teachings of Jesus and his apostles are preserved in the New Testament literature, we may say that literature, at least some of the content it contains, is divinely authoritative and inspired.

By the end of the first century and into the second, the early church viewed at least some of the New Testament literature as being divinely inspired. The canonical Gospels are "Scripture" because they contain the teachings of Jesus and were believed to have been written by either one of Jesus's disciples or by one of their associates. First Timothy 5:18 quotes from Deuteronomy 25:4 (LXX) and Luke 10:7, respectively, and refers to them as "Scripture": "For the Scripture says, 'You will not muzzle the

---

12. For a robust historical case for Jesus regarding Scripture as being authoritative and divinely inspired, see Craig L. Blomberg, "Reflections on Jesus' View of the Old Testament," in *The Enduring Authority of the Christian Scriptures*, ed. D. A. Carson (Grand Rapids: Eerdmans, 2016), 669–701.

13. See Licona, "Are the Gospels 'Historically Reliable'?"

ox while it is threshing' and 'The worker is worthy of his wage.'" Until recently, I refrained from using this text as evidence that 1 Timothy has the Gospel of Luke in mind, since I thought the saying "The worker is worthy of his wage" could also have been oral tradition about Jesus known by 1 Timothy. However, *Scripture* literally means "writing" or "writings"—in other words, *literature*. Therefore, it is highly probable that 1 Timothy is referring to either Luke's Gospel or, perhaps, another written source that has since been lost (e.g., *Q*). Second Peter 3:15–16 informs us that Paul's letters were regarded as Scripture. Second Clement 2:4 (second century, perhaps early-mid) repeats Jesus's words in Mark 2:17, "Again another Scripture says, 'I came not to call the righteous, but sinners,'" thereby regarding Mark's Gospel as Scripture.

Polycarp served as bishop of Smyrna (present-day Izmir, Turkey) and was later executed publicly by the Romans, probably in the middle of the second century when he was eighty-six years old. In the late second century (AD 174–189), Irenaeus asserted that Polycarp was instructed by the apostles, especially John with whom he had interacted, and also spoke with a number of others who had seen Jesus. Irenaeus claimed that, during his youth, he had seen Polycarp while he was bishop of Smyrna and had heard him speak about Jesus's miracles and teachings he had learned from the apostles and that the church had handed down.[14]

If Irenaeus is correct, Polycarp's writings become very important since he personally knew and followed one of Jesus's closest disciples. Polycarp wrote a letter to the church in Philippi for which copies still exist. Scholars usually date the letter between AD 110–120.[15] In that letter, Polycarp quotes Ephesians 4:26 and refers to it as belonging to "the sacred Scriptures" (Pol. *Phil.* 12.1).[16]

The apostles held great authority in the early church. Paul believed he

---

14. Irenaeus, *Haer.* (*Against Heresies*), 3.3.4; cf. Eusebius (*Ecclesiastical History* 5.20.5–8), who preserves a relevant fragment but that is no longer extant.

15. Some scholars think Polycarp's letter in its present form could be two of his letters combined by an editor at a later date.

16. This portion of Pol. *Phil.* has only been preserved in Latin. The term translated "sacred Scriptures" is *sacris literis* (lit. "sacred writings" or "sacred literature"). Polycarp's statement is of interest because most modern scholars tend to think that the apostle Paul did not write Ephesians. In my opinion, the typical arguments for denying Pauline authorship of Ephesians are not impressive. If Polycarp had been an associate of the apostle John, Polycarp's view of Ephesians as "sacred Scripture" would suggest he believed it was authored by Paul. Although this by no means establishes that the apostle John or any of the apostles believed Ephesians was written by Paul, that Polycarp may very well have been affiliated with one of Jesus's closest apostles renders his view of Ephesians as "Scripture" and, thus, probably Pauline, more valuable than in the absence of such affiliation.

had received authority from Jesus to teach (e.g., 1 Cor. 7:17; 14:37; 2 Cor. 13:10). And the apostolic leadership confirmed that the gospel message he was preaching was aligned with their own (Gal. 2:1–10; cf. Pol. *Phil.* 3:2). Those who are not from God do not listen to the apostolic teachings (1 John 4:6). Since the apostles had traveled with Jesus and/or seen the risen Jesus, the early church regarded their teachings as authoritative, because they were grounded in Jesus's teachings and had received authority from him.

I do not intend to go further on the matter and contend for the divine inspiration of all of the New Testament literature because that would take us off to the matter of the formation of the biblical canon.[17] What we have covered is enough to demonstrate that a cogent and plausible case can be made for the authority and divine inspiration of Scripture.[18]

It may be tempting for some to say, "I don't need any arguments for the divine inspiration of Scripture. The Bible says it. I believe it. And that settles it for me!" Although this approach may be sufficient for them, it will not be for many others, such as nonbelievers, fellow Christians who are struggling with doubt, and Christians who desire to hold theological positions that can be reasonably argued and are thus not inclined to approach the Bible with the presupposition that it is divinely inspired. After all, one can use the same argument for the Qur'an and the *Book of Mormon*: "It claims divine inspiration. I believe it. And that settles it for me!" If you would not accept such an argument from a Muslim or Mormon, why think another would or even should accept this type of argument from you?

HOW DID THE SCRIPTURES COME TO BE DIVINELY INSPIRED?

At the beginning of this chapter, I said we would examine the *why* and the *how* of divine inspiration: *Why* believe the Scriptures are divinely inspired, and *how* did they come to be divinely inspired? We have just examined the *why* and will now address the *how*. Since I and many readers regard

17. See Craig D. Allert, *A High View of Scripture? The Authority of the Bible and the Formation of the New Testament Canon* (Grand Rapids: Baker Academic, 2007). For those interested in the matter of the formation of the biblical canon, see my five video discussions with Lee Martin McDonald, *Formation of the Biblical Canon*, last updated November 20, 2020, https://bit.ly/3M5q0Fn.

18. There are other ways for contending that the Bible is divinely inspired. For a far more sophisticated case, see Craig, *Systematic Philosophical Theology*.

the Scriptures as being divinely inspired, how did inspiration occur? What was the mechanism of inspiration? And even more foundational, what does it mean to say Scripture is *divinely inspired*? We have seen that, at minimum, to say that Scripture is divinely inspired means it was given authority by God. But can we say more?

"The term 'inspiration' relates to that influence of the Holy Spirit by which human beings become organs to communicate the truth of God in words to others."[19] How should that divine influence be best described? Second Timothy 3:16 reads: "All Scripture is inspired by God and is beneficial for teaching, for reproof, for restoration, for training in righteousness." The Greek word often translated "inspired by God" is *theopneustos*, which literally means "God-breathed."[20] Scripture is "God-breathed." There are around 2,500 occurrences of *theopneustos* in ancient Greek literature.[21] The term may have been in use prior to the composition of 2 Timothy. *Theopneustos* appears twice in the *Sibylline Oracles*, "a complex and unsystematic compilation of reconstructed or fabricated prophecies ascribed to Sibyls but largely representing the ingenuity of Jewish and Christian compilers."[22] There are two collections of the oracles, one dating to the end of the fifth century AD and the other to the end of the seventh century.[23] However, some of the oracles are earlier than the collections in which they appear, though how much earlier is difficult to determine. Some could have been composed as early as 150 BC, thereby predating 2 Timothy. In one of the oracles, the foolish city of Cyme is said to have "*theopneustic* streams" (*Sibyl.* 5:308). In the other, we read of the "great God

19. Thomas D. Lea and Hayne P. Griffin, *1, 2 Timothy, Titus*, vol. 34, *The New American Commentary* (Nashville: B&H, 1992), 238. Paul Achtemeier offers this definition: "To say that the Bible is 'inspired' means, at least that, in some special way, the literature in that book owes its origin to God himself, and to the events behind which he has stood, which are reported in its pages, and that therefore the Bible occupies a central and irreplaceable position within the Christian faith." See Paul J. Achtemeier, *The Inspiration of Scripture: Problems and Proposals* (Philadelphia: Westminster, 1980), 21.

20. "Inspired by God" is the rendering of the NASB, NRSVue, NET, CSB, NABRE, NJB, NLT, CEB, WEB; "given by inspiration of God": KJV, NKJV; "inspired": REB; "God-breathed": NIV; "breathed out by God": ESV.

21. Search conducted using Thesaurus Linguae Graecae© Digital Library. Ed. Maria C. Pantelia. University of California, Irvine. http://stephanus-tlg-uci-edu.libproxy.hbu.edu.

22. Erich S, Gruen, "Sibylline Oracles," in *Oxford Classical Dictionary* (online), published December 22, 2016, https://doi.org/10.1093/acrefore/9780199381135.013.8134. A sibyl was a Greek prophetess.

23. David Porter, "Sibyl," in *Oxford Classical Dictionary*, gen. ed. Simon Hornblower and Antony Spawforth, assistant ed. Esther Eidinow, 4th ed. (Oxford: Oxford University Press, 2012), 1360–61.

begetter of all things *theopneustic*" (*Sibyl.* 5:406).[24] *Theopneustos* also appears in the *Testament of Abraham*, a pseudepigraphal writing, perhaps composed sometime between AD 75–125.[25] In the *Testament of Abraham* 20:11, the archangel Michael and a multitude of angels place "*theopneustic* ointments and perfumes" on Abraham's corpse until the third day after his death.

Sometime between the first century BC and the second century AD, someone composed a poem in the name of the poet Phocylides, who had lived in the sixth century BC. The poem is known as *Sentences* by Pseudo-Phocylides. *Theopneustos* appears in verse 129 and reads, "But the speech of *theopneustic* wisdom is best."[26] However, most scholars think verse 129 was added to the text later, perhaps even later than Origen.[27]

Theopneustos also appears in the *Anthologies*, a nine-book treatise on astrology written by Vettius Valens and composed sometime between AD 152–62.[28] Vettius writes that the aether (believed then to be an all-encompassing substance, which includes the air) exists in us and is a "*theopneustic* product."[29] In the late second century, Clement of Alexandria uses the term on three occasions in *Stromateis* (*Miscellanies*) and once in *Protrepticus* (*Exhortation to the Greeks*), each to describe Scripture.[30] *The Lives of Carpus, Papylus, and Agathonice*, 12.33–36 (circa AD 2–3 century) provides two occurrences of *theopneustos*. The first refers to the Scriptures as *theopneustos*. In the second, Carpus, who is a Christian, says to the Roman governor who will execute him, "What do you want, Proconsul? To resist the truth and suppose that you will prevail in spite of it? But if you want to give close attention to the *theopneustic* lessons of the church, you will become an heir of eternal truth."[31] In other words, the *teachings of the church* are *theopneustos*.

24. The text and surrounding context is too vague to determine whether "all things *theopneustic*" is saying everything is *theopneustic* or is referring only to some things that are *theopneustic*. An English translation of the Sibylline Oracles may be viewed at https://sacred-texts.com/cla/sib/sib.pdf. The text cited above as 5:406 has a different numbering of 5:546 in this older translation.

25. E. P. Sanders, "Testament of Abraham: A New Translation and Introduction," in *The Old Testament Pseudepigrapha*, vol. 1, *Apocalyptic Literature and Testaments*, ed. James H. Charlesworth (Peabody, MA: Hendrickson, 1983), 872–902.

26. John C. Poirier, trans., *The Invention of the Inspired Text: Philological Windows on the Theopneustia of Scripture*, Library of New Testament Studies 640 (New York: T&T Clark, 2021), 60.

27. Poirier, *The Invention of the Inspired Text*, 58.

28. Antony Spawforth, "Vettius Valens," in *Oxford Classical Dictionary*, 1547.

29. Vettius Valens, *Astrol.* 9.1.37 (frag. 1764.006); J. Heeg, *Codices Romani*, Catalogus Codicum Astrologorum Graecorum 5.3. (Brussels: Lamertin, 1910), 112, 117–18; D. Pingree, *Vettii Valentis Antiocheni anthologiarum libri novem* (Leipzig: Teubner, 1986), 1–348.

30. Clement of Alexandria, *Stromata* 1.21.124; 7.16.101, 103; *Protr.* 9.86.2–87.2.

31. Vitae Carpi, Papyli et Agathonicae, *Martyrium sanctorum Carpi, Papyli et Agathonicae* (BJG 294). H. Delehaye, "Les Actes des martyrs de Pergame," *Analecta Bollandiana* 58 (1940): 158–76.

Theopneustos appears forty-nine times in Origen's writings, more than by any other author in the first few centuries of the church. Origen clearly believed the Scriptures are divinely inspired, given all of the fulfilled prophecies contained in them.[32] However, he also held that the nature of divinely inspired Scripture allowed for minor errors in details though not in the message.[33] Finally, the term appears in a work falsely claimed to have been written by Plutarch (i.e., Pseudo-Plutarch) titled *Doctrines of the Philosophers*, actually written sometime between the second and fourth centuries. There it says interpreting dreams requires one to be *theopneustos*.[34]

We have just observed every time the term *theopneustos* appears in the extant ancient Greek literature within a period that possibly extends from before the time of Jesus through the end of the second century AD and perhaps later. There are eight and possibly as many as thirteen occurrences of the term within that period, three of which possibly predate 2 Timothy. *Theopneustos* then appears forty-nine times in the writings of Origen during the first half of the third century.

What have we learned in the process? The Scriptures are regarded as being *theopneustos*, as are the teachings of the church, which are based on the Scriptures. Other objects, such as certain streams, ointments, and aether can be *theopneustos*. The ability to interpret dreams is *theopneustos*. Perhaps the closest way of describing the meaning of *theopneustos* is to say the thing it describes *derives from God or that God is its ultimate and special origin*.[35] The term may have carried a fuller meaning during the earliest periods of its usage. However, we cannot know. Moreover, as we observed earlier on page 8, even at a later period when Origen uses *theopneustos* in relation to Scripture, he understands it in a sense that allows surface discrepancies between the Gospels

Because *theopneustos* literally means *God-breathed*, a surface understanding of the term would seem to suggest that it is the product of divine dictation, somewhat similar to how Muslims think the Qur'an is divinely inspired. Perhaps one imagines a biblical author, such as Paul sitting with reed in hand, writing on papyri while hearing a voice say, "This is God

---

32. Origen, *Of Principles*, Book 4, 1–7.

33. Origen, *Commentary on Gospel of John* 10.4.19–20.

34. Pseudo-Plutarch, *Doctrines of the Philosophers* 5.2 (904f).

35. Also see Douglas Mangum and E. Tod Twist, *2 Timothy*, ed. Douglas Mangum and Derek R. Brown, Lexham Research Commentaries (Bellingham, WA: Lexham, 2013), comment on 2 Tim. 3:16.

[or an angel coming to you by God's direction]. Write down what I am about to tell you, word-for-word." Philo, a prominent Hellenistic Jew who wrote in the second quarter of the first century AD, had something like this in mind for the inspiration of Scripture.

> A prophet *possessed by God* [*theophorētos*] will suddenly appear and give prophetic oracles. Nothing of what he says will be his own, for he that is truly under the control of *divine inspiration* [*enthusiōn*] has no power of apprehension when he speaks but serves as the channel for the insistent words of Another's prompting. For prophets are the interpreters of God, Who makes full use of their organs of speech to set forth what He wills.[36]

However, the matter is not so simple. The term *theophorētos* means to bear or carry a god, to be possessed by a god, and *enthusiōn* similarly refers to being possessed by a god or to being in a state of ecstasy. These terms are closer to what comes to the mind for many of us living in the twenty-first century when we think of Scripture being "God-breathed." So it is worth observing that Philo did not use the term *theopneustos* here or elsewhere, which could suggest complete divine control is not being implied in *theopneustos* in 2 Timothy 3:16. Moreover, since even the teachings of the church were thought by some to be *theopneustic*, understanding *theopneustos* as *proceeding from God, word-for-word, precisely as we have it* may be to go further than Paul intended for it to be understood.[37]

It would be very unusual to find an evangelical theologian or biblical scholar who thinks divine dictation was the mechanism of divine inspiration. In fact, as discussed in chapter 3, divine dictation cannot be the method of inspiration for most of the Scriptures because the human element in them is clearly present. Could divine dictation have occurred by God somehow dictating to the writers what to write while imitating their different personalities, writing styles, vocabularies, and education levels? God can do anything, of course. It is worth observing, however, that the

36. Philo, *The Special Laws*, 1:65 (emphases and transliterated Greek words are mine). See Philo, *On the Decalogue, On the Special Laws*, books 1–3, trans. F. H. Colson, LCL 320 (Cambridge: Harvard University Press, 1937), 136–37. See also Philo, *Who Is The Heir of Divine Things?*, 263–66, in Philo, *On the Confusion of Tongues, On the Migration of Abraham, Who Is the Heir of Divine Things? On Mating with the Preliminary Studies*, trans. F. H. Colson and G. H. Whitaker, LCL 261 (Cambridge: Harvard University Press, 1932), 418–19.

37. For further discussion on John C. Poirier's monograph *The Invention of the Inspired Text: Philological Windows on the Theopneustia of Scripture* (New York: T&T Clark, 2021) and the meaning of *theopneustos*, see the appendix below.

human element in Scripture also includes Mark's awkward grammar that Matthew and Luke apparently found undesirable and worked to improve. Surely, we are not to imagine the Holy Spirit reviewing Mark later and thinking, "I can do better than that! Let's say it this way in Matthew and Luke." The human element also includes Luke's editorial fatigue. Surely, we are not to imagine the Holy Spirit catching this at a later time and thinking, "How did I miss that?" Then there is Paul's memory lapse in 1 Corinthians 1:16 pertaining to whether he had baptized anyone outside the household of Stephanus. Surely, we are not to imagine the Holy Spirit asking Paul not to get ahead of him but instead to take a break while the Holy Spirit checked heaven's records, only to find the relevant one missing! Yet such occurrences would be required if the biblical authors wrote as the Holy Spirit was dictating to them what to write. After all, Paul may not have recalled everyone he had baptized. But the Holy Spirit knew. These observations clearly reveal a human element in Scripture; an element that includes imperfections and, thus, rules out divine dictation.

Although the process of divine inspiration is not described in Scripture, our interpretation of what it means to say Scripture is "divinely inspired" should be consistent with what we observe in Scripture and allow for human imperfections to be present in it, since they clearly are. Such imperfections would be present in the items said to be *theopneustos* in some of the other ancient literature we examined. Therefore, the term *theopneustos* in 2 Timothy 3:16 does not contribute as much to our discussion as we may have initially anticipated that it would.

We have observed that it is reasonable to believe Scripture is divinely inspired in the sense that it derives from God and is absolutely authoritative. However, since Scripture does not inform us *how* divine inspiration occurred, we can only consider possible scenarios. Back in 1999, William Lane Craig argued, in essence, that God, knowing all circumstances that could possibly occur, generated those circumstances whereby the biblical authors would write what they did at an appropriate time. In this sense, the biblical literature is divinely inspired because God guided certain circumstances and thereby approved the final product. How does this play out? Craig proposes,

> God knew, for example, that were He to create the Apostle Paul in just the circumstances he was in around AD 55, he would freely write to the Corinthian church, saying just what he did in fact say. It needs to be emphasized that those circumstances included not only Paul's background,

> personality, environment, and so forth, but also any promptings or gifts of the Holy Spirit to which God knew Paul would freely respond. . . . Perhaps some features of Paul's letters are a matter of indifference to God: maybe it would not have mattered to God whether Paul greeted Phlegon or not; perhaps God would have been just as pleased had Paul worded some things differently; perhaps the Scripture need not have been just as it is to accomplish God's purposes. We cannot know.[38]

Craig's view is not entirely new. B. B. Warfield articulated a similar view in 1915, which I quoted earlier toward the end of chapter 3. However, I will repeat it here. Warfield claimed that the process of inspiration was, in essence,

> to bring the right men to the right places at the right times, with the right endowments, impulses, acquirements, to write just the books which were designed for them. When "inspiration," technically so called, is superinduced on lines of preparation like these, it takes on quite a different aspect from that which it bears when it is thought of as an isolated action of the Divine Spirit operating out of all relation to historical processes. . . . If God wished to give His people a series of letters like Paul's He prepared a Paul to write them, and the Paul He brought to the task was a Paul who spontaneously would write just such letters.[39]

I will add that these processes will also have included secretaries with whom the biblical authors worked. Although neither scenario posited by Craig and Warfield can be proven, they are the best ways I have heard thus far for understanding what it means to say Scripture is divinely inspired, since they take into serious consideration the nature of Scripture as well as what Scripture says about itself, less preconceived ideas pertaining to its meaning. I would even add that there could have been a number of occasions when God acted upon the authors of Scripture in a manner that compelled them to write certain items in a specified manner. Some occasions could have included dictation, such as the giving of the Ten Commandments (Exod. 20:1–17). Throughout Leviticus, God dictates to Moses procedures for making a variety of offerings, becoming

---

38. Craig, "'Men Moved by the Holy Spirit Spoke from God' (2 Peter 1.21)." Craig offers a far more detailed presentation and defense of this view in chapter one of his *Systematic Philosophical Theology*.

39. Warfield, "Inspiration" in *The International Standard Bible Encyclopaedia* (1915), 3:1480.

ceremonially clean, various laws and punishments, and other items. On several occasions God tells the biblical author to "write this" (Exod. 17:14; 34:27; Deut. 31:19; Rev. 14:13; 19:9; 21:5). These are exceptions, however.

Philo and Josephus wrote about instances when God so acted upon others that they spoke the words God put in their mouths.[40] This seems to me to be in line with being "carried along by the Holy Spirit" in 2 Peter 1:20–21.[41] The Greek term translated "carried along" is *pherō*, which means to carry from one place to another, to move, to cause to follow a certain course in direction or conduct, of an impulse, to bring a thought or idea into circulation.[42] This allows for occasions, such as prophecies and oracles, when the Holy Spirit placed certain concepts in the thoughts of the biblical authors to which they provided the words. Such an action on God's part would not violate the will of the biblical authors if they desired to write what God wanted them to write. This would be similar to asking God to guide us when we share the gospel message with others. Freedom and guidance can both be present.

I imagine this is what Jesus had in mind when he said the following to his disciples: "But when they hand you over, do not worry about how or what you are to say; for what you are to say will be given you in that hour. For it is not you who are speaking, but the Spirit of your Father who is speaking in you" (Matt. 10:19–20). Jesus could have had dictation in mind, for example, "What you are to say will be given you in that hour. The Spirit of your Father will take control of you and cause you to speak the precise words he desires." But I think it is more probable that he had the following in mind: "What you are to say will be given you in that hour. The Spirit of your Father will guide your thoughts, mostly with the concepts and sometimes even the very terms you are to use, though any stuttering and unnecessary uses of 'ahs' and 'ums' will be yours." Either of these ways could be understood as his disciples being "carried along by the Holy Spirit."

Another text to contemplate related to the *how* of inspiration may be observed in one of Paul's letters to the church in Corinth. It seems that some in that church were standing against him by questioning his

40. Philo, *Moses* 1.283; *Laws* 1.65; Josephus, *Antiq.* 4.111, 118, 119.

41. Second Peter 1:20–21 may only be referring to prophecy from prophets and may not have the composition process of Scripture in view. Philo, *Laws* 1.65 may also be understood in this manner.

42. See the entry "φέρω" in *BDAG*. The term also appears twice in the immediate context (2 Peter 1:17–18).

credentials as an apostle and, therefore, his authority that came with it (see 1 Cor. 5–6). Paul responded, saying,

> I said before and I am saying now, when present [with you] the second time and now absent, to those who sinned previously and to all the rest, that if I come again I will not spare [anyone], since you seek proof that *Christ is speaking through me* [emphasis added]. He is not weak toward you but is powerful among you. (2 Cor. 13:2–3)

When Christ is speaking through Paul, in what sense is his action divinely inspired? If we view his letters in the same manner as his public speaking, memory lapse is present in 1 Corinthians 1:16. So if this text is an example of what it means to be "carried along by the Holy Spirit," the message derives from God in some sense. The authority vested in Paul as an apostle is also from God.[43] That said, we must acknowledge that the Scriptures are fairly silent on the *how* of inspiration. We can only speculate and attempt to have a coherent model of divine inspiration that takes seriously both the claims of Scripture about itself and the nature of Scripture.

VERBAL AND PLENARY INSPIRATION

Evangelicals commonly speak of the *verbal* and *plenary* inspiration of Scripture. *Verbal inspiration* means the very words of Scripture are divinely inspired. *Plenary inspiration* means the entirety of Scripture is divinely inspired. Take Paul's letter to the Christians in Philippi, for example. Verbal inspiration means the very words Paul used are inspired. Plenary inspiration means the entirety of Paul's letter is inspired as opposed to only portions of it. Some of what we have observed—editorial fatigue, memory lapse—are direct challenges to the verbal inspiration of Scripture as traditionally understood. Verbal and plenary inspiration can be defended only if we think of them in a nuanced manner, such as we see with Craig's and Warfield's views of divine inspiration or something similar to them. Because their models take into consideration the dual authorship or confluence of Scripture,[44] they can make sense of both the claims of Scripture

---

43. See also Acts 1:16; 4:25; Heb. 4:7.

44. A term similar to the confluence of Scripture is *organic inspiration*. "Organic inspiration means that the Spirit's witness has entered fully into the world of human creatureliness and found expression precisely in the limitations of a thoroughly human witness. Scripture is totally the work

about itself and the nature of Scripture. Accordingly, those models demonstrate that a coherent doctrine of Scripture can include divine inspiration that is verbal and plenary, if our concepts of verbal and plenary inspiration are thought of in a nuanced manner.

What might those nuanced views look like? Let's consider Craig's model of divine inspiration. Philosophers and philosophically inclined theologians sometimes speak of *possible worlds*. How would our world be different had the attempt by Claus von Stauffenberg to assassinate Adolf Hitler at the Wolf's Lair been successful? What if one of your direct ancestors had been killed in battle before his wife became pregnant? What would you be like if your mother had married someone else? Would *you* be different, perhaps even nonexistent? What would your life be like had you gone to a different college or chose a different vocation? Each of these would be a different world. The options are practically endless in relation to your life without even considering how our world would be if circumstances differed even slightly in reference to any person out of the nearly 100 billion people estimated to have lived. A slight change may not have resulted in a difference in your life, but it would impact the lives of others. As an all-knowing being, God was aware of all possible worlds prior to creation. Philosophers refer to this awareness as "middle knowledge."

Of all the possible worlds God could have chosen, he chose the one we have. He gave humans free will knowing that we would very often choose sin over holiness, that evil, pain, and suffering would result, and that this would require a great sacrifice from him.[45] Still, God approved of that specific world and actualized it. "And God saw that it was good" (Gen. 1:10, 12, 18, 21, 25, 31). By actualizing this world, does it mean that God approves of everything in it, including the Holocaust and human trafficking? Of course not. Scripture is clear that God opposes all evil and sin. God *approved* this world in the sense that he chose to actualize it with the knowledge that it would include certain elements within its fabric he finds undesirable.

---

of the Spirit yet at the same time is totally the work of human authors in history." Michael W. Goheen and Michael D. Williams, "Doctrine of Scripture and Theological Interpretation," in *A Manifesto for Theological Interpretation*, ed. Craig G. Bartholomew and Heath A. Thomas (Grand Rapids: Baker Academic, 2016), 69.

45. For excellent scriptural and philosophical defenses of human free will, see William Lane Craig, *The Only Wise God: The Compatibility of Divine Foreknowledge and Human Freedom* (Eugene, OR: Wipf and Stock, 2000); Leighton Flowers, *The Potter's Promise: A Biblical Defense of Traditional Soteriology* (Dallas: Trinity Academic Press, 2017); and Timothy A. Stratton, *Human Freedom, Divine Knowledge, and Mere Molinism* (Eugene, OR: Wipf and Stock, 2020).

Perhaps we may say something similar when speaking of the verbal and plenary inspiration of Scripture. There are many possible ways by which God could have given us the Scriptures. He could have delivered it to us by creating a book made of imperishable materials that contained everything he wants us to know. He could have had an angel dictate to the biblical authors what to write. But God did not choose either of those ways. The models proposed by Craig and Warfield may bring us closer to understanding divine inspiration, though neither may be the final word on the matter. Craig himself admits, "The doctrine of Scripture is as yet one of the most underdeveloped topics of contemporary philosophical theology."[46] What we can say is the way God chose for inspiration includes imperfections, memory lapse, and the New Testament authors employing the normal hermeneutical conventions of their day, repurposing various Old Testament Scriptures by assigning them meanings that differ, sometimes even radically, from what their original authors intended. Some of these phenomena make us moderns uncomfortable. However, if Scripture is truly inspired by God, these phenomena did not take him by surprise. In fact, he knew they would occur even before he created the universe. Even with the imperfections and peculiarities that accompany the human element in Scripture, God still placed his approval on the final product, though this does not mean he regards every word and argument in Scripture as being ideal. What we observe is the product of the unspecified method(s) that God chose. Scripture is as God intended it to be. *And God saw that it was good!*

Since Scripture is as God intended, followers of Jesus need not feel any sense of guilt when considering the matters we are discussing in this book. When we observe some editorial fatigue in Luke, we need not fear that God has become displeased with us because he was "found out" or because we are questioning Scripture. We are not questioning Scripture itself. We are questioning *our view of Scripture* and desiring to fine-tune it. Earlier in this book, I shared a principle by which I'm guided.

> **Principle 1:** My view of Scripture should be consistent with what I observe in Scripture.

I now commend to you a second principle:

46. William Lane Craig, *Systematic Philosophical Theology*, vol. 1 (forthcoming).

> **Principle 2:** If I truly have a high view of Scripture, I will embrace it as God has given it to us rather than insist that it conforms to a model shaped by how I think he should have given it. If I refuse to do this, I may sincerely believe that I hold a high view of Scripture when I actually hold a high view of my view of Scripture.

In conclusion, I am proposing a model of Scripture as divinely inspired that may bring us closer to reality than more popular models do: God, having foreknown all possible worlds, chose to actualize the one in which the biblical authors would write what they did. On some occasions, God may have planted ideas, concepts, perhaps even the very words they would write. However, the human element is present throughout and includes imperfections.

Up to this point we have observed several kinds of imperfections, such as memory lapse, awkward grammar, and editorial fatigue. But does the human element in Scripture go so far as to include factual errors? Does divine inspiration require that a text be without factual errors? How should we think about the doctrine of biblical inerrancy? This will be the subject of the next chapter.

WHY THIS IS IMPORTANT

A "high view" of Scripture regards it as being divinely inspired and authoritative. In contrast, a "low view" of Scripture views it as being entirely of human origin. According to a low view, while Scripture provides some teachings that are beneficial for living successfully and for treating others in a manner that promotes peace, it should not be an authoritative guide for how we should live.

What we have discussed in this chapter is important because it will assist us in fine-tuning our view of Scripture. While most Christians believe Scripture is divinely inspired, many of us have given little attention to *what* it means for Scripture to be divinely inspired and *how* it occurred. It then can be confusing when one observes clear human influence that was present when the Gospels were composed. Understanding that Scripture is confluent (i.e., Scripture has dual authorship: divine and human) clarifies how robust human elements can be present in divinely inspired Scripture. This opens the door for us to have a harmonious union of our view of Scripture and what we observe in Scripture.

SUMMARY

A reasonable case can be made that Scripture is divinely inspired. But what does it mean to say Scripture is divinely inspired? Scripture does not provide specific details on this matter. However, by observing certain phenomena in Scripture, we can infer what inspiration was not. We are then left to speculate what it involved. A plausible model appeals to God's middle knowledge, which is that God, having foreknown all possible worlds, chose to actualize the one in which the biblical authors would freely write what they did. On some occasions, God may have planted ideas, concepts, and perhaps even the very words they would write. However, the human element also is present and includes imperfections.

QUESTIONS FOR FURTHER THOUGHT

1. Prior to reading this chapter, how did you imagine divine inspiration to have occurred?
2. What do you think about the way God brought about Scripture proposed by Craig? Do you wish God would have done it differently? If so, why?
3. If you have a different view of divine inspiration, can it accommodate the items we have observed such as editorial fatigue, repurposing, and some of the compositional devices? If so, how?
4. Have some of the things discussed in this chapter made you feel uneasy or relieved? Why do you think that is?
5. God desires that we view Scripture as it truly is. How do you think some people have come to view Scripture differently?

CHAPTER 12

FINE-TUNING OUR DOCTRINE OF SCRIPTURE: INERRANCY

Since God inspired Scripture, it is reasonable to infer he would ensure that all he intended to communicate to us through Scripture has been preserved with no less than sufficient accuracy. But does the accuracy of God's message to us in Scripture go beyond "sufficient"? Since Scripture is confluent and God is one of the authors, would Scripture necessarily be without any errors? We observed in the previous chapter that, although Scripture informs us it is divinely inspired, it does not tell us specifically what that means or how inspiration occurred.[1] So we must be careful about concluding that the inerrancy of Scripture, or a certain view of it, is the logical implication of Scripture being divinely inspired.[2]

VIEWING SCRIPTURE THROUGH THE CORRECT LENS

When I hit my mid-forties, I noticed that reading had become increasingly more difficult. The words on a page were fuzzy, and each year I found myself pushing books farther from my eyes in order to read them

1. That the Bible does not provide us with a theory of inspiration is widely acknowledged. For a few examples, see Douglas K. Blount, "What Does It Mean to Say That the Bible Is True?," in *In Defense of the Bible: A Comprehensive Apologetic for the Authority of Scripture* (Nashville: B&H, 2013), 47–62, esp. 57n41. See also David S. Dockery and David P. Nelson, "Special Revelation," in *A Theology for the Church*, ed. Daniel L. Akin (Nashville: B&H Academic, 2007), 143; Ben Witherington III, *The Living Word of God* (Waco: Baylor University Press, 2007), 10; The Chicago Statement on Biblical Inerrancy, art. 7.

2. Craig Allert writes, "If the Bible does not give a theory of inspiration, we must be cautious about making inerrancy the logical conclusion of it." See Allert, *A High View of Scripture*, 172.

in focus. Shortly after I turned forty-eight, I took a vision test. I looked into a machine and observed letters. The optometrist would then change lenses, each time asking me whether the lens through which I presently peered or the one preceding it allowed me to see the letters with greater clarity. He continued to alter lenses in a finetuning process until he found the lens that allowed me to read the letters with the greatest clarity, then prescribed reading glasses with that lens strength.

In this chapter, I'm going to act in the role of a *scriptural optometrist*. We are going to look at Scripture through two lenses to see which allows us to view Scripture with the greatest clarity.

Lens 1: Traditional View of Inerrancy

The definition of biblical inerrancy familiar to most American evangelicals is the Chicago Statement on Biblical Inerrancy (CSBI). It was crafted in 1978 by three evangelical scholars, J. I. Packer, Norman Geisler, and R. C. Sproul, and subsequently signed by 334 evangelical leaders. The statement represents what I will refer to as *traditional inerrancy*. Similar definitions of inerrancy have been offered by the Lausanne Covenant and several individual evangelicals. But the CSBI is the most exhaustive, containing six pages that explain what biblical inerrancy is and is not. Although the CSBI allows for some flexibility in how events are reported in the Bible, such as approximations, the rounding of numbers, the use of hyperbole, and so on, it does not allow for any errors in the details reported.

Precisely how much wiggle room does CSBI allow? Matthew, Mark, and Luke report that Jesus predicted his death and resurrection, then said that anyone wanting to be his disciple must be willing to take up their cross and follow him. He then told them there were some standing there who would not die until they saw the kingdom of God. Matthew and Mark report that Jesus was transfigured six days after saying these things (Matt. 17:1; Mark 9:2) while Luke says it occurred "about eight days" later (Luke 9:28). "About eight days" is close enough to "six days" to be considered an approximation, especially in view of Luke's more exact statement that Jesus was circumcised "at the end of eight days" (Luke 2:21). According to CSBI, this is an allowable difference and does not involve a contradiction. However, if Luke was mistaken that the Roman Emperor Caesar Augustus conducted a census of the Roman Empire when Quirinius was governor of Syria (Luke 2:1–2), this would be an error in the details.

Those holding a *traditional view* of inerrancy contend that the inerrancy of the Bible is grounded in the nature and character of God. Therefore, the inerrancy of the Bible is the logical outcome of it being inspired by God.[3] Their argument often looks something like this:

> God is a perfect being. Being omniscient, he has perfect knowledge of how every event in history transpired and the names of the people involved in those events. Therefore, if God wrote a book, it would be error-free. The Bible is such a book. It is God's Word, having been "God-breathed" (2 Timothy 3:16). Therefore, the inerrancy of the Bible is the logical outcome of its divine inspiration, and our current Bible is error-free to the extent that it mirrors the original manuscripts.

This argument is very often stated using the following syllogism or one similar to it:

1. God cannot err.
2. The Bible is God's Word.
3. Therefore, the Bible cannot err.[4]

The first premise—God cannot err—is supported by an appeal to Scriptures stating that God's character is absolutely flawless and truthful (Num. 23:19; 1 Sam. 15:29; Ps. 119:160; Titus 1:2; Heb. 6:18).

The second premise—the Bible is God's Word—is also supported by numerous biblical texts in which the words of the Bible are said to be God's words. We observed several examples in the previous chapter.

---

3. Gleason L. Archer, *Encyclopedia of Bible Difficulties* (Grand Rapids: Zondervan, 1982), 28; Dockery and Nelson, "Special Revelation," 156; Norman L. Geisler and Thomas Howe, *The Big Book of Bible Difficulties: Clear and Concise Answers from Genesis to Revelation* (Grand Rapids: Baker, 1992), 13; Paul Helm, "The Idea of Inerrancy," in *The Enduring Authority of the Christian Scriptures*, ed. D. A. Carson (Grand Rapids: Eerdmans, 2016), 903, 917; R. Albert Mohler Jr., "When the Bible Speaks, God Speaks: The Classic Doctrine of Biblical Inerrancy," in *Five Views on Biblical Inerrancy*, ed. J. Merrick and Stephen M. Garrett, Counterpoints: Bible and Theology (Grand Rapids: Zondervan, 2013), 39. See J. I. Packer, *Fundamentalism and the Word of God* (Grand Rapids: Eerdmans, 1958), 95, where Packer applies this principle to the infallibility of the Bible.

4. See Steve W. Lemke, "The Inspiration and Authority of Scripture," in *Biblical Hermeneutics: A Comprehensive Introduction to Interpreting Scripture*, ed. Bruce Corley, Steve W. Lemke, and Grant I. Lovejoy, 2nd. ed. (Nashville: B&H, 2002), 176–93, esp. 188; Norman L. Geisler and F. David Farnell, *The Jesus Quest: The Danger from Within* (Maitland, FL: Xulon, 2014), loc. 577, 777, Kindle; and Norman L. Geisler and William C. Roach, *Defending Inerrancy: Affirming the Accuracy of Scripture for a New Generation* (Grand Rapids: Baker, 2012), loc. 2496, Kindle. See also Blount, "What Does It Mean to Say That the Bible Is True?," 56–60.

In *Inerrancy and the Gospels*, Vern Poythress writes, "The Bible is the word of God, God's speech in written form. What the Bible says, God says."[5] In support, he cites two texts we discussed in the previous chapter:

> All Scripture is *breathed out by God* and profitable for teaching, for reproof, for correction, and for training in righteousness, that the man of God may be complete, equipped for every good work. (2 Tim. 3:16–17)
>
> For no prophecy was ever produced by the will of man, but men *spoke from God* as they were *carried along by the Holy Spirit*. (2 Pet. 1:21)[6]

Scripture is "breathed out by God" or "God-breathed." It was not "produced by the will of man" or "borne of human impulse,"[7] but it came from men who were "carried along by the Holy Spirit." On their face, these verses appear to support interpreting the Word of God as "God's speech in written form." Many inerrantists understand the Word of God in this sense.[8]

Three Major Challenges to the Traditional View Considered

Three challenges to the traditional view of biblical inerrancy should be addressed.

1. The Traditional View Often Possesses Unstated Freight

If the first two premises of the syllogism are correct and the logic of the argument is valid, the conclusion—the Bible cannot err—is true. However, there is a problem with how the second premise is understood. What does it mean to say the Bible is the Word of God? There is a lot of freight in the second premise. Traditional inerrantists who use this syllogism mean by it that the statement "The Bible is the Word of God" is equivalent to saying that "the Bible is God's speech in written form," in the sense that God spoke all of the very words of Scripture. If they are correct, the logic of the syllogism is valid. However, we are going to observe serious problems with the argument.

---

5. Vern S. Poythress, *Inerrancy and the Gospels: A God-Centered Approach to the Challenges of Harmonization* (Wheaton, IL: Crossway, 2012), 14.

6. Poythress, *Inerrancy and the Gospels*, 14 (emphasis Poythress's, who quotes the ESV in his book).

7. This is how the NET Bible translates the phrase.

8. For example, see Dockery and Nelson, "Special Revelation," 133–34. John Wenham, *Christ and the Bible*, 3rd ed. (Grand Rapids: Baker, 1994), 195.

Understanding all of the words of Scripture to be as though God himself had spoken them assumes that the role played by the human writers in the composition of the biblical literature was minimal. It almost suggests some form of divine dictation, although most inerrantists are quick to deny that inspiration occurred via dictation.[9] Consider Article VIII of the Chicago Statement on Biblical Inerrancy (CSBI): "*WE DENY* that God, in causing these writers to use the very words that He chose, overrode their personalities." For the CSBI, which is the foremost guide among traditional inerrantists on how biblical inerrancy should be understood, God did not *dictate* the words to the biblical writers but somehow *caused* those writers to "use the very words that He chose." But in what sense could God be said to have caused the biblical writers "to use the very words that He chose"? In the previous chapter, we discussed the meaning of "God-breathed" (*theopneustos*) in 2 Timothy 3:16 and of the biblical writers being "carried along by the Holy Spirit" in 2 Peter 1:21. We observed that these texts are plausibly and perhaps best interpreted using a middle-knowledge model of inspiration: God, knowing all possible worlds, chose and actualized the one whereby the biblical authors would freely write what they did.[10] Accordingly, the authors did not act as secretaries transcribing word-for-word what God told them to write. Rather, it was mostly a combination of circumstances in the churches with the life experiences, personalities, raw emotions, and the thoughts of the authors, who wrote what they did to accomplish particular objectives they had in mind—objectives God knew they would have when he chose to make a particular possible world the actual one. There may have been occasions when God planted the concepts or thoughts in the mind of the biblical writer, though not causing them to write specific words.

Given a middle-knowledge view of inspiration, when we speak of the biblical writers using the very words God chose, we should not think of those words as being precisely the words God would have chosen had he written or directly dictated Scripture. Otherwise, God ends up improving his grammar and is guilty of occasional editorial fatigue and lapse of memory. It would also become difficult to avoid concluding that the

---

9. In the concluding chapter of their book *Five Views on Biblical Inerrancy*, editors J. Merrick and Stephen M. Garrett write that "the maxim, 'What Scripture says, God says,' is loaded with presumptions begging for clarification" (310).

10. It is possible that a theoretical world exists in which the human writers of Scripture, operating in complete freedom of their wills, never erred in the details they reported. Although *possible*, such a world may not be *feasible* any more than it is feasible that God could create a world of free beings, all of whom freely choose to act in complete holiness all of the time.

psalmist mirrored God's heart when expressing the following against his Babylonian captors: "Happy is the one who seizes your infants and dashes them against the rocks" (Ps. 137:9 NIV). It becomes apparent that the role of the human author was often greater than traditional inerrantists imagine. We have noted in the previous chapter that Scripture is confluent, having dual authorship: God and human. So Scripture should be thought of as the precise words God chose only insofar as he actualized the world in which the biblical writers would freely write what they did. God approved of the Scriptures we have. However, it is not necessarily the case that he regards every word, every analogy, and every illustration, as being ideal. Most often, the *Word of God* should be thought of in the broader sense of being God's message or God's teachings. In fact, it is used in this sense with great frequency in the New Testament where both Jesus's teachings and the message preached in oral form by his apostles and others is called the Word of God (Luke 5:1; 8:4–15; Acts 4:31; 6:2, 7; 11:1; 12:24; 13:7, 46; 2 Cor. 2:17; Col. 1:25; 1 Thess. 2:13; Rev. 1:9; 6:9). Surprisingly, while many of us modern Christians use the term *Word of God* exclusively to refer to Scripture, it is rarely ever used in that sense in the Bible.

This may cast light on an item we previously observed in chapter 2 whereby all three Synoptic Gospels quote Isaiah 40:3 as "make his paths straight." As noted earlier, this rendition of the Isaiah text differs from what we read in the Hebrew ("make straight in the desert a highway for our God" [NIV]) and in the Greek ("make straight the ways of our God" [LXX]). Which one is the divinely inspired text? All three are, as long as we understand inspiration to refer to God's message rather than the very words God would have used had he communicated his message without the use of a human writer.

This conclusion also provides some light in relation to another puzzle. The New Testament quotes or alludes to the Old Testament hundreds of times, the majority of which has the LXX in view. On many occasions, the LXX reads somewhat differently than the Hebrew text. When it does, which is the inspired reading? At first we might think the Hebrew text is, since it is the language in which the majority of the Old Testament texts were written. However, things are not that simple. For the LXX sometimes seems to be rooted in an earlier version of the original Hebrew text than the Hebrew Masoretic text, which is the dominant text used for translating the Old Testament. An observation that leads scholars to this conclusion is that the LXX and Samaritan Pentateuch were translated from the Hebrew texts independently of one another and are often closer to each other than they are to the Hebrew Masoretic text. In such cases, the LXX is often given more weight than the Hebrew Masoretic text. So which text is divinely inspired? Both, as long as we understand inspiration to refer to God's message rather than the very words God would have used had he communicated his message without the use of a human writer.

Let's now return to the standard syllogism used to support a traditional view of biblical inerrancy. I have added some words to clarify what goes unstated by those using it.

1. God cannot err *in any way, including the details.*
2. The Bible is God's Word. *All of the words in the Bible are the very words God spoke.*
3. Therefore, the Bible cannot err *in any way, including the details.*

Stated as such, the logic is valid, but the second premise is false given the reasons stated above—namely, it fails to take seriously the confluence or dual authorship of Scripture and, therefore, requires that God improves his own grammar, is guilty of editorial fatigue and memory lapse, and is happy when infants are killed against rocks. Let's now restate the syllogism with the second premise being revised to reflect a better understanding of *Word of God.*

1. God cannot err *in any way, including the details.*
2. The Bible is God's Word, *in the sense of being God's message (or God's teachings).*
3. Therefore, the Bible cannot err *in any way, including the details.*

In this revised syllogism, both premises are true. However, you can see that nothing in the relationship between the two premises justifies the conclusion that "the Bible cannot err *in any way, including the details.*" Neither syllogism works. The syllogism as understood by traditional inerrantists fails because the second premise is false as they understand it. The syllogism with the revised second premise fails because the logic is invalid.

Admittedly, when we read of Scripture being "God-breathed" and perhaps that its writers had been "carried along by the Holy Spirit," a view of inspiration that has God being more *hands-on*—a singular authorship whereby the biblical writers are practically viewed as transcribers—seems more intuitive than the middle-knowledge view, at least through modern

Western eyes. But the Bible was neither written nor originally read by those with modern Western eyes.[11] The Bible does not reflect a view of inspiration that severely limits the role of the human writers to the extent we find believed by most traditional inerrantists.

2. The Traditional View Is Very Limited in Its Scope

Despite disputes over how inspiration occurred and how inerrancy should be properly understood, there is a fact on which virtually all agree: The Bible we now possess contains some errors in its details. Consider the following discrepancy:

> So David prevailed over the Philistine with the sling and the stone: he struck the Philistine and killed him, and there was no sword in David's hand. (1 Samuel 17:50 NASB 2020)

> And there was war with the Philistines again at Gob, and Elhanan the son of Jaare-oregim the Bethlehemite killed Goliath the Gittite, the shaft of whose spear was like a weaver's beam. (2 Samuel 21:19 NASB 2020)

Who killed Goliath? First Samuel reports that David killed him, whereas 2 Samuel says it was Elhanan. What are we to make of this? Some scholars suggest the error was created by a later copyist of 2 Samuel.[12] They may be correct although other plausible explanations can be found in the commentaries.[13] The books of 1–2 Samuel were originally a single book that was later divided into two. It is unlikely that the author would have made such an error. Regardless of why the discrepancy exists, the matter yields

11. See E. Randolph Richards and Brandon J. O'Brien, *Misreading Scripture with Western Eyes: Removing Cultural Blinders to Better Understand the Bible* (Downers Grove, IL: InterVarsity Press, 2012); and E. Randolph Richards and Richard James, *Misreading Scripture with Individualist Eyes: Patronage, Honor, and Shame in the Biblical World* (Downers Grove, IL: IVP Academic, 2020).

12. Robert D. Bergen, *1, 2 Samuel*, The New American Commentary 7 (Nashville: B&H, 1996), 449; Geisler and Howe, *The Big Book of Bible Difficulties*, 176–77. Geisler and Howe also suggest copyist error as either a possible or probable reason for discrepancies in 1 Samuel 6:19; 2 Samuel 21:19; 1 Kings 4:21; Ezra 2:1ff.; Jeremiah 27:1; and Matthew 8:28–34. Several English translations have corrected 2 Samuel 21:19 and changed "Goliath" to "the brother of Goliath" on the premise that a copyist corrupted the text (NIV, NLT, NET, WEB, KJV, NKJV).

13. For example, see A. A. Anderson, *2 Samuel*, Word Biblical Commentary 11 (Dallas: Word, 1989), 255; A. Graeme Auld, *I & II Samuel: A Commentary*, ed. William P. Brown, Carol A. Newsom, and Brent A. Strawn, 1st ed., The Old Testament Library (Louisville: Westminster John Knox, 2012), 579; Joyce G. Baldwin, *1 and 2 Samuel: An Introduction and Commentary*, Tyndale Old Testament Commentaries 8 (Downers Grove, IL: InterVarsity Press, 1988), 305–6. P. Kyle McCarter Jr., *I Samuel: A New Translation with Introduction, Notes and Commentary*, Anchor Yale Bible 8 (New Haven, CT: Yale University Press, 2008), 291.

an interesting and important fact that requires our consideration: if the original manuscript of Samuel was inerrant in all details and subsequently corrupted in the copying process, we are faced with the knowledge that God allowed the biblical text to be corrupted and that the text we have in our hands today has an error in the details; in fact, several errors, since there are additional instances of discrepancies in Samuel, Kings, and Chronicles.[14]

Evangelical scholars who are strong proponents of a *traditional view* of inerrancy always agree that the doctrine of inerrancy only pertains to the original manuscripts. The CSBI acknowledges that inspiration applies only to the originals or autographs.[15] Here is article 10 of the CSBI:

> We affirm that *inspiration, strictly speaking, applies only to the autographic text of Scripture*, which in the providence of God can be ascertained from available manuscripts with great accuracy. We further affirm that copies and translations of Scripture are the Word of God to the extent that they faithfully represent the original.
>
> We deny that any essential element of the Christian faith is affected by the absence of the autographs. We further deny that this absence renders the assertion of Biblical inerrancy invalid or irrelevant.[16]

In agreement with the *traditional view* of inerrancy, the CSBI is quick to follow up, saying "the authority of Scripture is in no way jeopardized" by the fact that manuscript copies contain errors in the details.[17] I agree with these statements because it is reasonable to hold that God, who is perfect in knowledge, power, and a love so great that it resulted in the incarnation, would ensure everything he desires for us to know is preserved in Scripture with sufficient accuracy. Moreover, the wealth of manuscripts in our possession, especially those of the New Testament literature,[18] allows

---

14. See the following: 1 Kings 4:26 or 2 Chron. 9:25; 1 Kings 16:8 or 2 Chron. 16:1; 1 Chron. 21:1 or 2 Sam. 24:1; 1 Chron. 21:25 or 2 Sam. 24:24; 1 Sam. 31 // 1 Chron. 10 or 2 Sam. 1. Also 1 Sam. 13:1 is missing the portion of the text pertaining to the number of years. (English translations reconstruct as two years [ESV, KJV, NRSV, WEB], twenty-two years [REB], forty years [NET], and forty-two years [CEB, CSB, NIV, NLT, NASB-2020].). The NJB leaves the number blank.

15. The Chicago Statement on Biblical Inerrancy may be viewed at https://library.dts.edu/Pages/TL/Special/ICBI_1.pdf. See also Dockery and Nelson, "Special Revelation," 157; Paul D. Feinberg, "The Meaning of Inerrancy," in *Inerrancy*, ed. Norman L. Geisler (Grand Rapids: Zondervan, 1980), 296.

16. Emphasis added. The "Exposition" of the CSBI articulates the same message.

17. CSBI, Exposition, Transmission, and Translation.

18. The ground on which the Old Testament text rests is not nearly as secure as that on which the New Testament rests.

scholars to reconstruct a critical Greek text of the New Testament that is probably very close to the originals. Even the skeptical New Testament scholar Bart Ehrman, who now refers to himself as an "agnostic-atheist," opines that "scholars are convinced that we can reconstruct the original words of the New Testament with reasonable (although probably not 100 percent) accuracy."[19]

The fact remains, however, that errors in details are peppered throughout our present Bible. Again, it is important to recognize that all scholars who are traditional inerrantists do not claim that our present Bible is inerrant and acknowledge the presence of some errors in the details of it. For them, the Bible you and I read is only inerrant to the extent that it mirrors the originals.

> Most traditional inerrantists affirm the inerrancy of texts we no longer have while denying the inerrancy of the texts we have.

What we have discussed thus far pertains to errors we can identify. Traditional inerrantists sometimes claim that discrepancies are not problematic, since we know where they are located and have plausible solutions. But this overstates the matter. We are often able to identify a discrepancy when the same item appears in parallel texts. However, in the absence of a parallel text, no discrepancy can exist.[20] So a text without a parallel could contain a real error in a detail, and there would be no means for recognizing it. Moreover, since we can identify a few errors in details when a parallel text is present, we cannot rule out the possibility of the presence of errors in details in texts having no parallels, since there is no reason to think copyists lapsed in their focus only when they were aware of the existence of another text containing the same story they were reporting. So there is no way of knowing whether we have identified all of the errors in our current Bible.

There is more. Our current biblical texts contain details that have a reasonable chance of being incorrect despite the fact that a copyist error is unlikely to be the cause. In chapter 3, we observed that Mark 2:26 names

---

19. Bart D. Ehrman, *The New Testament: A Historical Introduction to the Early Christian Writings*, 3rd ed. (New York: Oxford University Press, 2003), 481.

20. Similarly, if all we had was one complete manuscript of the entire Bible, there would be no manuscript variants.

Abiathar as the high priest when David ate the consecrated bread, which appears to contradict the claim of 1 Samuel that it was Abiathar's father Ahimelech.[21] There are three occasions where Mark may be geographically confused.[22] And there are other details that are reasonable candidates for errors. Solutions have been proposed for some if not all of these differences, but they may or may not be correct.[23] However, if we cannot know if those solutions are correct, how can we affirm the inerrancy of those texts in terms of every detail being correct, especially when, as we have seen, the most popular argument for traditional inerrancy fails to yield its intended conclusion? At best, one could only say the Bible in the originals *may have been* inerrant in every detail.

One may ask why God would allow our present Bible to contain some errors in the details. Could he have prevented any errors from entering the texts during the transmission process? There are two ways we may answer.

The first way is to say, "No, God was not able to preserve a text inerrant in all details." But an omnipotent God would be able to preserve a text that's inerrant in every way, unless in doing so it would conflict with another objective he held as preferable. Let's suppose that, being fully aware of human weaknesses, God knew the only way entirely inerrant texts of the Bible could be preserved over the millennia would be for him to violate the free will of several very early copyists to ensure they would perfectly copy the originals or inerrant copies of them and that God would follow this by guiding a multiplicity of circumstances to ensure the preservation of these inerrant manuscripts. However, God preferred that

---

21. Mark 2:25–26 and 1 Samuel 21:1–6; 22:20. In the latter, Ahimelech was priest at the time, and Abiathar was his son. There is significant verbal agreement in the parallel texts of Matthew 12:3–4 and Luke 6:3–4, suggesting Mark is their source. Therefore, it is worth noting that both Matthew and Luke make no mention of Abiathar, which may suggest they were aware of the tension and chose to omit it.

22. The first one appears in Mark 5:1, 13 and pertains to the distance of Gerasa from the Sea of Galilee, since Gerasa is about thirty miles from the Sea of Galilee. Second, in Mark 6:45, Jesus commands his disciples to get in a boat and cross over to Bethsaida, which is on the northeast side of the lake, but they land at Gennesaret, which is on the northwest side (6:53). However, in Matthew 14:22, 34, he commands them to get in a boat and cross over to the other side, and they land in Gennesaret. And in John 6:16–21, his disciples get into a boat, begin to cross to Capernaum, which is also on the northwest side just north of Gennesaret, and land *where they had intended*. For more on this occasion of possible geographical confusion in Mark, see my online article, Mike Licona, "Was Mark Confused Pertaining to the Location of the Feeding of the 5,000?," *Risen Jesus* (blog), August 23, 2016, https://www.risenjesus.com/mark-confused-pertaining-location-feeding-5000. Third, in Mark 7:31, we read of an awkward journey from Tyre through Sidon to the Sea of Galilee in the midst of the region of the Decapolis.

23. For example, Archer, *Encyclopedia*; Geisler and Howe, *The Big Book of Bible Difficulties*; Poythress, *Inerrancy and The Gospels*.

these copyists would act without divine interference. In short, it may have been that God, preferring for all to act freely, could not preserve a text inerrant in every detail without violating the free will of the copyists and others who were involved in the process of preserving those texts (such as storing them in jars in desert caves to be forgotten for many centuries). It seems that something similar could apply to the writers of Scripture. For if God limited his own intervention in the copying process and permitted the copyists to work freely so that the preservation of an entirely inerrant text was not guaranteed, why think the composition process involving the biblical writers was necessarily different in principle? If it was not, we cannot rule out the possibility that the biblical writers unintentionally included some errors in the details within the texts they wrote.

The second way is to say, "Yes, God was able to preserve a text inerrant in all details." God was able to preserve an entirely inerrant text, with or without violating the free wills of the copyists. If this option is correct, it raises an important question: Why didn't he do so? And since it is acceptable to God that the biblical text we have today contains errors in some details, why would it not also have been acceptable to him for the originals to contain errors in some details? We can restate this challenge as follows: God could have preserved an entirely inerrant text. However, he allowed the text to be corrupted to a minor extent during the transmission process in which human elements were involved. Since Scripture is confluent, human elements were likewise present in the composition of Scripture. Thus, if the human element in the transmission process resulted in textual errors, one may reasonably suspect that the human element in the composition process could have resulted in some errors. Furthermore, *since God could have preserved a text without any errors in the details but did not, he must not have thought it was important for us to have such a text.*

In summary, the standard argument supporting traditional inerrancy imagines a role of the biblical writer that is too small and would not result in the Bible we have. Similar to inspiration, traditional inerrancy pertains only to the original manuscripts. Although the existence of parallel texts in the Bible have enabled scholars to identify several discrepancies, at least some of which are the result of copyist error, there may be others that have not been identified, because no parallel texts of them exist. And there are several details that are reasonable candidates for errors in details, despite the best efforts of textual critics. Accordingly, since the Bible we have suggests that the role of the human authors of Scripture was greater than a traditional view of inerrancy imagines, we can say, at most, that the originals *may have been inerrant* in a traditional sense. Finally, since God does not think it's important for us to have Scripture that is inerrant in all of the details it includes, he may not have ensured that the original texts of Scripture were inerrant in all of the details they included.

3. The Traditional View Can Go Too Far

Some traditional inerrantists place an unjustified amount of importance on the doctrine of biblical inerrancy. Norman Geisler held it as being fundamental to the Christian faith.

> By almost any count of fundamentals of the faith, the infallibility and inerrancy of Scripture is to be included, as it is the foundation of all other doctrines. Every other fundamental of the Christian faith is based on the Scripture—if it does not have divine authority, then we have no divine authority for any doctrine to which we adhere. As the basis of all other doctrines, the inerrancy of the Bible is a fundamental of the Fundamentals, and if a fundamental of the Fundamentals is not fundamental, then what is fundamental? The answer is: fundamentally nothing.[24]

Albert Mohler sounds out a dire warning on the dangers of rejecting biblical inerrancy in a traditional sense.

> I do not believe that evangelicalism can survive without the explicit and complete assertion of biblical inerrancy. Given the pressures of late modernity, growing ever more hostile to theological truth claims, there is little basis for any hope that evangelicals will remain distinctly evangelical without the principled and explicit commitment to the inerrancy of the Bible.
>
> Beyond this, inerrancy must be understood as necessary and integral to the life of the church, the authority of preaching, and the integrity of the Christian life.[25]

Many, perhaps most, evangelical scholars, however, would not agree. Michael Bird, an Australian New Testament scholar opines,

> The American inerrancy tradition is not an essential facet of the faith, because most of us outside of North America get on with our mission

---

24. Geisler, *Systematic Theology*, 377.

25. R. Albert Mohler Jr., "When the Bible Speaks, God Speaks," in *Five Views on Biblical Inerrancy*, 31.

> without it, and we are none the worse for not having it! Our churches uphold Scripture as the inspired Word of God. We therefore study it, teach from it, and preach it, but without the penchant to engage in bitter divisions over which nomenclature best suits our theological disposition. While the contexts for the international evangelical church are varied, in no place has it been necessary to construct a doctrine of inerrancy as a kind of fence around evangelical orthodoxy. In what I have observed, such doctrinal fences, far from preserving orthodoxy, tend to divide believers, inhibit Christian witness by assuming a default defensive stance, and risk making the Bible rather than Christ the central tenet of Christian faith. What best represents the international view, in my opinion, is a commitment to the *infallibility* and *authority* of Scripture, but not necessarily a doctrine of Scripture conceived in the specific terms of the American inerrancy tradition as represented in the Chicago Statement on Biblical Inerrancy (CSBI).[26]

Not all traditional inerrantists hold the doctrine of biblical inerrancy with the importance Geisler and Mohler assign to it.

Lens 2: Flexible View of Inerrancy

Traditional inerrantists believe every detail was correct in the originals. Given what we have discussed above, *traditional inerrancy* might be correct. However, we cannot know that it is since we do not have the original manuscripts and the standard argument for *traditional inerrancy* has serious challenges that prevent a justified confidence in its conclusion. Others, like myself, hold what I will refer to as *flexible inerrancy*, which is less extensive than *traditional inerrancy*. Here is a definition of flexible inerrancy to which I can subscribe: *the Bible is true, trustworthy, authoritative, and without error in all that it teaches.* Flexible inerrancy does not concern itself over whether there were errors in details in the original manuscripts. To fret over such is not a profitable exercise, since we do not have any of the originals and have not had them for a very long time, not to mention the other challenges articulated previously. Still, traditional and flexible inerrantists have what is most important in common—that is, both have faith that since God loved us enough to bring about the incarnation, he would ensure that the Scriptures that have come down to

26. Michael F. Bird, "Inerrancy Is Not Necessary for Evangelicalism outside the USA," 146. See also Feinberg, "The Meaning of Inerrancy," 269. For a robust, fair, and well-deserved critique of the more rigid traditional approach to inerrancy, see J. P. Holding and Nick Peters, *Defining Inerrancy: Affirming a Defensible Faith for a New Generation*, 2nd ed. (Orlando, FL: Tekton E-Bricks, 2021).

us in their present form are sufficiently accurate in all that they teach and that God intends for us to know.

Flexible inerrancy fits hand-in-glove with a model of inspiration that includes the confluence of Scripture, that is, its dual authorship. This model of inspiration can be open to the possibility of the presence of some errors *in the autographs*. How? Humans were involved in both the composition and preservation of the biblical texts. God allowed the human element to introduce errors in the text during the transmission process while ensuring that the integrity of Scripture's message was preserved. Similarly, God could have allowed the human element to introduce errors during the composition process while ensuring that the integrity of Scripture's message was preserved.

In fact, this model receives support from the apostle Paul. In the previous chapter, we looked briefly at 2 Corinthians 13:2–3 where Paul mentions Christ speaking through him: "If I come again, I will not spare [anyone], since you seek proof that Christ is speaking through me. He is not weak toward you but is powerful among you." This text appears to be referring to a type of divine inspiration no less than 2 Timothy 3:16, only it is doing so in the sense of Paul's oral communications. This raises some thoughts worth pondering: When Christ was speaking through Paul, in what sense were Paul's utterances divinely inspired? If Paul could experience a memory lapse when writing divinely inspired Scripture (1 Cor. 1:16), there is no reason to think he could not have done so when Christ was speaking through him while preaching. Given all of Paul's preaching over a period of about thirty years, are we to demand that, while he preached, he never once attributed a text to the wrong prophet or unintentionally mislocated an event in the life of Jesus? If Paul's statement "Christ is speaking through me" is an example of what it means to be *theopneustos* ("God-breathed") or "carried along by the Holy Spirit," then *the message* Paul preached derives from God and is approved by God. But to insist that every last word in Paul's preaching was always inerrant in the strictest sense is not something most would want to argue. Now if minor errors of detail could be present *in Paul's preaching* when Christ was speaking through him, why could they not also be present *in Paul's writing* when Christ was speaking through him? This is not to say there were errors in the autographs. It is to say that we cannot know if there were.

Flexible inerrancy is a more modest concept of biblical inerrancy than the traditional view. I prefer it to traditional inerrancy because it is consistent with what we observe in Scripture—imperfections resulting from the human authors, such as Matthew and Luke improving Mark's grammar, editorial fatigue, and memory lapse. Moreover, flexible inerrancy applies to both the originals *and to our present Bible.* Remember that virtually all traditional inerrantists believe that only the original manuscripts of the biblical literature (and those that reflect them perfectly) were inerrant. So when I am having a friendly dispute on the matter of inerrancy with a traditional inerrantist, I like to say, "You may not like the way I define inerrancy, but of the two of us, I'm the only one who believes that our present Bible, the Bible you and I hold in our hands and study, is inerrant."[27]

Four Challenges to the Flexible View Considered

Four challenges to the flexible view of biblical inerrancy need to be addressed, although most of them concern the implications of a flexible view rather than internal problems to the view. I articulate them here in the form of questions and answers.

1. If the Bible Is Not Inerrant in the Traditional Sense, Why Should I Trust Its Theological Statements?

Paul Feinberg was an evangelical theologian and philosopher. He argued that if one admits that the historical statements in the Bible contain some errors, then one has no reason to trust the theological statements in it. For "you stretch the bounds of credulity in asking me to believe all the things that I have no possible way of confirming while at the same time allowing that there are numerous errors in areas that I *can* confirm."[28] But his argument does not follow. Let's say that my wife, Debbie, bumps into one of my friends at the mall who asks her to tell me he has two tickets to Saturday's Atlanta Braves game and is inviting me to go with him. After returning home, she tells me Carl has two tickets to Saturday's Braves game and wants to know if I'd like to go. When I call Carl to accept his invitation, he tells me he didn't see Debbie because he's out of town. When I ask Debbie about it, she tells me she meant to say it was Carlin she saw, and he's inviting me to Saturday's game. I then call Carlin and accept his invitation. A few hours later, Debbie tells me she would really like to go to the local Mexican food restaurant for dinner that evening. I would not be justified in replying, "*Un momento, por favor!* I can't always trust you to report facts with accuracy, facts I am capable of confirming.

27. For translations of the Bible, this definition requires that the critical Hebrew and Greek biblical texts have been translated accurately.

28. Feinberg, "The Meaning of Inerrancy," 281.

Therefore, I also can't always trust you to report things I am incapable of confirming, such as your palatal preference for tonight's dinner." One can make occasional errors in minor details and still be regarded as a reliable source. All of us conduct our lives knowing this. If your parents and your spouse (if you have one) are good people, it is very unlikely that they have always reported details in an inerrant manner. Yet that has not resulted in everything they say being suspect in your eyes. You do not find yourself unable to trust them on anything they report as a result. In fact, you still trust a large majority of everything they report.

Something similar can be said pertaining to the integrity of the Greek text behind English translations of the New Testament. I am not aware of any New Testament scholar who believes that our present critical Greek New Testament text is an exact representation of the original texts. Notwithstanding, a unanimous consensus of scholars believe the text is extremely close to the originals and is an essentially faithful representation of them, though not perfect. Even the iconoclast Bart Ehrman writes,

> The manuscripts of the New Testament do indeed have large numbers of variations in them. . . . But the problem is not of such a scope as to make it impossible to have any idea what the ancient Christian authors wrote. If we had no clue what was originally in the writings of Paul or in the Gospels, this objection might carry more weight. But there is not a textual critic on the planet who thinks this, since not a shred of evidence leads in this direction. . . . As a result, in the vast majority of cases, the wording of these authors is not in dispute.[29]

Ancient and modern historians alike are occasionally guilty of reporting details erroneously while preserving an accurate picture or portrait of an event and what a person had said and even their motives. If an author misstated where an event had occurred or had a confused memory resulting in attributing a statement to a different person, that would not place readers in a position where they could not trust anything else that author had written. Despite the fact that ancient biographers often wrote in a creative manner that goes beyond modern literary conventions, classicists do not despair, thinking they are unable to trust anything the ancient biographers wrote.

---

29. See Bart D. Ehrman, *Did Jesus Exist? The Historical Argument for Jesus of Nazareth*, New York: HarperOne, 2012, 181.

Furthermore, proponents of traditional inerrancy like Feinberg do not recognize that they are already on the wrong side of the conversation. Since Feinberg acknowledges that inerrancy only applies to the originals, he is already in a spot where he must acknowledge the existence of errors of detail in our present Bible.[30] The same argument he offers could easily be applied to the present Bible: if one admits to errors in the historical statements in our present Bible, which I can confirm, there is no reason to trust the theological statements in our present Bible, statements having no possible way of being confirmed. Feinberg anticipates this reply and asserts that it fails since we can usually determine what the originals said with a fair amount of clarity through the use of textual criticism.[31] He is correct—to an extent. But we have already observed that we cannot be confident we have located all copyist errors, and the biblical text contains several instances that have a reasonable chance of being errors of detail for which copyists are probably not the cause.

Even if we knew that all of the historical statements in the Bible are true, that would not ensure that all of the theological statements in it are true. There is simply no method for confirming the theological claims of the Bible. For example, one cannot confirm that Jesus's death atones for sins or that God exists in three persons (i.e., Trinity). Of course, that does not imply we should reject those items that cannot be confirmed, whether historical or theological. It only means that the truth of those items cannot be verified. So my relation to the Bible is one of trust, a trust grounded in the belief that God loves us and desires for us to know him and to live in a holy manner. I trust that God preserved everything we need with sufficient accuracy, just as traditional inerrantists, who acknowledge errors of detail in our present Bible, trust that God preserved everything we need with sufficient accuracy.

One might ask, "Why not just have faith that the Bible is without any error, no matter how small or insignificant?" God nowhere promises us an inerrant Bible. Since the Bible does not describe for us the process(es) of inspiration, we cannot be assured that inspiration did not allow for errors of detail.

30. Feinberg, "The Meaning of Inerrancy," 296.
31. Feinberg, "The Meaning of Inerrancy," 296.

Furthermore, we are not left arbitrarily picking which reports are correct and which are not. Modern historians of antiquity can often discern at least a broad outline of an event or of a person's life. Many times they are even able to verify specifics. Many items in the life and teachings of Jesus can be verified historically, including his resurrection from the dead![32] Moreover, we have good reasons to think the Gospels are historically reliable.[33] So we are by no means left without hope of being able to discern what is true in the New Testament if there are errors in the Bible. Nor are we left with an arbitrary picking and choosing what to accept in the Bible.

2. Is a Flexible View of Inerrancy Based on a Lower View of Scripture than What Traditional Inerrantists Have?

The highest view of Scripture is the one that most accurately reflects Scripture, just as the highest view of God is the one that most accurately reflects God. Jesus taught that not everyone will be saved (Matt. 7:13–14, 21–23; 25:31–46; John 8:21–24). If someone said they have a higher view of God because they believe God will save everyone, I would reply, "The highest view of God is the one that most accurately reflects him rather than a view that reflects how you prefer him to be."

However we may describe Scripture—divinely inspired, infallible, authoritative, or inerrant (however defined)—we should prefer a view consistent with what we observe in Scripture. So if a flexible view of inerrancy is the correct view of Scripture, a traditional view of inerrancy would be a wrong view of Scripture, not a higher view. The correct view of Scripture is the highest view of Scripture.

3. Is a Flexible View of Inerrancy a Step Down a "Slippery Slope" toward Rejecting the Bible?

Those who use "slippery slope" objections almost always do so from a point *they think* is at the top of the hill. Some Christians only read the King James Version and think they stand at the top of the hill because those reading modern English translations have already started down the slope toward rejecting the Bible. Young earth creationists who read modern English

---

32. See my book *The Resurrection of Jesus*.

33. For introductory level reading, see Peter J. Williams, *Can We Trust the Gospels?* (Wheaton, IL: Crossway, 2018); and Paul Barnett, *Is the New Testament Reliable?*, 2nd ed. (Downers Grove, IL: IVP, 2003). For an intermediate level reading, see Craig L. Blomberg, *The Historical Reliability of the Gospels*, 2nd ed. (Downers Grove, IL: IVP Academic, 2007). For a foundational discussion on the reliability of the Gospels, see Michael R. Licona, "Are the Gospels 'Historically Reliable'?," 148.

translations think they stand at the top and that old earth creationists have already started down the slope, while also thinking that those who either embrace or are open to theistic evolution are only a hair's breadth away from denying Jesus's deity! No one thinks they are half-way down the slope.

We should also keep in mind that a hill has more than one slope. Going down the other side of the hill could likewise result in tragedy. A well-meaning but rigid commitment to literal interpretations of some biblical texts resulted in some men in the early church castrating themselves after reading Jesus's statement too literally about some who made themselves eunuchs for God's kingdom (Matt. 19:12; see also 5:29; 18:9). Hermeneutical blunders can have tragic consequences!

Some people who embraced traditional views of inerrancy have gone down a slippery slope that ended with their rejection of the Bible and their embrace of agnosticism or atheism because their view of inerrancy was not in concert with what they observed in the Bible. Because they placed an unjustified amount of importance on inerrancy, the slope was a lot steeper than the grade on the other side of the hill. Rather than a gradual change, taking a single step threw them off balance quickly, causing them to tumble down the hill. They ended up giving up their belief in inerrancy *and their Christian faith*. Michael Bird warns of a danger inherent in a rigid view of inerrancy.

> My point is that if your doctrine of inerrancy means you cannot explain why the evangelists do not agree on the details of Jesus's entrance into Jericho, then your inerrancy model will not last the winter of its own peculiarities or survive the summer of simple queries. Did Jesus heal one blind man on the way out of Jericho (Mark 10:46) or on the way into Jericho (Luke 18:35), or was it two blind men (Matthew 20:29–30)? Can you address these issues without fanciful suggestions like Jesus healed one blind man on the way into Jericho and two blind men on the way out of Jericho? Or can we accept that the evangelists felt free to amend the details in the storytelling? By seeking to define the precise way in which Scripture is true, or not untrue, you risk defining it so narrowly that the first time you find something in Scripture that does not seem to fit, you end up having to choose between a true Bible and a falsified Bible. Inerrancy should not be posed as an alternative to unbelief. As if one is asked: Do you believe in either (a) biblical inerrancy with Mosaic authorship of the Pentateuch, six literal twenty-four-hour days of creation, the historical existence of Jonah and Job, that all the psalms were written by David, the

> four Gospels were written independently, Paul wrote Hebrews, and the book of Revelation should be interpreted in a strictly literal fashion; or (b) a bunch of atheist, Marxist, liberal, secularized, Christ-hating, sacrilegious blasphemy of God's holy word? Trust me, there is an option (c), which I'm trying to lay out for you. Be that as it may, well intentioned as some are in trying to fortify their own doctrine of Scripture with naked assertions of its truthfulness and how it is true, they can inadvertently shatter other people's confidence in the Bible and even shipwreck their faith.[34]

Bird's description of an either-or scenario, which is not uncommon among adherents of the traditional view of inerrancy, is very real and has played out as he describes much more often than we would like to admit. I received the following email within a few hours of my 2019 debate with Christian philosopher Richard Howe on the question of how biblical inerrancy is best understood:[35]

> Hi Professor Licona,
>
> I just stayed up late watching your recent discussion on inerrancy with Richard Howe. I used to be a passionate Christian youth leader. I used to be into apologetics a lot. I still believe in Christ but my convictions about the Bible being inerrant weren't solid and I just slowly walked away from the church. I haven't attended church in a long time.
>
> Maybe I didn't read better books about this whole issue. But the general responses to "contradictions" in the Bible were the same ones Howe kept mentioning in the discussion, even by my pastors. I am currently a graduate student at Johns Hopkins University and I'm not trying to sound cocky but, in all honesty, the responses that Howe gave simply don't meet my expectations of academic rigor. They don't get to the heart of the issue. They just don't satisfy my mind. However, your position on this issue, . . . your view, your rationale makes complete sense to me. You have rejuvenated my trust in the Bible as God's Word. Thank you very much.
>
> James Lopez

---

34. Michael F. Bird, *Seven Things I Wish Christians Knew about the Bible* (Grand Rapids: Zondervan Reflective, 2021), 62–63. I highly recommend Bird's book for further reading on the topic of this chapter.

35. Shared with permission. Richard Howe is brother to Norman Geisler's coauthor Thomas Howe of *The Big Book of Bible Difficulties*. Richard and I publicly debated the topic of how inerrancy is best understood on October 11, 2019. The debate may be viewed at https://youtu.be/rLwnjx6-5dc?si=HuPWD1CmIC7vZWUm.

I thanked Mr. Lopez for his encouraging comments. Two years later, I sent a follow-up email inquiring as to how he was doing. He replied saying that his faith in Christ has been thriving ever since.

Ricardo Mora is a high school teacher in California. In September 2019, he sent me an email telling me he had lost his faith while attending USC but got it back later. He then attended a major Christian university that requires students to embrace a traditional view of inerrancy and earned a master's degree there that focused on Christian apologetics. Gospel differences especially troubled him. He read books on resolving Bible difficulties by Gleason Archer, Norman Geisler, and Thomas Howe. But he found himself unpersuaded by many of their proposed solutions, saying that "a lot of times their explanations of the Bible difficulties were more difficult than the difficulty itself." In September 2019, Mr. Mora was listening to William Lane Craig's podcast and heard him recommend my 2017 book on differences in the Gospels. He bought it, read it, and then sent me an email saying how my book had helped him profoundly. Having his permission, I share how he ended his email:

> I am so thankful for what you have done here Mr. Licona. I am crying right now as I write these words, and I'm a guy; I don't usually cry. It's been 22 years of searching for an answer, praying for some form of insight, hoping that my mind would one day be at peace. It is finally at peace. . . . Now the very differences that caused me so much worry and doubt are turning into markers of authenticity. I can finally trust these accounts again. . . . Your work is crucial for young adults to know as they enter college! What happened to me can be avoided. Please don't stop doing what you do.

Many others have sent me similar comments. When they read the Gospels in view of the compositional devices classicists and many New Testament scholars have mentioned for decades, they gained a better sense of what the Evangelists were doing that resulted in the differences in how they report the same events. The differences troubled them because they had placed too much importance on a traditional view of inerrancy, especially a more rigid form of it. When strained harmonizations failed to satisfy, their faith weakened, and the vitality of their Christian life evaporated. But then they learned about the use of compositional devices by ancient biographers and the four Evangelists. They learned that a flexible understanding of inerrancy makes more sense of the biblical text that we have than more traditional understandings of inerrancy. The experience revitalized their faith and invigorated their walk with Christ. It turns out that a traditional view of inerrancy has been a dangerous doctrine for some readers of the Bible.

But the converse is also true: taking a flexible view of inerrancy could lead some who place too much weight on a traditional view of inerrancy and have a rigid view of truth-telling to lose their confidence in the Bible and abandon their faith. Still, I think there is greater safety for believers in taking a flexible approach. There is a difference between *insulating* and *inoculating* others. Many traditional inerrantists insulate their fellow believers by ignoring the differences, downplaying or denying that they exist, discouraging others from discussing them, or saying we may not know the answer but can trust that Scripture is inerrant in every detail. They may also address some of the more easily explained discrepancies in the Gospels and lead others to assume all discrepancies are addressed as effortlessly.

Inoculation differs from insulation. When I was fifty-seven years old, I received two vaccination shots for shingles. The pharmacist injected me with the varicella-zoster virus so that my immune system would learn to deal with the virus effectively and prevent me from getting shingles, a viral infection related to varicella (chicken pox). The immediate side-effects from each shot were unpleasant. However, the shots have prevented me from getting shingles. Exposing my brothers and sisters in Christ to the various compositional devices used by ancient biographers, a middle-knowledge model of inspiration, and a flexible view of inerrancy could cause one to feel some initial discomfort, especially if they have embraced a more rigid form of the traditional view of inerrancy. But given a little time, the mind can process these things and build immunity against skeptics when they raise the matter of differences in the Gospels. Once one understands the nature of the differences in the Gospels and why they are there, they are not nearly as troublesome. In fact, they may not bother you at all. If they do, you may just need some time to process. Instead of insulating my fellow believers from difficult matters, I prefer to inoculate them by exposing them to the matters and helping them think through them. I know that such an approach would have been helpful to me when I was first troubled by differences in the Gospels.[36]

Embracing a flexible view of inerrancy should by no means result in giving up the Bible and Christianity. *Christianity is true because of the person of Jesus and his resurrection. If Jesus rose from the dead, it's game, set, match.*

---

36. See my account of this experience at the beginning of chapter 1.

Christianity is true—period! Thousands became followers of Jesus during the decades before any of the New Testament literature was written. If none of the New Testament literature had ever been written, Christianity would still be true. We just would not know much about Jesus.

4. Is *Inerrant* the Best Term to Describe the Bible?

The doctrine of biblical inerrancy was the theme of the 2013 Annual Meeting of the Evangelical Theological Society. During that conference, there was a panel discussion featuring contributors to the book *Five Views on Biblical Inerrancy*.[37] Panelists were asked whether it was still important to use the term *inerrant* to describe the Bible. Four of the five contributors were present.[38] Al Mohler answered that it is still important to use the term *inerrant*, while Michael Bird, John Franke, and Peter Enns stated that they thought the term was useful but needed to take on a more nuanced meaning.[39] Although the fifth contributor, Kevin Vanhoozer, was absent, in the book he writes, "I regularly refuse to say whether I hold to inerrancy until my interlocutor defines the term (or allows me to do so)."[40]

In the book *The Lost World of Scripture: Ancient Literary Culture and Biblical Authority*, John Walton and Brent Sandy assert that "we need to adjust our understanding of inerrancy to the evidence we find in Scripture."[41] Some conservative biblical scholars prefer other terms to *inerrant*. N. T. Wright says he does not like describing the Bible using any terms that begin with *in-* (e.g., inerrant, infallible). Instead, Wright prefers to describe the Bible as *reliable*.[42] Ben Witherington prefers *truthful* and *trustworthy*.[43] Michael Bird and Kevin Vanhoozer prefer *infallible* but define the term differently.[44] I also prefer these terms to *inerrant*. In my opinion, we have

---

37. Merrick and Garrett, *Five Views on Biblical Inerrancy*.

38. Kevin Vanhoozer was absent.

39. An MP3 sound recording of the panel discussion may be purchased from WordMp3 at http://www.wordmp3.com/details.aspx?id=15848.

40. See Kevin J. Vanhoozer, "Augustinian Inerrancy: Literary Meaning, Literal Truth, and Literate Interpretation in the Economy of Biblical Discourse" in *Five Views on Biblical Inerrancy*, 206.

41. John H. Walton and D. Brent Sandy, *The Lost World of Scripture: Ancient Literary Culture and Biblical Authority* (Downers Grove, IL: IVP Academic, 2013), 196; cf. 303.

42. See "Ask N. T. Wright Anything 7: Bible Infallibility, Sola Scriptura and Slavery," on *Unbelievable* (podcast), by Justin Brierley, timestamp 4:19–5:48, https://www.premierunbelievable.com/ask-nt-wright-anything/ask-nt-wright-anything-7-bible-infallibility-sola-scriptura-and-slavery/12214.article.

43. Ben Witherington III, "The Truth Will Out: An Historian's Perspective on the Inerrancy Controversy," in *Journal of the Evangelical Theological Society* 57, no. 1 (2014): 20, https://www.etsjets.org/files/JETS-PDFs/57/57-1/JETS_57-1_19-27_Witherington.pdf.

44. Michael F. Bird, "Saving Inerrancy from the Americans," *Word from the Bird* (blog), posted

arrived at a time when *inerrant* may not be the best term for describing the Bible. Many like myself still use it but do so in nuanced terms.

TOP-DOWN AND BOTTOM-UP APPROACHES TO SCRIPTURE

What we mean when we say, "Scripture is inspired," should be informed by the claims of Scripture about itself *and* by the nature of Scripture. Too often, the nature of Scripture is considered only superficially while Scripture's claims about itself are loaded with preconceived ideas of what divinely inspired Scripture should look like. The resulting view of Scripture then fails to line up with what we observe in Scripture. Nevertheless, that view of Scripture ends up being freeze-dried, prepackaged, approved by certain authorities, and sold for consumption. Consumers in the pews are then told, "This is what you will eat. It's good for you!" But it's missing important ingredients that were overlooked.

We are not obligated to purchase a view of Scripture that lacks literary sensitivity. Known worldwide as the "dean of evangelical scholarship,"[45] F. F. Bruce was no theological liberal or progressive. J. I. Packer, one of the three theologians who crafted the Chicago Statement on Biblical Inerrancy, wrote of Bruce, "No man ever did more to demonstrate how evangelical faith and total academic integrity may walk hand in hand."[46] Bruce's comments on divine inspiration are worth pondering.

> I should not find the career of a Bible teacher so satisfying as I do if I were not persuaded that the Bible is God's word written. The fact that I am so persuaded means that I must not come to the Bible with my own preconceptions of what the Bible, as God's word written, can or cannot say. . . . Occasionally, when I have expounded the meaning of some biblical passage in a particular way, I have been asked, "But how does that square with inspiration?" But inspiration is not a concept of which I have a clear understanding before I come to the study of the text, so that I know in advance what limits are placed on the meaning of the text by the requirements of inspiration. On the contrary, it is by the patient study

---

November 10, 2021, at https://michaelfbird.substack.com/p/saving-inerrancy-from-the-americans?; Kevin J. Vanhoozer, "Response to Michael F. Bird," in *Five Views on Biblical Inerrancy*, 188.

45. Quoted from website devoted to F. F. Bruce's legacy at https://www.ffbruce.com/.

46. J. I. Packer, "Foreword" in F. F. Bruce, *In Retrospect: Remembrance of Things Past*, Paternoster / Baker, 1980; revised edition, Marshall Pickering / Baker, 1993; Ebook, Kingsley Books, 2017, Kindle Edition, loc. 5093–5104.

> of the text that I come to understand better not only what the text itself means but also what is involved in biblical inspiration. My doctrine of Scripture is based on my study of Scripture, not *vice versa*.
>
> The question, "How does that square with inspiration?" is perhaps asked most insistently when one part of Scripture seems to conflict in sense with another. I suppose much depends on the cast of one's mind, but I have never been bothered by "apparent discrepancies," nor have I been greatly concerned to harmonize them. My faith can accommodate such "discrepancies" much more easily than it could swallow harmonizations that place an unnatural sense on the text or give an impression of special pleading.[47]

Ben Witherington expresses similar thoughts: "I take it as a fundamental axiom that I should not bring my theology to the text, and then tell the text what it must say in order to be consistent with my presuppositions about the Bible being God's word and being truthful."[48]

Bruce and Witherington take what we can refer to as a *bottom-up approach*. They begin by looking at Scripture, observing it carefully for what it is and what it says about itself, and then forming a view of Scripture that is consistent with both. In contrast, many well-meaning followers of Jesus take a *top-down approach*.[49] They begin with certain assumptions (e.g., how *Word of God* must be understood), form a model of what divinely inspired Scripture must be like, and then read Scripture in view of that model. But then they run into numerous items in the Gospels that do not quite fit with their model. When this occurs, they appeal to mystery and resort to harmonization efforts that are sometimes so strained that it can be seen as subjecting Matthew, Mark, Luke, and John to hermeneutical waterboarding until each yields to the harmonizer and tells him or her what they want to hear. This is not treating Scripture with reverence or to have a high view of it. This is a good time to reiterate principle 2, which I commended to you in the previous chapter:

> If I truly have a high view of Scripture, I will embrace it as God has given it to us rather than insist that it conform to a model shaped by how I think he should have given it. If I refuse to do this, I may sincerely believe that I hold a high view of Scripture when I actually hold a high view of my view of Scripture.

---

47. F. F. Bruce, *In Retrospect: Remembrance of Things Past*, loc. 5093–5104 (Kindle).
48. Witherington, *The Living Word of God*, xv. See also 60–61, 72.
49. I am indebted to Mark L. Strauss for suggesting that I contrast these two approaches.

WHY THIS IS IMPORTANT

During the time for audience questions after my lectures on the topic of Gospel differences, I have often been asked how my approach is compatible with the inspiration and inerrancy of Scripture. Many are comfortable with the authors of the Gospels rounding numbers, using approximations and minor paraphrasing. They are even comfortable with attributing a message or action to a specific person when it had actually been an emissary of that person who had delivered the message or performed the action. After all, these devices are typical in today's reporting, and we use them in our everyday communications without giving them any thought.

But what about other devices, such as telling a story in a manner that gives the impression that an event had occurred over a shorter period of time or even at a different time or location than it actually had occurred? What about knowingly attributing a statement made by one person to another? Some are uncomfortable with these moves because they bend the raw facts differently, sometimes further than the other devices they accept. Because they do not use such devices in their communications, they lack familiarity with them and struggle to acknowledge when ancient authors used them. Some may even assert, "Since God is the ultimate author, he would not have allowed the use of certain compositional devices because doing so would be to deceive readers." In making this assertion, however, the person is assuming what God would and would not do. But would it not be prudent to observe Scripture carefully to see what God, in fact, did?

> *To have faith in God's Word does not mean that we stand firm on our particular church's traditions or on our theoretical presuppositions about how God should have inspired Scripture (how we would have done it ourselves, we mean, had we been infinite) rather than on careful examination of how he chose to do so. It means that we trust whatever God speaks as reliable, and, because we share the view that Scripture is God-inspired (see 2 Tim 3:16; 2 Pet 1:20–21), that we stand in awe of it (Ezra 10:3; Ps 119:120, 161; cf. Isa 66:2, 5), and therefore devote our most diligent interpretive effort to honestly discerning and embracing its message (Ezra 7:10).*
>
> —Craig Keener[50]

50. Craig S. Keener, *Spirit Hermeneutics: Reading Scripture in Light of Pentecost* (Grand Rapids: Eerdmans, 2016), 198.

Our view of divine inspiration should not require the Evangelists to write about Jesus using modern conventions of truth-telling in biography. For if the literary conventions of ancient biography permitted biographers to employ compositional devices that altered some details while preserving an essentially faithful representation of what occurred, and if the Gospel authors used compositional devices to this effect, then this is what truth-telling in divinely inspired Scripture looks like, and those who make accusations of deceit end up unintentionally pointing their fingers at God. We must keep in mind that the Gospels were written nearly two millennia before we were born. They have not since changed. However, the objectives and rules for writing biography have. We should no more fault the ancient authors for having different conventions than we would want historians living a thousand years from now faulting us for doing things differently than they. Because the Evangelists and their readers belonged to a different culture than our own, we will benefit from keeping the following statement in mind: the Bible was written *for us* but not *to us.*

I do not think the compositional devices examined in this book create errors in the texts of the Gospels any more than an abbreviated version of recalling words and events creates errors. There is the occasional contradiction in surface details. But the essential elements of the stories remain the same. Nevertheless, just as some object to how an abbreviated version can be somewhat loose with nonessential details when recalling events, some can be averse to the proposal that the Evangelists would alter nonessential details when using the various compositional devices that were in the toolbox of every other biographer in that era. After all, we are talking about Holy Scripture. Therefore, I have discussed the topics of inspiration and inerrancy so you may see that even if one regards such editorial work to have produced errors, this would only threaten some traditional views of inspiration and inerrancy that are already on unstable ground. I believe the views of inspiration and inerrancy I have proposed in this book are on far more solid ground, being consistent with both the claims and nature of Scripture. These views easily accommodate all of the compositional devices we have examined, including the more radical ones (such as composite citations and the repurposing of Scripture).

What I have presented in these two chapters is not intended to be an exhaustive treatment of the doctrines of the inspiration and inerrancy of Scripture. Neither am I proposing that they should be the final words on these subjects. What I have offered is intended only to show that the compositional devices I have examined and demonstrated to have been used by the Evangelists do not challenge the doctrines of the inspiration and inerrancy of Scripture, although doubt is cast on some ways of understanding those doctrines.

The views of the inspiration and inerrancy of Scripture being proposed in this book may not be as tight as some prefer. They do not answer the matter of whether there were errors in details in the originals and are, in fact, quite open to them. As I have encouraged throughout this book, we should hold a view of Scripture that is consistent with what we observe in Scripture and with the teachings of Scripture about itself. Because we cannot offer, what is to my thinking at least, a conclusive argument that the originals were inerrant in every detail, it would be prudent to refrain from defining inspiration and inerrancy more precisely than Scripture does.[51] That said, when we view the Scriptures through the lenses of the traditional and flexible views of biblical inerrancy, it is the flexible view that brings the Scriptures into greater focus, having far more harmony between what Scripture says about itself and the phenomena we observe in it.

SUMMARY

We have viewed Scripture through two lenses in this chapter—traditional inerrancy and flexible inerrancy. *Traditional inerrancy* holds that the Bible is inerrant in every detail in the original manuscripts. This view is grounded in the nature and character of God and contends that Scripture is necessarily without error in all of its details because it proceeds from God, who cannot err. However, the argument fails to deliver the desired conclusion. To assert that the Bible is God's speech in written form and that every word in it is ideally how God would have written it oversimplifies a complex matter, which can be beneficial if not taken too far. However, problems often arise when it is.

51. Lest one suspect that I have been toying with a progressive form of Christianity, I wish to be clear that I am an evangelical Christian without apology. Because there is no standard definition of *evangelical*, let me be clear that I believe God exists, that he created all things, that Jesus was born of a virgin and is deity as God's uniquely divine Son whose death on the cross has atoning qualities, that he rose bodily from the dead and will return, and that the Bible is divinely inspired, true, trustworthy, authoritative, and without error in all that it teaches. While I acknowledge that a traditional understanding of biblical inerrancy is possibly true, I do not think it is. Instead, I hold a flexible view of inerrancy, which I have described and defined in this chapter. I believe that I have a vibrant relationship with God and so can others without holding a traditional view of inerrancy. In fact, I know of many who have a vibrant walk with the Lord and do not claim to be an inerrantist in any sense.

To say the Bible is "God's speech in written form" assigns too small a role to its human authors and assumes a type of inspiration that would not result in the Bible we have. *And* an incorrect concept of inspiration begets an incorrect concept of inerrancy. Scripture is confluent, having both divine and human authors. Moreover, traditional inerrancy limits the inerrancy of the biblical text to the original manuscripts. Although copyist errors plausibly account for many errors in details in the present biblical texts, several details are present that have a reasonable chance of being errors in the original manuscripts. Therefore, the most that traditional inerrantists are justified in claiming is that the original manuscripts *may have been inerrant* in every detail.

Flexible inerrancy holds that the Bible is inerrant in all that it teaches. It is preferable to traditional inerrancy because it is consistent with what we observe in Scripture—imperfections resulting from the human authors, such as Matthew and Luke improving Mark's grammar, editorial fatigue, and memory lapse. Flexible inerrancy is more encompassing than the traditional view since it applies to the originals and to our present Bible, whereas the traditional view of inerrancy only applies to the originals, which we no longer have. Moreover, the flexible view of inerrancy is entirely consistent with a middle-knowledge model of divine inspiration.

It is time to recalibrate our thinking about biblical inerrancy. It is indisputable that God could have preserved a text that is inerrant in every way and chose not to. Because he did not preserve an inerrant text, he must not regard it as being important for us to have a Bible that is inerrant in every way. It seems then that the doctrine of biblical inerrancy in a traditional sense is far less important to God than it is to some of its proponents. Many evangelical scholars are now calling for nuanced definitions of *inerrancy* or for abandoning the term altogether in favor of others. I mentioned a few alternatives above, such as *reliable*, *infallible*, *truthful*, *trustworthy*, and *authoritative*.

The intentional use of compositional devices by an ancient author resulted in details being altered. Sometimes this created surface inconsistencies while the essence of the reports remained the same. This is entirely consistent within a flexible view of inerrancy. Even if one were to think the Bible contains some errors in details, this need not diminish one's faith in the message and teachings of Jesus, since much of them, including his resurrection, can be verified with reasonable confidence using the tools of historians. We are now in a position where we can have a harmonious union of our view of Scripture and what we observe in Scripture.

QUESTIONS FOR FURTHER THOUGHT

1. What are your thoughts about the definition of inerrancy I offered? *The Bible is true, trustworthy, authoritative, and without error in all that it teaches.* (Flexible inerrancy applies to the original manuscripts *and* to our present Bible.)
2. Do you think the doctrine of biblical inerrancy as understood by traditional inerrantists is fine as it stands, or should it be nuanced or abandoned? Why or why not?
3. If you knew for certain that the Bible contained some errors in the originals, would that impact your faith in a negative manner? Why or why not?
4. Would you describe the Bible as *inerrant* or do you prefer a different term, such as *reliable*, *truthful*, *trustworthy*, *infallible*, or *authoritative*? If you prefer *inerrant*, do you describe yourself as an inerrantist in a traditional or flexible sense?

CHAPTER 13

FINAL THOUGHTS

For my final semester in college as a music major, I used my remaining elective to take a course in Koine Greek, the language in which the New Testament was written. I recall that, after learning how to pronounce Greek, I read the words of Jesus in one of the Gospels out loud and had the thought, "This must be how it sounded when Jesus said these exact words!" It was a nice thought. But I was naïve. Although Jesus very likely was conversant in Greek, when he was speaking to other Jews, which was most of the occasions reported in the Gospels, he spoke in Aramaic. So, at the very most, what I am reading in the Gospels is more often than not the remembered words of Jesus having been translated into Greek. And that is when I am reading my Greek New Testament. When I am reading my English New Testament, I am reading a translation of a translation.

One need not feel alarmed by this. For although nuance is sometimes lost in translation, translations usually get it right, and good Bible commentaries provide insights lost in both the translation process and from not understanding the cultural settings in which the biblical literature were written.[1] My point, however, is that I had a very literal or rigid view of what I was reading in the Gospels that began to crack when I realized that most of the time I was not reading the actual words Jesus had uttered. Further cracks in such a view became visible when I compared what Jesus and other characters in the Gospels say in their parallel accounts and observed differences in them. It becomes very clear that, at least most of the time, the Gospels are not precise transcripts of what was said. And we have observed that the same can be said about Jesus's actions.

1. One notable exception is the *New World Translation*, which is published and used by the Jehovah's Witnesses. It is often a very poor English translation that is largely influenced by the theological beliefs of the translators.

OVERPLAYING ONE'S HAND

So what are we to make of the differences in the Gospels? Skeptics are often quick to answer, "Error," and then judge the Gospels as being unreliable in their historical reporting. But that response makes too much of the differences. Many of the same sorts of differences exist between reports in other ancient historical literature. We observed in chapter 7 that the numerous ancient accounts of Julius Caesar being assassinated are rife with differences, even inconsistencies. Who delayed Antony from entering the theatre where the senate was to meet with Caesar? Where did the first strike by a conspirator land on Caesar? What did Caesar then say? How many speeches did Brutus give in the aftermath and when did he give them or it? How many times did the senate meet to discuss what had occurred and how best to respond? Did Cicero play a major or minor role in those meetings? Why did the people turn against the conspirators? What did Antony do with Caesar's robe during his eulogy?

Ancient sources answer these questions with conflicting details. However, I am not aware of any historian who questions whether Caesar was assassinated on the Ides of March, 44 BC. I am not aware of any historian who thinks the accounts are so hopelessly contradictory that, although they acknowledge Caesar was assassinated on that day, they are reluctant to assert we can be assured of little else about what happened on that day and on those that immediately followed. I am not aware of any historian who claims the accounts do not provide readers with an accurate gist, an essentially faithful representation of what happened on that day and its immediate aftermath. As Christopher Pelling, the foremost authority on Plutarch, has stated, such reports are "true *enough*."[2] Well, what's sauce for the goose is sauce for the gander. If differences among the Gospels, which are no more excessive than those observed among other ancient histories and biographies, render them historically unreliable sources, the same must be said of virtually all other ancient histories and biographies. Only the more radical of postmodern historians may be willing to take such a pessimistic view of the historian's ability to know about the past.

We have observed some of the same types of differences between parallel accounts in Plutarch's *Lives* that we observe in the Gospels.

---

2. Christopher Pelling, *Plutarch and History: Eighteen Studies* (Swansea: Classical Press of Wales, 2002), 160.

And we came to understand how many of the differences were introduced. Plutarch edits his sources according to the standard literary conventions he and others of his era were taught. The Evangelists, or more probably the secretaries who assisted them, would also have learned these literary conventions and edited their sources accordingly. This accounts for many of the differences in both Plutarch's *Lives* and the Gospels. When peering through the lens of compositional devices, virtually all of the differences between the Gospels cited by skeptics seem inconsequential. Ben Witherington rightly observes that "rumors of the [New Testament] being riddled with errors are greatly exaggerated. Indeed, when all is properly taken into consideration, we are hard pressed to find any real or significant errors at all."[3]

Though our focus throughout this book has been differences in the Gospels, there is another matter that should not be overlooked: similarities. When one compares how Matthew and Luke use and edit Mark with how Plutarch edits his sources, the similarities in how the Synoptic Gospels report the same events are nothing short of stunning. Matthew and Luke exercise far less editorial freedom than do Plutarch or the Jewish authors Philo and Josephus.

BEHOLD THE LOG IN YOUR EYE

Just as skeptics can go too far with their assessments, so too can pious believers. Views of Scripture that are incongruent with what we observe in Scripture are all too common and often result from top-down approaches to forming a doctrine of Scripture. These approaches often prefer to harmonize differences, sometimes even to a strained extent. When God affirmed Jesus at his baptism, did he speak to Jesus or to the crowd? Those committed to harmonizing may suggest that he spoke twice. Did the centurion go to Jesus directly to request that he heal his servant, or did he send emissaries? Those committed to harmonizing may suggest that both are true: he sent emissaries then soon after decided to go to Jesus and make his request in person. Although harmonizations should not be ruled out automatically, they often have the appearance of being created with the objective of rescuing a Bible that is in trouble.

---

3. Witherington, *The Living Word of God*, 81.

STANDING ON BETTER GROUND

There is a ground on which we can read Scripture without being naïve. Operating on that ground involves understanding the cultural settings and literary conventions for writing biography that were in play in the first century. A biographer in the first century writing for others living in the first century about a person who had lived in the first century is going to use the standard literary conventions for writing biography in the first century rather than those that would not come into play until more than a thousand years later.

The Gospels are ancient biographies of Jesus, largely rooted in the testimonies of eyewitnesses and those who had known them. The Gospels do not belong to the genre of modern biography. The importance of this statement makes it worth repeating: *the Gospels do not belong to the genre of modern biography*. They participate in the genre of ancient biography, and that genre had literary conventions that differ from modern versions. Classicists and New Testaments scholars alike are unanimous in their opinion that ancient biographers enjoyed a greater flexibility for reporting details than modern biographers are allowed. So we should approach the texts with this expectation in mind.

As Craig Keener opines, "Unless we artificially impose on the Gospels the standards of modern genres that did not yet exist in their day and that barely anyone expected, such variations are not problematic."[4] Ben Witherington similarly comments,

> One must judge a document on the basis of what it intends or attempts to accomplish, and within the contexts of the conventions it is observing. When one does that, it is not hard to say with a straight face that, yes, these books deserve to be considered words of God preserved in human words, written up according to existing standards and conventions so they would be a truthful and fruitful word on target for their original audiences.[5]

David Dockery and David Nelson state:

---

4. Craig S. Keener, *Spirit Hermeneutics: Reading Scripture in Light of Pentecost* (Grand Rapids: Eerdmans, 2016), 196.

5. Witherington, *The Living Word of God*, 61.

> When the Bible reports matters as history, they are intended to be understood as historical—though not necessarily with the kind of precisions expected of modern historiography. We should, however, expect and even require a precision that is in keeping with the standards of the time when the text was written.[6]

Judging ancient historical literature by modern standards is like judging a fish negatively for its inability to fly, a bird because it cannot swim, a portrait painted in the seventeenth century because it includes items not present at the sitting, and parables because they are not recollections of historical events and actual conversations.

We do not suggest the psalmist is mistaken when saying God was asleep (Ps. 44:23). Neither do we think the teacher believed that Wisdom is an actual woman who shouts in the streets and square, encouraging people to listen to her and warning them of the consequences of neglecting to do so (Prov. 1:20–33). Nor do we think Jesus was in error when mentioning fictitious characters in his parables. The reason is because we understand that wisdom literature and parables are not intended to be understood in a historical sense.

In contrast, we expect accuracy of great precision in modern histories and transcripts of legal depositions and court trials. But we do not fault movies such as *Gone With The Wind* (1939) and *Titanic* (1997) for combining truth and fiction. We understand upfront that the genre in which the movie is cast permits it, so we adjust our expectations accordingly. In other movies we find a closer affinity with what we would have seen had we been there. For example, the movie *Apollo 13* (1995) has been praised by critics for its accurate portrayal of events. Still, some dramatic license was taken by director Ron Howard.[7] In one of its most memorable scenes, the team members at Mission Control were discussing how to get the astronauts back to Earth safely when they realized that the CO^2 filters in the lunar module were not built to accommodate the unanticipated third astronaut. The flight director Gene Kranz was played by actor Ed Harris. In the movie Harris (as Kranz) told the team to work the problem because "Failure is not an option!" This line became an unforgettable tagline for

---

6. David S. Dockery and David P. Nelson, "Special Revelation" in *A Theology for the Church*, ed. Daniel L. Akin (Nashville: B&H Academic, 2007), 118–74, esp. 148.

7. See the *Apollo 13* DVD special features on Disc 1, "Lost Moon: The Triumph of Apollo 13," including feature commentary with director Ron Howard and feature commentary with Jim and Marilyn Lovell (Howard, 1995). The 1995 motion picture is based on the book *Lost Moon: The Perilous Voyage of Apollo 13* by Jim Lovell and Jeffrey Kluger (Boston: Houghton Mifflin, 1994).

the movie, epitomized the attitude of the entire team at Mission Control, and was selected to be the title of a subsequent book written by Kranz.[8] However, Kranz did not utter that statement on that occasion. Neither did it originate with him.

In September 2022, I spoke at a church in the Houston area where my friend Gary Hamrick was a pastor at the time. Knowing of my longtime fascination with the Apollo program and that as a kid I had dreamed of being an astronaut, Gary asked if I would like to meet Charles "Chuck" Gruby, who was Kranz's best friend. My eyes lit up and I said, "Absolutely!" We went to Gruby's home. When he answered the door, Chuck's face exhibited his excitement at seeing Gary whom he knew well. He invited us in. Chuck was eighty-seven years old and had been struggling with his health, which now required him to carry an oxygen tank everywhere. As I entered his home, I looked around and observed all sorts of photographs and memorabilia from his career with NASA. As we talked about his time with Apollo, I could see that his mind was still sharp. At one point, he took Gary and me into a small room, which was his home office. He showed us several thick binders with the very notes he and others at Mission Control had used during the Gemini and Apollo missions. He then showed us several photographs of a plane he had built. On his wall was a document signed by all those who had worked the Apollo missions at Mission Control. My eyes were then drawn to a photograph of Gruby and Kranz. I asked him about Kranz. He said Ed Harris had played him in an impressive manner that captured Kranz with uncanny accuracy. I said, "I want to ask you about a statement attributed to Kranz in the movie *Apollo 13*: 'Failure is not an option!'" Chuck chimed in before I could go further. "Ah, yes. I asked Gene if he had said that, and he said, 'No. But I wish that I had!'" The three of us laughed and chatted some more. After spending more than an hour with Chuck, he gave me his contact information and invited me to contact him anytime I would like to chat. Sadly, Chuck had a further setback in health only a few days later, was admitted into the local hospital, and died exactly one week after our visit.

So what is the origin of the statement "Failure is not an option"? In his autobiography, Kranz describes the efforts of the Mission Control team to formulate "workaround" options during the Apollo 13 flight: "These three astronauts were beyond our physical reach. But not beyond the reach

8. Gene Kranz, *Failure Is Not an Option: Mission Control from Mercury to Apollo 13 and Beyond* (New York: Simon & Schuster, 2001).

of human imagination, inventiveness, and a creed that we all lived by: 'Failure is not an option.'"[9] Was this a formalized creed or more of an unstated attitude shared by all?

Jerry Bostick, NASA's flight dynamics officer for Apollo 13, provides the answer. In a conversation with NASA engineer Jerry Woodfill, Bostick said the following when recounting his interview by the scriptwriters of *Apollo 13*:

> One of their questions was "Weren't there times when everybody, or at least a few people, just panicked?" My answer was "No, when bad things happened, we just calmly laid out all the options, and failure was not one of them. We never panicked, and we never gave up on finding a solution." I immediately sensed that Bill Broyles wanted to leave and assumed that he was bored with the interview. Only months later did I learn that when they got in their car to leave, he started screaming, "That's it! That's the tag line for the whole movie, Failure is not an option. Now we just have to figure out who to have say it." Of course, they gave it to the Kranz character, and the rest is history.[10]

Gene Kranz did not utter "Failure is not an option" on the occasion portrayed in the movie. Instead, it was assigned to him by the scriptwriters (transferal) who had the task of telling the story of events spanning six days in less than two and a half hours. Sometimes precision was sacrificed to communicate the essence of what occurred. That is good writing, and it is an accurate portrayal of Kranz and his team, though not in a precise sense.

How about one more example. In Mel Gibson's epic movie *The Passion of the Christ*, we understand that when Jesus stomps on the snake in Gethsemane, it's a nice allusion to Genesis 3:15 where God tells the serpent that the offspring of Eve will crush its head. But we are not put off by the fact that Jesus probably did not fulfill prophecy in Gethsemane that evening by killing a snake. One of the most touching scenes in that movie is when Jesus stumbles while carrying his cross, his mother runs to him and he tells her, "Behold, I am making all things new." Then he picks up the cross, embraces it in an almost loving manner, and moves on

9. Gene Kranz, *Failure Is Not an Option*, New York: Simon & Schuster, 2001, 12.

10. Recounted by Jerry Woodfill in an interview with Nancy Atkinson. See Nancy Atkinson, "13 More Things That Saved Apollo 13, Part 12: The 'Trench' Band of Brothers," *Universe Today: Space and Astronomy News*, May 5, 2015, https://www.universetoday.com/120114/13-more-things-that-saved-apollo-13-part-12-the-trench-band-of-brothers/.

toward Golgotha. That event never happened. But viewers understand that it is an allusion to Revelation 21:5 where Jesus makes that statement and Hebrews 12:2 which tells us that Jesus endured the cross for the *joy* set before him, despising its shame! Once again, that is good writing for the movie, and it is an accurate portrayal of Jesus and what he accomplished, though not in a precise sense.

The Gospels were written nearly 2,000 years before you and I were born. They have not changed. However, the objectives and conventions for writing biography have. To ignore this fact is to be guilty of anachronistic thinking. In the early 1400s, Spitz Master painted *The Way to Calvary* in which Jesus is depicted carrying his cross. He and the Roman soldiers accompanying him are wearing elegant attire of the early fifteenth century. Are we not guilty of similar anachronistic thinking when assuming biographers in the first century wrote using the same conventions we use today?

Earlier in this book, I quoted Robert Stein and repeat some of his words here.

> It is evident from source criticism that the individual Evangelists "*do not intend to provide us with a record of the precise literal words of Jesus.*" Quite the contrary, they felt free to paraphrase, modify certain terms, and add comments in order to help their readers understand the "significance" of what Jesus taught. The Evangelists had no obsession with the *ipsissima verba* [i.e., the very words], for they believed that they had authority to interpret these words for their audience.[11]

The Gospels are not modern biographies. They are ancient biographies. A failure to recognize this fact can lead one down the wrong path, resulting in making wrong assumptions and asking wrong questions.[12]

When differences in the Gospels are observed, the question very often asked has been, "How can these texts be harmonized?" While it is appropriate to ask that question, I suggest the more appropriate one, and the one more likely to provide greater light, is, "Why are the differences there?" There are many possible causes: normal variation in memory, normal variation when passing along oral tradition, erroneous memory, the source used was incorrect—just to name some of the major ones. This book has attempted to bring light to another possible cause: compositional

---

11. Stein, *Studying the Synoptic Gospels*, 168, emphasis in the original.
12. Witherington, *The Living Word of God*, 53.

devices that were commonly employed by ancient authors. These devices can easily account for more than 90 percent of all differences between the Gospels, although this does not mean compositional devices are responsible for all of those they can explain. That said, this book and the preceding one I wrote on the topic present what I assess to be some of the clearer cases in which an author employed compositional devices.

Few scholars today hesitate to recognize the use of some compositional devices in the Gospels, such as spotlighting (e.g., to explain why Matthew and Mark mention one angel at the tomb while Luke and John mention two). Even today we often use compositional devices in normal communication. They are so common that we often use them without ever thinking about them, sometimes describing an event as though occurring over a shorter period of time than it had actually occurred, sometimes conflating events, sometimes mentioning only one person saying or doing something while having knowledge of others who were involved. We do these things to abbreviate, to make a point more clearly, or merely because we are not concerned with precision at that moment. We do not regard these as errors or deceit. Perhaps you may not even want to call them "compositional devices" because they are so common. Whatever you call them, we use them with and without conscious thought in both written and oral communications. This does not make us unreliable or deceitful. Recognizing that the Gospel authors used compositional devices allows us to understand why the differences are there. It assists us in avoiding appeals to creative harmonizations that may be false. And it provides a more plausible reason than error for many of the differences.

"STICKS AND STONES MAY BREAK MY BONES . . ."

The matter of the best way to approach differences in how the Gospels report the same events will continue to be debated. Many have strong convictions about how they view Scripture. Skeptics and many of those on the theological left have a low view of Scripture: Scripture is entirely of human origin and should not be an authoritative guide for how we should live or for influencing how society operates. These do not believe much of what Scripture teaches and many do not care. So they often prefer to think of the differences as being errors.

Then there are those on the theological right who have a high view of Scripture: Scripture is divinely inspired and authoritative. A portion of these will think of the inspiration of Scripture in terms that are not far from divine dictation, though they deny the theory. For them, the nature of God would not permit even the slightest deficiency of detail in anything attributed to being the "Word of God," despite the observation that the New Testament often refers to the apostolic preaching of the gospel as the "Word of God," which no doubt included occasional misstatements of details within the thousands of sermons the apostles delivered and the discussions in which they had engaged over the decades that followed the resurrection of Jesus.[13] Many have a rigid concept of truth-telling that does not allow for some of the compositional devices I have articulated throughout this book.

Unfortunately, strong convictions, though often justified, have frequently resulted in infighting among Christians, especially conservative Christians who criticize their fellow believers on theological matters that are outside of the essential doctrines of the Christian faith. This can have a negative impact on unity in the church. Ammianus Marcellinus was the last major Roman historian. Writing in the latter half of the fourth century, he had witnessed the brutal acts of the Romans and, though he was a pagan, condemned the intolerance of the Emperor Julian toward the Christians.[14] Having also witnessed how Christians acted toward one another when they had disagreements on theological matters, he opined that "no wild beasts are such dangerous enemies to man as Christians are to one another."[15]

In a sense, not much has changed in 1,600 years. Michael Bird mentions how, as a scholar in Australia, he is up against other scholars there who promote a low view of Scripture, contending that Scripture carries no authority over us and that God does not speak through it. He then comments:

> So when I look at the American evangelical scene, where people want to divide denominations over "infallible" versus "inerrancy," the whole thing looks kind of piddly and pathetic in comparison. It's like I'm fighting the barbarians at the gate while some of you guys back in your mega-seminary sanctuaries are engaging in a ferocious fratricide over the proper length of church candles.[16]

---

13. See Acts 4:31; 6:2, 7; 8:14; 11:1; 12:24; 13:46; 17:13; 18:11; 1 Thess. 2:13; Rev 1:9; 6:9.

14. Ronald Mellor, *The Roman Historians* (New York: Routledge, 1999), 121.

15. Ammianus Marcellinus, *Roman History*, 22.5. English translation by Mellor, *The Roman Historians*, 123.

16. Michael F. Bird, "Response to R. Albert Mohler Jr.," in *Five Views on Biblical Inerrancy*, 68n52.

"How good and pleasant it is for brothers to live in unity!" (Ps. 133:1)

With Western culture becoming increasingly left leaning and hostile toward those holding biblical ethics, unity among followers of Jesus is growing increasingly vital to the health and stability of the church in the West. Although debates will continue over a variety of Christian doctrines, we should place a premium on unity in the body of Christ, standing firmly on the essential doctrines while tolerating differences of opinion on nonessential doctrines.

> *In essentials, unity, in non-essentials, liberty, in all things charity.*
> —Rupertus Meldenius (early seventeenth century)

The apostle Paul often encouraged unity among believers. In Romans 15:5–6, he writes, "May the God who gives endurance and encouragement give you the same attitude of mind toward each other that Christ Jesus had, so that with one mind and one voice you may glorify the God and Father of our Lord Jesus Christ" (NIV).[17] We cannot control how others act. But, as individuals, you and I can resolve not to be an active source of division in the church. Still, every one of us is flawed and will fail many times. I have apologized on more than one occasion for the unjustified harshness of my responses to others. Patience and forgiveness must flow in abundance (Matt. 6:12, 14; 18:21–36 / Luke 17:3–4; Eph. 4:1–3; Col. 3:12).

Paul was a wonderful example for us all. He was in prison when he wrote his letter to the church in Philippi (Phil. 1:7, 13, 14, 17). His words inform us that some who were preaching the gospel were doing so with impure motives, promoting themselves to a point where they hoped to replace Paul's position of prominence in the hearts of the Philippian believers and cause distress for him (Phil. 1:15–17). Why would Paul feel distress? The Philippian believers were dear to his heart. He was their spiritual father, having started the church in their city. He referred to them as "my dear brethren, whom I long to see, my joy and crown" (Phil. 4:1). Paul loved the Philippian believers, and they returned his affection, even

17. See also Rom. 12:18; 14:19; 1 Cor. 1:10–14; 2 Cor. 13:11; Eph. 4:1–3; Phil. 2:2; Col. 3:14; 1 Thess. 5:13.

supporting him financially as he preached the gospel elsewhere (Phil. 4:10, 14–18). Now imprisoned in a different city, he was aware of those who were working to supplant him and was unable to go to his beloved Philippians. Paul must have felt similar to a man unjustly incarcerated away from his hometown while knowing that another man was actively trying to win over his wife's heart. How would you feel in such circumstances? Distress? You bet! So we can at least empathize with Paul. And we can be all the more impressed by Paul's next statement: "But what does it matter? The important thing is that in every way, whether from false motives or true, Christ is preached. And because of this I rejoice" (Phil. 1:18 NIV). Despite the fact that some were preaching the gospel out of self-interest and rivalry to Paul, he rejoiced that the gospel was being preached.

What is our takeaway from this? If Paul can rejoice because the gospel was being preached by those believers who stood against him, we should be quick to rejoice when those with whom we disagree on nonessential matters are proclaiming Christ. As sons and daughters of the living God, let's be determined not to argue among ourselves over nonessentials to a point of division, like two children in the backseat of the car yelling at and hitting each other because one touched the other's side. It is fine to disagree on nonessentials as long as charity is present and accusations are absent. Whether you prefer to harmonize or appeal to compositional devices, whether you are or are not an inerrantist, if we are in agreement on the essential doctrines of the Christian faith, let us work harder to live according to Paul's instructions:

> As a prisoner for the Lord, then, I urge you to live a life worthy of the calling you have received. Be completely humble and gentle; be patient, bearing with one another in love. Make every effort to keep the unity of the Spirit through the bond of peace. (Eph. 4:1–3 NIV)

> Do all things without grumbling or arguing in order that you may be blameless and innocent, children of God, without fault, in the midst of a crooked and perverted society among which you shine as lights in the world. (Phil. 2:14–15)

If this book has helped you, please let me know by sending me a note through my website: https://www.risenjesus.com/contact.

APPENDIX

In the 2021 monograph *The Invention of the Inspired Text: Philological Windows on the Theopneustia of Scripture*, John Poirier states his objective: "The pages that follow do not attempt to dismiss the doctrine of inspiration *in spite of* Scripture's supposed claim, but rather to show that Scripture really *makes no such claim* in the first place."[1] He argues that *theopneustos* meant "life-giving" until Origen gave it a new meaning: "divinely inspired."

However, Poirier's thesis suffers from several weaknesses. First, Tertullian (*De cultu feminarum* 1.3, late AD 2 c. / early 3 c.), who writes in Latin and prior to Origen, is clearly aware of 2 Timothy 3:16 and translates *theopneustos* as *divinitus inspirari*. Poirier attempts to downplay this (120–23)—ineffectively, in my view. Tertullian knew Greek well enough that he wrote some of his treatises in Greek. So it is clear enough that Tertullian understood *theopneustos* to mean "divinely inspired."

Second, whereas *theopneustos* is relatively rare in the ancient literature written prior to the third century and only in 2 Timothy 3:16 in the Bible, *zōapoiéō* (to make alive, to give life to) is common, even in Paul's letters (see Rom. 4:17; 8:11; 1 Cor. 15:22, 36, 45; 2 Cor. 3:6; Gal. 3:21; also in the New Testament, see 1 Pet. 3:18; John 5:21 [2x]; 6:63; and in the LXX, see Judg. 21:14; 2 Kgs. 5:7; Neh. 9:6; Psa. 70[71]:20). If Paul had meant "life-giving" in 2 Timothy 3:16, he had another term he had used widely to communicate the thought. One could respond that Paul did not write 2 Timothy, which is the majority opinion of modern scholars. Still, if Paul is not the author, the writer is using Pauline thought and is familiar with at least some of Paul's letters. Thus, he likely knows the far more common term *zōapoiéō*, whereas *theopneustos* is a relatively rare term that appears in only three texts that are *possibly* earlier than 2 Timothy.

1. See John C. Poirier, *The Invention of the Inspired Text Philological Windows on the Theopneustia of Scripture* (New York: T & T Clark, 2021), 3.

Third, a majority of the occurrences of *theopneustos* and its cognate *theopnoos* are used in a neutral sense (i.e., a clear sense of the term is not provided, perhaps because it is assumed that its meaning is known by the readers). Several of Poirier's examples where he thinks the term is used in the sense of "life-giving" can also be both easily and reasonably understood in the sense of "inspiration," including 2 Timothy 3:16. Thus, the matter is sometimes not nearly as clear as Poirier imagines. Ambiguity is present. For example, *theopneustos* appears four times in the writings of Clement of Alexandria. All four refer to Scripture. Two are used in a neutral sense, referring to Scripture without giving readers a clear sense of the meaning other than its surface meaning of "God-breathed" (see *Strom.* 1.21.124; 7.16.103). Poirier asserts that the other two occurrences carry the sense of "life-giving" (*Strom.* 7.16.101; *Protr.* 9.86.2–87.2). While both may be read in that sense, they may also and without any forcing whatsoever be read in the sense of inspiration.

Fourth, even if those in the non-Christian world used *theopneustos* with the meaning "life-giving," the Christian community of that day may have conveniently found it useful to employ the term with its face meaning (*God-breathed*). Even today, the term *racist* carries different senses within different communities. Moreover, many are seeking ways of redefining *male* and *female*, *man* and *woman*, in a manner that is quite different than how they have been traditionally understood.

Fifth, perhaps the weakest part of the fabric of Poirier's case is that he misses the forest for the trees. For prior to our discussion of the meaning of *theopneustos* in chapter 11, we observed several reasons from Scripture itself that strongly suggest the historical Jesus and several New Testament authors, including the apostle Paul, viewed the bulk of Old Testament literature as being divinely inspired and divinely authoritative. Moreover, even in the first century and into the second, several leaders in the early church, including a few authors of the New Testament literature, viewed at least some of the New Testament literature as being divinely authoritative and divinely inspired, since they contain the teachings of Jesus and/or were either written by an apostle or closely rooted in their eyewitness testimony (e.g., 1 Tim. 5:18 quotes Luke 10:7; 2 Pet. 3:16 mentions Paul's letters as "Scripture"). Accordingly, even if Poirier is correct pertaining to the meaning of *theopneustos* in 2 Timothy 3:16, good reasons still exist for holding that Scripture makes claim to being divinely inspired.

BIBLIOGRAPHY

Ancient Sources

The Ante-Nicene Fathers. Edited by Alexander Roberts and James Donaldson. American ed. 10 vols. Buffalo, NY: Christian Literature Company, 1885–96.

Augustine. "Agreement among the Evangelists (*De consensu Evangelistarum*)." Translated by Kim Paffenroth. In *Saint Augustine, The New Testament: I and II*, edited by Boniface Ramsey, 131–348. The Works of Saint Augustine. Part 1. Vols. 15–16. Hyde Park, NY: New City, 2014.

———. *The Harmony of the Gospels*. In *Saint Augustin: Sermon on the Mount, Harmony of the Gospels, Homilies on the Gospels*, edited by Philip Schaff, translated by S. D. F. Salmond. Vol. 6 of *A Select Library of the Nicene and Post-Nicene Fathers of the Christian Church*. First Series. New York: Christian Literature Company, 1888.

———. *Sermones*. "Sermons on Selected Lessons of the New Testament." In *Saint Augustin: Sermon on the Mount, Harmony of the Gospels, Homilies on the Gospels*, edited by Philip Schaff, translated by R. G. MacMullen. Vol. 6 of *A Select Library of the Nicene and Post-Nicene Fathers of the Christian Church*. First Series. New York: Christian Literature Company, 1888.

———. *Against Faustus the Manichaean*.

———. *Letter to Jerome*.

Chrysostom, John. *Homiliae in Matthaeum*.

———. *Homilies on the Gospel of John*. John Chrysostom, "Homilies of St. John Chrysostom, Archbishop of Constantinople, on the Gospel of St. John." In *Saint Chrysostom: Homilies on the Gospel of St. John and Epistle to the Hebrews*, edited by Philip Schaff, translated by G. T. Stupart, 123–24, vol. 14 of *A Select Library of the Nicene and Post-Nicene Fathers of the Christian Church*, First Series. New York: Christian Literature Company, 1889.

Cicero. *Epistulae ad familiares* (*Letters to Friends*). *Cicero: Letters to Friends*. Edited and translated by D. R. Shackleton Bailey. Vol. 1. Loeb Classic Library 205. Cambridge: Harvard University Press, 2001.

Dio, Cassius. *Roman History*.

Ephrem the Syrian, *Commentary on Tatian's Diatessaron*. In *Saint Ephrem's Commentary on Tatian's Diatessaron: An English Translation of Chester Beatty Syriac MS 709 with Introduction and Notes* by Carmel McCarthy. Journal of Semitic Studies Supplement 2. Oxford: Oxford University Press on behalf of the University of Manchester, 1993.

Eusebius. *Historia ecclesiastica* (*Ecclesiastical History*).
Hippolytus. *De Duodecim Apostolis.*
Irenaeus, *Adversus Haereses* (*Against Heresies*).
Jerome. *Ad Damascus.*
Jerome. *De viris illustribus.*
Josephus. *Jewish Antiquities.*
———. *Jewish War.*
———. *The Essential Works: A Condensation of* Jewish Antiquities *and* The Jewish War. Translated and edited by Paul L. Maier. Grand Rapids: Kregel, 1994.
Justin. *Dialogue with Trypho.*
Lucian. *How to Write History.* Vol. 6 of *Lucian.* Translated by K. Kilburn. Loeb Classical Library 430. Cambridge: Harvard University Press, 2006.
Maximus, Valerius. *Facta et dicta memorabilia* (*Memorable Deeds and Sayings*).
Origen. *Commentary on the Gospel of John, Books 1–10.* Translated by Ronald E. Heine. Vol. 80 of *The Fathers of the Church.* Washington, DC: The Catholic University of America Press, 1989.
———. *Origenous ta euriskomena panta = Origenis opera omnia*, patrologiae cursus completus, series graeca, t. 13. Paris: Apud J. P. Migne, 1862.
———. *Of Principles.*
Papias, *Frag.*
Philo. *On the Decalogue. On the Special Laws, Books 1–3*, Translated by F. H. Colson. Loeb Classic Library 320. Cambridge, MA: Harvard University Press, 1937.
———. *Who Is The Heir of Divine Things?* In *On the Confusion of Tongues. On the Migration of Abraham. Who Is the Heir of Divine Things? On Mating with the Preliminary Studies*, translated by F. H. Colson and G. H. Whitaker, 263–66. Loeb Classic Library 261. Cambridge: Harvard University Press, 1932.
———. *On the Life of Moses.*
———. *The Special Laws.*
Plutarch. *Life of Alexander.*
———. *Life of Antony.*
———. *Life of Brutus.*
———. *Life of Cato Minor.*
———. *Life of Caesar.*
———. *Life of Cicero.*
———. *Life of Cimon.*
———. *Life of Crassus.*
———. *Life of Lucullus.*
———. *Life of Nicias.*
———. *Life of Pompey.*
Polybius. *The Histories, Books 9–16.* Translated by W. R. Paton, Frank W. Walbank, and Christian Habicht. Loeb Classic Library 159. Cambridge: Harvard University Press, 2011.
Progymnasmata: Greek Textbooks of Prose Composition and Rhetoric. Translated by George A. Kennedy. Writings from the Greco-Roman World 10. Atlanta: Society of Biblical Literature, 2003.

Pseudo-Plutarch. *Doctrines of the Philosophers*.
Quintilian. *The Institutio oratoria of Quintilian*. Translated by H. E. Butler. 4 vols. Loeb Classical Library 124–27. London: Heinemann, 1921–22.
———. *The Orator's Education*.
Sallust. *The War with Catiline. Sallust: The War with Cataline, The War with Jugurtha*. Translated by J. C. Rolfe. Edited by John T. Ramsey. Loeb Classic Library 116. Cambridge: Harvard University Press, 2013.
Seneca the Younger. *Epistulae morales*. In *Seneca: Epistles 1–65*. Translated by Richard M. Gummere. Loeb Classic Library 75. Cambridge: Harvard University Press, 1917.
Suetonius. *Divus Julius*. *Suetonius*. Vol. 1. Translated by J. C. Rolfe. Loeb Classic Library 31. Cambridge: Harvard University Press, 1998.
———. *Nero*.
Tacitus. *The Annals: The Reigns of Tiberius, Claudius, and Nero*. Translated by J. C. Yardley. New York: Oxford University Press, 2008.
Tertullian. *Adversus Marcionem* (*Against Marcion*).
Theon. *Progymnasmata* (*Preliminary Exercises*). In "The Progymnasmata of Theon: A New Text with Translation and Commentary." By James R. Butts. PhD diss., Claremont Graduate School, 1986.

Contemporary Sources

Achtemeier, Paul J. *The Inspiration of Scripture: Problems and Proposals*. Philadelphia: Westminster, 1980.
Adams, Sean A. *Greek Genres and Jewish Authors: Negotiating Literary Culture in the Greco-Roman Era*. Waco: Baylor University Press, 2020.
Adams, Sean A., and Seth M. Ehorn, eds. *Composite Citations in Antiquity*. Vol. 1, *Jewish, Graeco-Roman, and Early Christian Uses*. Library of New Testament Studies 525. London: Bloomsbury T&T Clark, 2016.
———. *Composite Citations in Antiquity*. Vol. 2, *New Testament Uses*. New York: T&T Clark, 2018.
Aland, Kurt, ed. *Synopsis of the Four Gospels: Greek-English Edition of the* Synopsis Quattuor Evangeliorum. 15th ed. Stuttgart: German Bible Society, 2013.
Alexander, Loveday. *The Preface to Luke's Gospel: Literary Convention and Social Context in Luke 1.1–4 and Acts 1.1*. Society for New Testament Studies Monograph Series 78. New York: Cambridge University Press, 1993.
———. "What Is a Gospels?" In *The Cambridge Companion to The Gospels*, edited by Stephen C. Barton and Todd Brewer, 9–28. New York: Cambridge University Press, 2021, 9-28.
Allert, Craig D. *A High View of Scripture? The Authority of the Bible and the Formation of the New Testament Canon*. Grand Rapids: Baker Academic, 2007.
Anderson, A. A. *2 Samuel*. Word Biblical Commentary 11. Dallas: Word, 1989.
Anderson, Paul N. *Riddles of the Fourth Gospel: An Introduction to John*. Minneapolis: Fortress, 2011.

Anderson, Paul N., Felix Just, SJ, and Tom Thatcher. *John, Jesus and History*. Vol. 1 of *Critical Appraisals of Critical Views*. Atlanta: Society of Biblical Literature, 2007.

———. *John, Jesus and History*. Vol. 2 of *Aspects of History in the Fourth Gospel*. Atlanta: Society of Biblical Literature, 2009.

———. *John, Jesus and History*. Vol. 3 of *Glimpses of Jesus through the Johannine Lens*. Atlanta: Society of Biblical Literature, 2016.

Archer, Gleason L. *Encyclopedia of Bible Difficulties*. Grand Rapids: Zondervan, 1982.

Arndt, William, F. W. Danker, and W. Bauer. *A Greek-English Lexicon of the New Testament and Other Early Christian Literature*. 3rd ed. Chicago: University of Chicago Press, 2000.

Auld, A. Graeme. *I & II Samuel: A Commentary*. Edited by William P. Brown, Carol A. Newsom, and Brent A. Strawn. 1st ed. The Old Testament Library. Louisville: Westminster John Knox, 2012.

Bailey, Kenneth E. *Poet and Peasant*. Grand Rapids: Eerdmans, 1976.

Baldwin, Joyce G. *1 and 2 Samuel: An Introduction and Commentary*. Tyndale Old Testament Commentaries 8. Downers Grove, IL: InterVarsity Press, 1988.

Barclay, William. *The Gospel of John*. Daily Study Bible Series 1. Philadelphia: Westminster John Knox, 1975.

Barnett, Paul. *Is the New Testament Reliable?*, 2nd ed. Downers Grove, IL: InterVarsity Press, 2003.

Bauckham, Richard. *The Christian World around the New Testament*. Grand Rapids: Baker Academic, 2017.

———. *Jesus and the Eyewitnesses: The Gospels as Eyewitness Testimony*. 2nd ed. Grand Rapids: Eerdmans, 2017.

Bayer, Hans F. *Jesus' Predictions of Vindication and Resurrection: The Provenance, Meaning and Correlation of the Synoptic Predictions*. Tübingen: Mohr Siebeck, 1986.

Beasley-Murray, George R. *John*. Word Biblical Commentary 36. Dallas: Word, 1999.

Bergen, Robert D. *1, 2 Samuel*. The New American Commentary 7. Nashville: B&H, 1996.

Bernard, J. H. *A Critical and Exegetical Commentary on the Gospel according to St. John*. Edited by Alan Hugh McNeile. Vol. 2. International Critical Commentary. New York: Scribner's, 1929.

Bird, Michael F. "Inerrancy Is Not Necessary for Evangelicalism outside the USA." In *Five Views on Biblical Inerrancy*, edited by J. Merrick and Stephen M. Garrett, 145–73. Grand Rapids: Zondervan, 2013.

———. "Saving Inerrancy From The Americans." *Word from the Bird* (blog), November 10, 2021. https://michaelfbird.substack.com/p/saving-inerrancy-from-the-americans?.

———. *Seven Things I Wish Christians Knew about the Bible*. Grand Rapids: Zondervan Reflective, 2021.

Blomberg, Craig L. *Jesus the Purifier: John's Gospel and the Fourth Quest for the Historical Jesus*. Grand Rapids: Baker Academic, 2023.

———. "Reflections on Jesus' View of the Old Testament." In *The Enduring Authority of the Christian Scriptures*, edited by D. A. Carson, 669–701. Grand Rapids: Eerdmans, 2016.

———. "Dealing with Gospel Differences: Can We Still Believe the Bible?" Response presented in "Synoptic Gospels: Issues in the Gospels," Annual Meeting of the Evangelical Theological Society, Atlanta, GA, November 18, 2015.

———. *Historical Reliability of the Gospels*. 2nd ed. Downers Grove, IL: IVP Academic, 2007.

———. *Historical Reliability of John's Gospel*. Downers Grove, IL: IVP Academic, 2001.

———. *The Historical Reliability of the New Testament: Countering the Challenges to Evangelical Christian Beliefs*. B&H Studies in Christian Apologetics. Nashville: B&H Academic, 2016.

———. *Matthew: An Exegetical and Theological Exposition of Holy Scripture*. New American Commentary 22. Nashville: B&H, 1992.

Blount, Douglas K. "What Does It Mean to Say That the Bible Is True?" In *In Defense of the Bible: A Comprehensive Apologetic for the Authority of Scripture*, edited by Steven B. Cowan and Terry L. Wilder, 47–62. Nashville: B&H, 2013.

Bock, Darrell L. "Different Depictions of Christ | Highlight." Mike Licona (channel). June 3, 2021. YouTube video. 8:36 (begins at 6:33). https://youtu.be/u0O7GzyAxyo?t=393. Original conversation from "Explaining Differences in the Gospels – Michael Licona, Mikel Del Rosario and Darrell L. Bock." *The Table* (podcast). Dallas Theological Seminary. March 26, 2021. https://youtu.be/-6Unz9iMAHg.

———. "Greco-Roman and Jewish Historiography as Backdrop for the Gospels." In *Fountains of Wisdom: In Conversation with James H. Charlesworth*, edited by Gerbern S. Oegema, Henry W. Morisada Rietz, and Loren Stuckenbruck, 241–56. London: T&T Clark, 2022.

———. "Luke, Acts." In *The Holman Apologetics Commentary on the Bible: The Gospels and Acts*. Edited by Jeremy Royal Howard. Nashville: B&H Academic, 2013.

———. *Luke*. Vol. 1, *1:1–9:50*. Baker Exegetical Commentary on the New Testament. Grand Rapids: Baker Academic, 1994.

Bock, Darrell L., and J. Ed Komoszewski, eds. *Jesus, Skepticism, and the Problem of History: Criteria and Context in the Study of Christian Origins*. Grand Rapids: Zondervan Academic, 2019.

Bond, Helen. *The First Biography of Jesus: Genre and Meaning in Mark's Gospel*. Grand Rapids: Eerdmans, 2020.

Borchert, Gerald L. *John 1–11*. New American Commentary 25A. Nashville: B&H, 1996.

Boring, M. Eugene. "The Gospel of Matthew." In *New Interpreter's Bible*, edited by Leander E. Keck. Nashville: Abingdon, 1994–2004.

Bovon, François. *Luke 1: A Commentary on the Gospel of Luke 1:1–9:50*. Hermeneia. Edited by Helmut Koester. Minneapolis: Fortress, 2002.

Brown, Jeannine, K. *The Gospels as Stories: A Narrative Approach to Matthew, Mark, Luke, and John*. Grand Rapids: Baker Academic, 2020.

Brown, Michael L., and Rabbi Daniel Freitag. "Is Jesus the Jewish Messiah?" YouTube video. March 23, 2017. Kennesaw State University. 2:09:09. https://youtu.be/t_oCkfe4ivQ.

Brown, Raymond E. *The Birth of the Messiah: Commentary on the Infancy Narratives in the Gospels of Matthew and Luke*. Updated ed. New York: Doubleday, 1993.

———. *The Gospel according to John (I–XII): Introduction, Translation, and Notes*. Anchor Yale Bible Commentaries 29. New Haven, CT; London: Yale University Press, 2008. Originally published 1966 by Doubleday.

Bruce, F. F. *In Retrospect: Remembrance of Things Past*. Grand Rapids: Eerdmans, 1980; rev. ed., London: Marshall Pickering; Grand Rapids: Baker, 1993; Kingsley Books, 2017, Kindle Edition.

———. *The Gospel and Epistles of John: Introduction, Exposition, and Notes*. Grand Rapids: Eerdmans, 1983.

Burridge, Richard A. *What Are the Gospels? A Comparison with Graeco-Roman Biography*. 25th anniversary ed. Waco, TX: Baylor University Press, 2018. First ed. published 1992 by Cambridge University Press.

Byrskog, Samuel. *Story as History, History as Story: The Gospel Tradition in the Context of Ancient Oral History*. Boston: Brill Academic, 2002.

Carlson, Stephen, C. *Papias of Hierapolis* Exposition of Dominical Oracles*: The Fragments, Testimonia, and Reception of a Second-Century Commentator*. Oxford, UK: Oxford University Press, 2021.

Carson, D. A., ed. *The Enduring Authority of the Christian Scriptures*. Grand Rapids: Eerdmans, 2016.

———, ed. *The Gospel according to John*. Pillar New Testament Commentary. Grand Rapids: Eerdmans; Leicester: Inter-Varsity Press, 1991.

———. "Matthew." In *The Expositor's Bible Commentary: Matthew–Mark*. Edited by Tremper Longman III and David E. Garland. Vol. 9. Rev. ed. Grand Rapids: Zondervan, 2010.

Cheney, Johnston M. *The Life of Christ in Stereo: The Four Gospels Combined as One*. Rev. ed. Portland: Western Baptist Seminary Press, 1969.

Craig, William Lane. "'Men Moved by the Holy Spirit Spoke from God' (2 Peter 1.21): A Middle Knowledge Perspective on Biblical Inspiration." *Philosophia Christi* 1, no. 1 (1999): 45–82.

———. *The Only Wise God: The Compatibility of Divine Foreknowledge and Human Freedom*. Eugene, OR: Wipf & Stock, 2000. Originally published in 1987 by Baker.

———. *The Son Rises: The Historical Evidence for the Resurrection of Jesus*. Eugene, OR: Wipf & Stock, 2001. Originally published 1981 by Moody Press.

———. *Systematic Philosophical Theology*. Vol. 1. Forthcoming.

Davies, W. D., and Dale C. Allison Jr. *A Critical and Exegetical Commentary on the Gospel according to Saint Matthew*. Vol. 2, *Commentary on Matthew XIX–XVIII*. International Critical Commentary. London; New York: T&T Clark International, 2004.

Dockery, David S., and David P. Nelson. "Special Revelation." In *A Theology for the Church*, edited by Daniel L. Akin, 118–74. Nashville: B&H Academic, 2007.

Downing, F. Gerald. "Compositional Conventions and the Synoptic Problem." *Journal of Biblical Literature* 107, no. 1 (1988): 69–85. https://doi.org/10.2307/3267825.

Dunn, James D. G. *Jesus Remembered: Christianity in the Making*. Vol. 1. Grand Rapids: Eerdmans, 2003.

Edwards, James R. *The Hebrew Gospel and the Development of the Synoptic Tradition*, Grand Rapids: Eerdmans, 2009.

Ehrman, Bart D. *Did Jesus Exist? The Historical Argument for Jesus of Nazareth*. New York: HarperOne, 2012.

———. *The New Testament: A Historical Introduction to the Early Christian Writings*. 3rd ed. New York: Oxford University Press, 2003.

Enns, Peter. *Inspiration and Incarnation: Evangelicals and the Problem of the Old Testament*. 2nd ed. Grand Rapids: Baker Academic, 2015.

Evans, Craig A. *Jesus and the Manuscripts: What We Can Learn from the Oldest Texts*. Peabody, MA: Hendrickson Academic, 2020.

———. *Matthew*. New Cambridge Bible Commentary. New York: Cambridge University Press, 2012.

Farmer, William R. *The Synoptic Problem: A Critical Analysis*. 2nd ed. Macon, GA: Mercer University Press, 1976.

Feinberg, Paul D. "The Meaning of Inerrancy." In *Inerrancy*, edited by Norman L. Geisler, 267–304. Grand Rapids: Zondervan, 1980.

Feldman, Louis H. *Philo's Portrayal of Moses in the Context of Ancient Judaism*. Notre Dame, IN: University of Notre Dame Press, 2007.

Flowers, Leighton. *The Potter's Promise: A Biblical Defense of Traditional Soteriology*. Dallas, TX: Trinity Academic Press, 2017.

France, R. T. *The Gospel of Mark: A Commentary on the Greek Text*. New International Greek Testament Commentary. Grand Rapids: Eerdmans; Carlisle: Paternoster, 2002.

———. *The Gospel of Matthew*. New International Commentary on the New Testament. Grand Rapids: Eerdmans, 2007.

Gangel, Kenneth O. *John*. Holman New Testament Commentary 4. Nashville: B&H, 2000.

Garland, David E. *Reading Matthew: A Literary and Theological Commentary on the First Gospel*. Macon, GA: Smyth & Helwys, 2001.

Geisler, Norman L. *Systematic Theology: In One Volume*. Grand Rapids: Bethany House, 2011.

Geisler, Norman L., and F. David Farnell. *The Jesus Quest: The Danger from Within*. Maitland, FL: Xulon, 2014.

Geisler, Norman L., and Thomas Howe. *The Big Book of Bible Difficulties: Clear and Concise Answers from Genesis to Revelation*. Grand Rapids: Baker, 1992.
Geisler, Norman L., and William C. Roach. *Defending Inerrancy: Affirming the Accuracy of Scripture for a New Generation*. Grand Rapids: Baker, 2012.
Geldenhuys, Norval. *Commentary on the Gospel of Luke: The English Text with Introduction, Exposition and Notes*. New International Commentary on the Old and New Testament. Grand Rapids: Eerdmans, 1952.
Gilderhus, Mark T. *History and Historians: A Historiographical Introduction*. 7th ed. Upper Saddle River, NJ: Prentice Hall, 2010.
Goheen, Michael W., and Michael D. Williams. "Doctrine of Scripture and Theological Interpretation." In *A Manifesto for Theological Interpretation*, edited by Craig G. Bartholomew and Heath A. Thomas, 48–71. Grand Rapids: Baker Academic, 2016.
Goodacre, Mark. "The Farrer Hypothesis." In *The Synoptic Problem: Four Views*, edited by Stanley E. Porter and Bryan R. Dyer, chap. 3. Grand Rapids: Baker Academic, 2016.
———. "Fatigue in the Synoptics." In *New Testament Studies* 44 (1998): 45–58. http://www.markgoodacre.org/Q/fatigue.htm.
———. *The Synoptic Problem: A Way through the Maze*. New York: Continuum, 2001.
Gregory, Andrew. "Jewish-Christian Gospels." In *The Non-Canonical Gospels*, edited by Paul Foster, 54-67. New York: T&T Clark, 2008.
Guelich, Robert A. "The Gospels: Portraits of Jesus and His Ministry." *Journal of the Evangelical Theological Society* 24, no. 2 (June 1981): 117–25. https://www.etsjets.org/files/JETS-PDFs/24/24-2/24-2-pp117-125_JETS.pdf.
Gundry, Robert H. *Matthew: A Commentary on His Handbook for a Mixed Church under Persecution*. 2nd ed. Grand Rapids: Eerdmans, 1994.
Habermas, Gary R. *On the Resurrection*. Vol. 1, *Evidences*. Nashville: B&H Academic, 2024.
Habermas, Gary R., and Michael R. Licona. *The Case for the Resurrection of Jesus*. Grand Rapids: Kregel, 2004.
Haenchen, Ernst, Robert Walter Funk, and Ulrich Busse. *John 1: A Commentary on the Gospel of John, Chapters 1–6*. Translated by Robert W. Funk. Edited by Robert W. Funk and Ulrich Busse. Hermeneia. Philadelphia: Fortress, 1984.
Hagner, Donald A. *Matthew 1–13*. World Biblical Commentary 33A. Nashville: Nelson, 1993.
Hahn, Roger L. *Matthew: A Commentary for Bible Students*. Indianapolis: Wesleyan, 2007.
Harrington, Daniel J., ed. *The Gospel of John*. Vols. 1 and 4. Sacra Pagina Series. Collegeville, MN: Liturgical, 1998.
———, ed. *The Gospel of Matthew*. Sacra Pagina Series 1. Collegeville, MN: Liturgical, 2007.
Hays, Richard B. *Reading Backwards: Figural Christology and the Fourfold Gospel Witness*. Waco: Baylor University Press, 2014.

Helm, Paul. "The Idea of Inerrancy." In *The Enduring Authority of the Christian Scriptures*, edited by D. A. Carson, 899–919. Grand Rapids: Eerdmans, 2016.

Hemer, Colin J. *The Book of Acts in the Setting of Hellenistic History*. Edited by C. H. Gempf. Winona Lake, IN: Eisenbrauns, 1990.

Hill, Charles E. "The Fragments of Papias." In *The Writings of the Apostolic Fathers*, edited by Paul Foster, 42–51. New York: T&T Clark, 2007.

"Hill Cumorah." Mormon Stories. https://www.mormonstories.org/truth-claims/the-books/the-book-of-mormon/hill-cumorah.

Holding, J. P., and Nick Peters. *Defining Inerrancy: Affirming a Defensible Faith for a New Generation*. 2nd ed. Orlando, FL: Tekton E-Bricks, 2014. Kindle.

Hooker, Morna D. *The Gospel according to Saint Mark*. Black's New Testament Commentary. London: Continuum, 1991.

Horsfall, Nicholas. "The Ides of March: Some New Problems." *Greece and Rome* 21, no. 2 (1974): 191–99.

Howard, George. *The Gospel of Matthew according to a Primitive Hebrew Text*. Macon, GA: Mercer University Press, 1987.

Kaiser, Walter C., Jr., Peter H. Davids, F. F. Bruce, and Manfred T. Brauch. *Hard Sayings of the Bible*. Downers Grove, IL: InterVarsity Press, 1996.

Keener, Craig S. *Christobiography: Memory, History, and the Reliability of the Gospels*. Grand Rapids: Eerdmans, 2019.

———. *The Gospel of John: A Commentary*. Vol. 1. 2 vols. Peabody, MA: Hendrickson, 2003.

———. *The Gospel of Matthew: A Socio-Rhetorical Commentary*. Grand Rapids: Eerdmans, 2009.

———. *The Historical Jesus of the Gospels*. Grand Rapids: Eerdmans, 2009.

———. *Spirit Hermeneutics: Reading Scripture in Light of Pentecost*. Grand Rapids: Eerdmans, 2016.

Keener, Craig S., and Edward T. Wright, eds. *Biographies and Jesus: What Does It Mean for the Gospels to Be Biographies?* Lexington: Emeth, 2016.

Keith, Chris, and Anthony Le Donne, eds. *Jesus, Criteria, and the Demise of Authenticity*. London: T&T Clark, 2012.

Kelber, Werner H., and Samuel Byrskog, eds. *Jesus in Memory: Traditions in Oral and Scribal Perspectives*. Waco: Baylor University Press, 2009.

Kloppenborg Verbin, John S. *Excavating Q: The History and Setting of the Sayings Gospel*. Minneapolis: Fortress, 2000.

Kroll, Wilhelm. *Vettii Valentis anthologiarum libri*. Berlin: Weidmann, 1973. Originally published 1908 by Weidmann (Berlin).

Lea, Thomas D., and Hayne P. Griffin. *1, 2 Timothy, Titus*. The New American Commentary 34. Nashville: B&H, 1992.

Lemke, Steve W. "The Inspiration and Authority of Scripture." In *Biblical Hermeneutics: A Comprehensive Introduction to Interpreting Scripture*, edited by Bruce Corley, Steve W. Lemke, Grant I. Lovejoy, 176–93. 2nd ed. Nashville: B&H, 2002.

Licona, Michael R. "Are the Gospels 'Historically Reliable'? A Focused Comparison of Suetonius's *Life of Augustus* and the Gospel of Mark." *Religions*, Special Issue: Current Trends in New Testament Study 10, no. 3, 148 (2019): 18 pages. https://doi.org/10.3390/rel10030148.

———. "Behold, I Stand at the Door and Knock: What to Say to Mormons and Jehovah's Witnesses When They Knock on Your Door." 1998. PDF file. 52 pages. https://www.risenjesus.com/wp-content/uploads/behold-i-stand-at-the-door-and-knock.pdf.

———. "Compositional Techniques within Plutarch and the Gospel Tradition." In *Christian Origins and the Establishment of the Early Jesus Movement*, edited by Stanley E. Porter and Andrew W. Pitts. Texts and Editions for New Testament Study 12. Boston: Brill, 2018.

———. *The Resurrection of Jesus: A New Historiographical Approach*. Downers Grove, IL: IVP Academic, 2010.

———. "Viewing the Gospels as Ancient Biographies Resolves Many Perceived Contradictions." In *Biographies and Jesus: What Does It Mean for the Gospels to Be Biographies?*, edited by Craig S. Keener and Edward T. Wright, 323–28. Lexington: Emeth, 2016.

———. *Why Are There Differences in the Gospels? What We Can Learn from Ancient Biography*. New York: Oxford University Press, 2017.

Licona, Michael R., and Lee Martin McDonald. *Formation of the Biblical Canon*. Last updated November 20, 2020. https://bit.ly/3M5q0Fn.

Liddell, Henry George, Robert Scott, Henry Stuart Jones, and Roderick McKenzie. *Greek-English Lexicon*. Oxford: Clarendon, 1996.

Liefeld, Walter L., and David W. Pao, "Luke." In *The Expositor's Bible Commentary: Luke–Acts*. Edited by Tremper Longman III and David E. Garland. Vol. 10. Rev. ed. Grand Rapids: Zondervan, 2007.

Lincoln, Andrew T. *The Gospel according to Saint John*. Black's New Testament Commentary. London: Continuum, 2005.

Lindsell, Harold. *The Battle for the Bible*. Grand Rapids: Zondervan, 1976.

Loke, Andrew. *Investigating the Resurrection of Jesus Christ: A New Transdisciplinary Approach*. London: Routledge: 2020.

Lorenz, Chris. "Historical Knowledge and Historical Reality: A Plea for 'Internal Realism.'" In *History and Theory* 33, no. 3, 1994, 297–327.

Luz, Ulrich. *Matthew 8–20: A Commentary on Matthew 8–20*. Translated by James E. Crouch. Edited by Helmut Koester. Hermeneia. Minneapolis: Augsburg, 2001.

Maier, Paul L. *In the Fullness of Time: A Historian Looks at Christmas, Easter, and the Early Church*. Grand Rapids: Kregel, 1997. First published 1991 by Kregel.

Mangum, Douglas, and E. Tod Twist. *2 Timothy*. Edited by Douglas Mangum and Derek R. Brown. Lexham Research Commentaries. Bellingham, WA: Lexham, 2013.

Marshall, I. Howard. *The Gospel of Luke: A Commentary on the Greek Text*. New International Greek Testament Commentary. Carlisle: Paternoster; Grand Rapids: Eerdmans, 1978.

McCarter Jr., P. Kyle. *I Samuel: A New Translation with Introduction, Notes and Commentary*. Anchor Yale Bible 8. New Haven, CT: Yale University Press, 2008.

McGing, Brian. "Philo's Adaptation of the Bible in His *Life of Moses*." In *The Limits of Ancient Biography*, edited by Brian McGing and Judith Mossman, 117–40. Swansea: Classical Press of Wales, 2006.

McGrew, Lydia. *The Mirror or the Mask: Liberating the Gospels from Literary Devices*. Tampa, FL: DeWard, 2019.

McHugh, John F. *A Critical and Exegetical Commentary on John 1–4*. Edited by Graham N. Stanton. International Critical Commentary. New York: T&T Clark, 2009.

McIver, Robert K. *Memory, Jesus and the Synoptic Gospels*. Atlanta: Society of Biblical Literature, 2011.

Mellor, Ronald. *Roman Historians*. New York: Routledge, 1999.

Merrick, J., and Stephen M. Garrett, eds. *Five Views on Biblical Inerrancy*. Grand Rapids: Zondervan, 2013.

Metzger, Bruce M. *Breaking the Code: Understanding the Book of Revelation*. Nashville: Abingdon, 1993.

———. *A Textual Commentary on the Greek New Testament*. 2nd ed. New York: United Bible Societies, 1994. First published 1971 by United Bible Societies.

Mohler, R. Albert, Jr. "When the Bible Speaks, God Speaks: The Classic Doctrine of Biblical Inerrancy." In *Five Views on Biblical Inerrancy*, edited by J. Merrick and Stephen M. Garrett, 29–58. Grand Rapids: Zondervan, 2013.

Moles, J. L. *Plutarch: The Life of Cicero*. Eastbourne, UK: Aris and Phillips, 1988.

Morris, Leon. *The Gospel according to Matthew*. Pillar New Testament Commentary. Grand Rapids: Eerdmans; Leicester, England: Inter-Varsity Press, 1992.

Mounce, Robert H. "John." In *The Expositor's Bible Commentary: Luke–Acts*. Edited by Tremper Longman III and David E. Garland. Vol. 10. Rev. ed. Grand Rapids: Zondervan, 2007.

Noll, Mark. *The Princeton Theology*. Grand Rapids: Baker, 1983.

Nolland, John. *The Gospel of Matthew: A Commentary on the Greek Text*. Grand Rapids: Eerdmans, 2005.

Osborne, Grant. *The Gospel of John*. Philip W. Comfort and Wendell C. Hawley. *1–3 John*. Cornerstone Biblical Commentary 13. Carol Stream, IL: Tyndale House, 2007.

Osborne, Grant R. *Matthew*. Zondervan Exegetical Commentary on the New Testament 1. Grand Rapids: Zondervan, 2010.

Packer, J. I. *Fundamentalism and the Word of God*. Grand Rapids: Eerdmans, 1958.

Pelling, Christopher. *Plutarch and History: Eighteen Studies*. Swansea: Classical Press of Wales, 2002.

———, trans. *Plutarch: Caesar*. Oxford: Oxford University Press, 2011.

Pfeifer, Daniel J. "Temporal Continuity and Discontinuity in the Narrative Sequence of the Synoptic Gospels." PhD diss., Department of New Testament Studies, Dallas Theological Seminary, 2021.

Poirier, John C. *The Invention of the Inspired Text Philological Windows on the Theopneustia of Scripture*. Library of New Testament Studies 640. New York: T&T Clark, 2021.

Porter, David. "Sibyl." In *The Oxford Classical Dictionary*. 4th ed. Edited by Simon Hornblower and Antony Spawforth. New York: Oxford University Press, 2005.

Porter, Stanley E., and Andrew W. Pitts, eds. *Christian Origins and the Establishment of the Early Jesus Movement*. Texts and Editions for New Testament Study 12. Boston: Brill, 2018.

Poythress, Vern S. *Inerrancy and the Gospels: A God-Centered Approach to the Challenges of Harmonization*. Wheaton, IL: Crossway, 2012.

Qureshi, Nabeel. *Seeking Allah, Finding Jesus: A Devout Muslim Encounters Christianity*. Grand Rapids: Zondervan, 2014.

Ramsey, John. "At What Hour Did the Murderers of Julius Caesar Gather on the Ides of March 44 B.C.?" In *In Pursuit of Wissenschaft: Festschrift für William M. Calder III zum 75, Geburtstag*. Edited by Stephan Heilen, Robert Kirstein, R. Scott Smith, Stephen M. Trzaskoma, Rogier L. van der Wal, and Matthias Vorwerk, 351–63. Spudasmata 119. New York: Olms, 2008.

Richards, E. Randolph. *Paul and First-Century Letter Writing: Secretaries, Composition and Collection*. Downers Grove, IL: InterVarsity Press, 2004.

Richards, E. Randolph, and Brandon J. O'Brien. *Misreading Scripture with Western Eyes: Removing Cultural Blindness to Better Understand the Bible*. Downers Grove, IL: IVP Books, 2012.

Richards, E. Randolph, and Richard James. *Misreading Scripture with Individualist Eyes: Patronage, Honor, and Shame in the Biblical World*. Downers Grove, IL: IVP Academic, 2020.

Russell, D. A. "Plutarch." In *The Oxford Classical Dictionary*. 4th ed. Edited by Simon Hornblower and Antony Spawforth. New York: Oxford University Press, 2005.

Sanders, E. P. "Testament of Abraham: A New Translation and Introduction." In *The Old Testament Pseudepigrapha: Volume One: Apocalyptic Literature and Testaments*, edited by James H. Charlesworth, 872–902. Peabody, MA: Hendrickson, 1983.

Skinner, Christopher W. "The Gospel according to John." In *The Cambridge Companion to The Gospels*, edited by Stephen C. Barton and Todd Brewer, 2nd ed., 199–218. New York: Cambridge University Press, 2021.

Sorabella, Jean. "Portraiture in Renaissance and Baroque Europe." The Met Museum. August 2007. https://www.metmuseum.org/toah/hd/port/hd_port.htm.

Stein, Robert H. *Luke*. New American Commentary 24. Nashville: B&H, 1992.

———. *Studying the Synoptic Gospels: Origin and Interpretation*. 2nd ed. Grand Rapids: Baker Academic, 2001.

Stone, A. M. "*Pro Milone*: Cicero's Second Thoughts." *Antichthon* 14 (1980): 88–111.

Storr, Gottlob C. *Über den Zweck der evangelischen Geschichte und der Briefe Johannis*. Tübingen: Herrbrandt, 1786.

Stratton, Timothy A. *Human Freedom, Divine Knowledge, and Mere Molinism*. Eugene, OR: Wipf and Stock, 2020.

Strauss, Mark L. *Mark*. Zondervan Exegetical Commentary on the New Testament 2. Edited by Clinton E. Arnold. Grand Rapids: Zondervan, 2014.

Thompson, Marianne Meye. *John: A Commentary*. New Testament Library. Louisville: Westminster John Knox, 2015.

Tuckett, Christopher M. *Luke*. T&T Clark Study Guides. New York: T&T Clark, 2000. Originally published 1996 by JSOT.

———. *The Revival of the Griesbach Hypothesis: An Analysis and Appraisal*. Society for New Testament Studies 44. Cambridge: Cambridge University Press, 1983.

Turner, David L. *Matthew*. Baker Exegetical Commentary on the New Testament. Grand Rapids: Baker Academic, 2008.

Vanhoozer, Kevin J. "Augustinian Inerrancy: Literary Meaning, Literal Truth, and Literate Interpretation in the Economy of Biblical Discourse." In *Five Views on Biblical Inerrancy*, edited by J. Merrick and Stephen M. Garrett, 199–235. Grand Rapids: Zondervan, 2013.

———. "Response to Michael F. Bird." In *Five Views on Biblical Inerrancy*, edited by J. Merrick and Stephen M. Garrett, 186–91. Grand Rapids: Zondervan, 2013.

Wallace, Daniel B. "John 5,2 and the Date of the Fourth Gospel." *Biblica* 71 (1990): 177–205.

Walton, John H., and D. Brent Sandy. *The Lost World of Scripture: Ancient Literary Culture and Biblical Authority*. Downers Grove, IL: IVP Academic, 2013.

Warfield, Benjamin B. "Inspiration." In *The International Standard Bible Encyclopaedia*, edited by James Orr, 3:1473–83. Chicago: Howard-Severance, 1915.

Wenham, David, and Steve Walton. *Exploring the New Testament: A Guide to the Gospels and Acts*. 2nd ed. Vol. 1. Downers Grove, IL: IVP Academic, 2011.

Wenham, John. *Christ and the Bible*. 3rd ed. Grand Rapids: Baker, 1994.

Wilkins, Michael. "Matthew." In *The Holman Apologetics Commentary on the Bible: The Gospels and Acts*. Edited by Jeremy Royal Howard. Nashville: B&H Academic, 2013.

Williams, Peter J. *Can We Trust the Gospels?* Wheaton, IL: Crossway, 2018.

Witherington, Ben, III. *The Individual Witnesses*. Vol. 1 of *The Indelible Image: The Theological and Ethical World of the New Testament*. Downers Grove, IL: IVP Academic, 2009.

———. *John's Wisdom: A Commentary on the Fourth Gospel*. Louisville: Westminster John Knox, 1995.

———. *The Living Word of God*. Waco: Baylor University Press, 2007.

———. *Matthew*. Smyth & Helwys Bible Commentary. Edited by P. Keith Gammons and R. Alan Culpepper. Macon, GA: Smyth & Helwys, 2006.

———. "The Truth Will Out: An Historian's Perspective on the Inerrancy Controversy" (plenary 3). *Journal of the Evangelical Theological Society* 57, no. 1 (2014): 19–27.

Wright, N. T. *Following Jesus: Biblical Reflections on Discipleship*. 2nd ed. Grand Rapids: Eerdmans, 2014.

———. *The Resurrection of the Son of God*. Minneapolis: Fortress, 2003.

Yarbrough, Robert W. "The Date of Papias: A Reassessment." *Journal of the Evangelical Theological Society* 26, no. 2 (June 1983). https://www.etsjets.org/files/JETS-PDFs/26/26-2/26-2-pp181-191_JETS.pdf.

GENERAL INDEX

ANCIENT SOURCES INDEX

SCRIPTURE INDEX

Luke

John